Representing Development

Representing Development presents the different social representations that have formed the idea of development in Western thinking over the past three centuries. Offering an acute perspective on the current state of developmental science and providing constructive insights into future pathways, the book draws together twelve contributors with a variety of multidisciplinary and international perspectives to focus upon development in fields including biology, psychology and sociology.

Chapters and commentaries in this volume present a variety of perspectives on social representations and development, addressing their contemporary enactments and reflecting upon future theoretical and empirical directions. The first part of the book provides an historical account of early representations of development that, having come from life science, have shaped the way in which developmental science has approached development. Part II focuses upon the contemporary issues of developmental psychology, neuroscience and developmental science at large. The third and final part offers a series of commentaries pointing to the questions opened by the previous chapters, looking to outline the future issues of developmental thinking.

This book will be of particular interest to child psychologists, educational psychologists and sociologists or historians of science, as well as academics and students interested in developmental and life sciences.

David Carré is PhD research fellow at the Niels Bohr Professorship Centre for Cultural Psychology, Faculty of Humanities, Aalborg University, Denmark.

Jaan Valsiner is Niels Bohr Professor of Cultural Psychology, Department of Communication and Psychology, Aalborg University, Denmark.

Stefan Hampl is Vice Rector for Teaching and Deputy Head of the Faculty of Psychology, Sigmund Freud University, Austria.

The series **Cultural Dynamics of Social Representation** is dedicated to bringing the scholarly reader new ways of representing human lives in the contemporary social sciences. It is a part of a new direction – cultural psychology – that has emerged at the intersection of developmental, dynamic and social psychologies, anthropology, education, and sociology. It aims to provide cutting-edge examinations of global social processes, which for every country are becoming increasingly multicultural; the world is becoming one 'global village', with the corresponding need to know how different parts of that 'village' function. Therefore, social sciences need new ways of considering how to study human lives in their globalizing contexts. The focus of this series is the social representation of people, communities and – last but not least – the social sciences themselves.

In this series

Representing Development

The social construction of models of change

Edited by David Carré, Jaan Valsiner and Stefan Hampl

Routledge
Taylor & Francis Group

LONDON AND NEW YORK

First published 2017
by Routledge
2 Park Square, Milton Park, Abingdon, Oxon OX14 4RN

and by Routledge
711 Third Avenue, New York, NY 10017

Routledge is an imprint of the Taylor & Francis Group, an informa business

British Library Cataloguing in Publication Data
A catalogue record for this book is available from the British Library

Library of Congress Cataloging in Publication Data
A catalog record for this book has been requested

ISBN: 978-1-138-85338-6 (hbk)
ISBN: 978-1-315-72279-5 (ebk)

Typeset in Times New Roman
by Swales & Willis, Exeter, Devon, UK

MIX
Paper from
responsible sources
FSC
www.fsc.org   FSC® C013604   Printed and bound by CPI Group (UK) Ltd, Croydon, CR0 4YY

In memory of Robert 'Bob' Cairns,
for inspiring this project.

Contents

Figures

Tables

Contributors

Gerhard Benetka, Univ.-Prof. Mag. Dr., is a titular professor at the Department of Psychology in the Sigmund Freud Private University Wien, Austria. His research interests focus on the philosophy and history of psychology. On this subject he has published *Psychologie in Wien. Sozial- und Theoriegeschichte des Wiener Psychologischen* [Psychology in Vienna: Social and theoretical history of the Vienna Psychological Institute from 1922 to 1938] (1995) and *Denkstile der Psychologie. Das 19. Jahrhunder* [Thinking styles of psychology: The 19th century] (2002), among others.

Agnes E. Dodds is an associate professor in medical education at the University of Melbourne, Australia. Her research interests are in medical education, with specialization in the evaluation of medical teaching and learning. She has developmental interests in emerging adulthood, particularly the developmental experiences of young adults who are on demanding professional career tracks, and in the convergence of university education with developmental tasks and goals.

Abigail Graves is a graduate student in the clinical programme at the University of Victoria. Her research focuses on the different aspects of parenting in families with typically and atypically developing children as well as parenting factors that influence early social development.

Jeanette A. Lawrence is an honorary associate professor in developmental psychology at The University of Melbourne, Australia. Her research interests are in personal and social development across life-course, particularly intergenerational relations in young and late adulthood and inheritance arrangements. She has a particular interest in the developmental experiences of children and young people from refugee backgrounds and their need for a suitable voice for expressing their well-being. She has expertise in developing culturally appropriate research methods, specializing in the development of computer-assisted interview techniques.

Vanessa Lux is a post-doctoral research fellow in genetic psychology at Ruhr University Bochum. In 2011, she received her PhD in psychology at the Free

University Berlin. From 2011 to 2015 she was a post-doctoral research fellow at the Center for Literary and Cultural Research Berlin, with the research projects *Cultural Factors of Inheritance* and *Neuropsychoanalysis: Neuroscience between Science and Humanities*. Her research interests are: the epigenetic regulation of psychobiological development and stress, developmental theory, embodiment theories and conceptual issues in empathy research. She is especially interested in methodological and epistemological issues at the intersections of psychology and other life sciences.

Eduardo Martí is Professor of Developmental and Educational Psychology at the University of Barcelona, Spain. He collaborated with Piaget at the Center of Genetic Epistemology, University of Geneva. His research area and publications concern cognitive development and the acquisition of external systems of representation. His most recently published books are *Representar el Mundo Externamente* [Representing the World Externally] (2003), *Desarrollo, Cultura y Educación* [Development, Culture and Education] (2005) and *After Piaget*, co-edited with C. Rodríguez (2012).

Ulrich Müller, PhD, is a professor at the University of Victoria, Department of Psychology. His research focuses on cognitive and social development in early childhood. He edited, among others, the *Cambridge Companion to Piaget* (2009), and serves as Associate Editor of *New Ideas in Psychology*.

Felipe Munoz-Rubke is a PhD student at the joint programme in Cognitive Science and Neuroscience at Indiana University. He is MS in Applied Statistics from Indiana University. His main research topics are tool use and manipulation, mechanical problem solving, and word meaning and language understanding. He has conducted research in these areas using behavioural experimentation, functional Magnetic Resonance Imaging (fMRI), and Transcranial Magnetic Stimulation (TMS).

Pablo Rojas is an associate researcher at École des hautes études en sciences sociales (EHESS) in Paris, France. He works at the Centre for Linguistic Anthropology and Sociolinguistics (LIAS), at the Marcel Mauss Institute. His dissertation work focused on the development of skill in instrumental musical practices. Among his research interests are anthropology of perception, skill development, technical activity (craftsmanship), and the affinities between practical and aesthetic dimensions of experience.

Leslie Smith is a freelance researcher based in the Lake District. He is Professor Emeritus at Lancaster University, Fellow of the British Psychological Society, and Associate Editor of *New Ideas in Psychology*. His international work has included membership of the Board of Directors of the Jean Piaget Society, and the International Scientific Committee of the Jean Piaget Archives in Geneva. His published work includes a dozen books and a hundred papers. His main interest is in Piaget's developmental epistemology, and especially in the normativity central to the formation of necessary knowledge.

Aaro Toomela is Professor of Cultural Neuropsychology at the Tallinn University, Estonia. His research interests cover all the main fields of psychology – cognitive, developmental, cultural, social, personality, biological, evolutionary and applied – as well as philosophy, history, and methodology of psychology. He has authored scientific papers in all these fields. He is a member of the editorial boards of several journals (including *Culture & Psychology* and *Integrative Psychological and Behavioral Science*).

Martin Wieser studied psychology and philosophy at the University of Vienna and the Free University Berlin. From 2010 to 2014 he was a research fellow at the doctoral college at the University of Vienna. Since October 2015, he has been a scientific assistant at the Sigmund Freud Private University Berlin and a staff member of the project *Psychology during National Socialism*, which is funded by the Austrian Science Fund. His main research topics are found in and between the areas of theory and history of psychology, media studies, cultural psychology and critical psychology.

Acknowledgements

The editorial work of this book was supported by a Niels Bohr Professorship grant from the Danske Grundforskningsfond, and by the Becas Chile – Doctorado en el Extranjero programme from the National Commission of Scientific and Technologic Research of Chile (CONICYT – Chile).

Introduction

Going backwards to move forwards – understanding the shortcomings of developmental science

Stefan Hampl, David Carré and Jaan Valsiner

Any science is built upon the basis of a set of social representations. In turn, as a knowledge-making enterprise, any science is also a vehicle for represent*ing* knowledge—to itself and to the whole of humankind. Such representing process is inevitably embedded in its social–historical frame: for example, it made sense to medieval alchemists to try to make gold out of any other substance. Nowadays we might chuckle over the "naïve" efforts of the alchemists—just to fall short in noticing our own simplicity. In this way, it makes perfect sense for our contemporary educational sciences to search for precursors of children's future academic success in early infancy and childhood. The inevitable fact that an exact prediction of such success is unrealistic on axiomatic grounds—given the open-systemic nature of development—does not stop us all from thinking in terms of predictions. The socially desirable, common-sense goal of wishing the best for our offspring makes us blind to the reality that the future is continuously being constructed by relating with our environments.[1] The accepted social representation of *prediction*—which has led the advance of material sciences—has guided our thinking away from another social representation: *construction*.

The two representations are deeply different in their provision of a feeling of certainty for us. While prediction implies that the world is a well-ordered system, of which we have only to discover its particular order, construction implies that no specific order is prevalent *a priori*, but that it needs to be created under conditions of uncertainty. The feeling of comfort related to order—together with its counterpart, the social representation of *control* (of what is not yet found out to be predictable[2])—makes the social representation of prediction commonly preferable to that of the muddy waters of construction. And so the whole discipline of psychology parts from the utopian trail, guided by the social expectation that it can "discover" the underlying order in the place where it is actually undergoing construction. The newly emerged direction of developmental science has a history in its preceding areas of child and developmental psychology as well as education; and it is a history defined for being captured by societal demands through the network of core social representations inherently accepted by a consensus within the larger society.

Developmental science: what is it?

First of all, developmental science is a label; and it certainly is an appealing one. If compared with its possible (but non-existent) counterpart—which could be *degenerative science*—it has all the reasons to make us feel positive by discussing and doing it.[3]

Behind the label is a large set of intellectual efforts to make sense of the processes of development—in nature (evolution), in organisms (embryogenesis), in the human psyche (developmental psychology), and in societies (community development). In its programmatic form, developmental science has been described as referring to,

> a fresh synthesis that has been generated to guide research in the social, psychological, and biobehavioral disciplines. It describes a general orientation for linking concepts and findings of hitherto disparate areas of developmental inquiry, and it emphasizes the dynamic interplay of processes across time frames, levels of analysis, and contexts. Time and timing are central to this perspective. The time frames employed are relative to the lifetime of the phenomena to be understood. Units of focus can be as short as milliseconds, seconds, and minutes, or as long as years, decades, and millennia. In this perspective, the phenomena of individual functioning are viewed at multiple levels—from the subsystems of genetics, neurobiology, and hormones to those of families, social networks, communities, and cultures.
>
> (Carolina Consortium on Human Development, 1996, p. 1)

Interestingly, this description of developmental science does not include any representation of development as such. The notion of "dynamic interplay of processes across time frames" does not characterize the developmental processes in such "interplay". The perennial theoretical issue at stake—how change is linked with development—remains hidden in this description. The description is an institutional look—that of various disciplines—at the general range of phenomena that undergo development, rather than a conceptual effort to provide new perspectives for the study of development itself. Its only substantive contribution is the emphasis on the joint functioning of the developing organism at multiple levels. Yet how to understand such relations between levels remains unclear. In fact, there have been very few consistently developmental theories in the field of developmental science (Shanahan, Valsiner & Gottlieb, 1996).

In the present book we look at developmental science from the perspective of cultural psychology, with a focus on how different aspects of development are socially represented in parallel in two worlds. On the one hand, there are those of public discourses; on the other, there are those of scientific discussions, as they struggle with the difficult issues of transformation of structures in irreversible time. In this effort there have been notable predecessors to the recent focus on developmental science. However, these perspectives have often overlooked the open-systemic nature of development, concentrating on inherent individual development instead. Furthermore what is developmental in these perspectives is often represented in non-developmental ways. As an example, Jean Piaget's focus (see Martí, 2016, Chapter 5 in this volume) on individual development through the mechanism of *equilibration majorante* (progressing equilibration) involving constant mutuality of assimilation and accommodation has been habitually replaced by the focus on his description of stages in individual cognitive advancement over age—while presenting the sequence of stages *as if this* were Piaget's "developmental theory". It could not possibly be so, as any description of sequence of stages in time is equivalent to a categorization (without time). Thus social representations of Piaget's work have defaced his developmental theory building efforts (that notably failed) into a non-developmental account of stages (Valsiner, 2001).

A similar situation has occurred around the theoretical efforts of Erik Erikson. His theory of *psychosocial development* has been majorly understood as a mere sequence of stages (or crises) every individual has to go through—neatly presented through a 4×4 chart to undergraduate students. This narrow reception by scientific psychology has largely neglected the interactive aspects of human development that Erikson himself was well aware of. The following quote demonstrates that revisiting Erikson from the perspective of 21st-century cultural psychology could be very fruitful for the developmental advance of the discipline. According to Erikson, the individual is never going through stages all by itself, but always in close reference to and in exchange with the people in its environment. In fact, Erikson conceived development as a reciprocal process within the group of people involved, thus overtly questioning a simple causality to individual development:

> A baby's presence exerts a consistent and persistent domination over the outer and inner lives of every member of a household. Because these members must reorient themselves to accommodate his presence, they must also grow as individuals and as a group. It is as true to say that babies control and bring up their families as it is to say the converse. A family can bring up a baby only by being brought up by him. His growth consists of a series of challenges to them to serve his newly developing potentialities for social interaction.
>
> (Erikson, 1959, p. 56)

Today we could take Erikson's idea of development within groups even one step further and speculate about the future of our society with regard to the influx of large numbers of outsiders, refugees, guest workers, beggars etc. If we understand Erikson's model of psychosocial development as one substantially based on social interaction, it becomes evident that large-scale transformations of society can very well effect new paths and patterns of development in individuals.

A representational trap: the need for teleology, and its avoidance

Development is a term that implies some form of teleology. At the same time, teleology is a deeply despised term in contemporary science. It sounds like a subtle hint to religion—at least as it is usually presented—and hence is a notion usually kept far away from science. Non-developmental sciences—dealing with the ontology of their objects—could easily avoid the notion. But this is different for developmental sciences—including evolutionary theory and embryology (see Valsiner, Chapter 2 in this volume, on the work of Hans Driesch). The general notion of teleology *in some form* is inevitable for developmental science. The only question is: in what kind of form?

It is clear that the open-ended (i.e. open-systemic) nature of development would not allow theoreticians to posit the existence of fixed future goals for it, the reaching of which could "complete" development. Yet a present focusing towards some possible goal in the future is not only commonly ordinary ("I want my child to succeed in life"—a common teleological claim by parents) but also theoretically necessary in case of cultural–psychological processes that transcend the border of the present, moving from the past towards the indeterminate (but in the process of being constructed) future. What can be posited is goals *orientation*, i.e. a set of possible future goals for striving towards, in contrast to other ones, not positively valued or willingly avoided. Furthermore, a version of developmental teleology can be expressed in the form of teleo*genesis*: along the ongoing process of development, the organism constructs its own potential goals to strive towards, even if these are never reached. Nor do they need to be reachable—utopian future promises have shaped the development of societies for long periods of times.

The paradox of developmental methodology: capturing emergence

As development involves emergence of new forms, the study of such processes is complicated—both in practice and in theory. In this respect, a view of reconstructive research methodology can be fruitful. The use of the *documentary* method puts a special empirical focus on human practice—but one that has already emerged, not one that is in the process of emerging. If you look at any human practice (as opposed to theorizing about attitudes and motives), it is clear that every one has developed in the sense that it has a specific history. However, even though there is the notion in cultural psychology and qualitative/reconstructive research that every phenomenon we are looking at has a history, this does not automatically imply that we can know how this phenomenon will develop in the future, nor how it came into being.

Thus we end up speculating about the frame within which development will be conceivable. Hence a limitation on what has emerged already (and is observable) is actually leading into something that is not yet visible, but will become so in some moment in the future; in this sense developmental science cannot be primarily "empirical science", since it deals with the duality in each of its phenomena. It is not a "miracle of emergence" but a systematic future-oriented synthesis of the new that requires the use of theoretical concepts that capture both real and imaginary (i.e. not–yet developed) aspects of the phenomena. Very few of such efforts exist in developmental science; the efforts of the Dynamic Systems Theory to posit the existence of *attractors* in the future state (van Geert, 2003) and Lev Vygotsky's original notion of the Zone of Nearest Development (Valsiner & van der Veer, 2014) are some examples.

Relativity in change between levels: persons in societies

Karl Mannheim (1980) once pointed out that human culture is not a result of cognitive decisions, but develops out of conjunctive experience (i.e. practice) with others. But the others are fellow human beings who are also developing in parallel—albeit at a different pace. Adolescent "growth spurt" of two or so years' duration is out of synchrony with the development of their parents—usually in their middle ages—over the same few years. In contrast, some aspects of development proceed under the conditions of minimal visible changes in the immediate life-worlds. For instance, the phenomena of life-long learning are guaranteed to never arrive, as the end of the learning process here (moment of death) eliminates the results of such learning, at least from the given person's acquired wisdom. A person might seem not to learn anything day by day, but nevertheless by the end of their life has arrived at a state of wisdom that could be useful for others in society. But to communicate that wisdom requires a move from the person-centered to the society-based look at the development of knowledge.

Here is the question of inter-levels relations—how can individual life-long learning become appropriated by others within the society? And how does a society develop as a result of such appropriation? These are practical questions, worked out in reality within everyday lives of ordinary human beings. According to Mannheim (1980) understanding (in an existential sense) is never primarily theoretical, but mainly practical. What a society can learn from its individuals is particularly the practices that they have brought into life or action. While thoughts are invisible and might die, practices are visible and therefore can be observed and replicated by other individuals, leading to further new ways of thinking. While this might appear like a disturbing result for traditional psychologists at first, it fits in remarkably well with Bandura's (1971) well-established social learning theory. Social learning, according to Bandura, is a cognitive process following the observation of behavior *and* the observation of the consequences of behavior. The development of societies could therefore be understood as the introduction of new practices, their consequences, and as a result the construction of new cultural mediation practices. Technical constraints like the 140 characters in a Twitter message, or 30-second time slots in television advertisements, are likely to change political discourse in our contemporary societies. Development of consuming as the main social practice leads persons to think in terms of choices between ready-made products, rather than about how to make a better product for themselves. The market orientation in economics leads to ways of thinking that mask the tele-ogenetic efforts of the market-makers behind the appealing social representation of "*free* market". Even though the "freedom" of the market is organized by the legal constraints on trading.

Presenting this book: from history to future

Any book is a conglomerate of social presentations of the topics covered. This book consists of three parts, which cover the past, present and future of developmental science. Part I is related to the emergence of representations of development, Part II to the study of development in its move to the 21st century, and Part III consists of ideas for new pathways into developmental science.

The reader will encounter much that is known—or known-yet-forgotten—and ripe for (re)discovery in the present book. However, there are gaps—hopefully to be filled in the next publications in this direction. First of all, this book is missing a clear and systematic program for the re-launch of a development science inspired by cultural psychology. However, as the Introduction proposes, it might be worthwhile revisiting some of the old classics like Piaget and Erikson in order to connect them with a modern understanding of psychology. Second, the book consists for the most part of academic, theoretical discussions on the subject of development. It would have been fruitful to integrate empirical findings and practical implications with theoretical coverage. Of course the fact that developmental science up to today is narrowly oriented towards children and adolescence in its empirical work, and even fails to cover the whole human life course (as critiqued by Zittoun et al., 2013), does not help. While declaring that developmental science covers all the levels of organization of human lives, we acknowledge that it fails to do so at the level of human interdependence with community and society at large. For example, the general theme of social representation of transformations in communities, cities and societies as wholes has not yet been covered in the social sciences. A book dedicated to that theme would integrate the knowhow of sociologists, historians and economists around the issue of social transformations of the existing social systems. How do societies change through insurgencies, revolutions, counter-revolutions, stock market crashes and famines? How do new technologies—guillotines, Twitters, and suicide bombings—mediate such societal changes, or eventually their development? The absence of coverage of these topics in terms of social representations leads us to suspect that stronger, meta-level representations are in place in social practices to block our coverage of these topics. Yet these need to be covered—and hopefully the present book sets the stage for such future elaboration.

Notes

1   This follows from the basic set of axioms of the open systems, namely those that their existence is fully dependent upon the exchange relationship with their environments. As a result, the actual trajectory of their development is in principle not predictable using the sole organism as basis. Notwithstanding this unpredictability, it is necessary to remember that open systems are the only kind of organization capable of development.
2   In the behaviorist tradition of defining psychology, the whole enterprise is conceived as a science of prediction and control of behavior.
3   This also fits at the level of societal transformations. Consider the field of "transformational studies": they are used to describe the political and/or economic shifts of countries, for instance. Also the term transformational (just like developmental) has been considered more and more as a good in itself. For example—a country has transformed well if it has turned from a totalitarian regime into a "democracy" based on market economy. We do not really know if the latter is welcomed by the citizens of such country, but in our representation of such change we are positively impressed.

References

Bandura, A. (1971). *Social Learning Theory*. New York, NY: General Learning Corporation.

Carolina Consortium on Human Development (1996). Developmental science: A collaborative statement. In R. B. Cairns, G. Elder & E. J. Costello (Eds.), *Developmental Science* (pp. 1–6). New York, NY: Cambridge University Press.

Erikson, E. (1959). *Identity and the Life Cycle*. New York, NY: International Universities Press.

Mannheim, K. (1980). *Structures of Thinking*. London, UK: Routledge & Kegan Paul. (Original work published in 1922–24)

Shanahan, M., Valsiner, J. & Gottlieb, G. (1996). The conceptual structure of developmental theories. In J. Tudge, M. Shanahan & J. Valsiner (Eds.), *Comparative Approaches in Developmental Science* (pp. 13–71). New York, NY: Cambridge University Press.

Valsiner, J. (2001). Constructive curiosity of the human mind: Participating in Piaget. Introduction to the Transaction Edition of Jean Piaget's *The Child's Conception of Physical Causality* (pp. ix–xxii). New Brunswick, NJ: Transaction Publishers.

Valsiner, J. & van der Veer, R. (2014). Encountering the border: Vygotsky's zona blizaishego razvitya and its implications for theory of development. In A. Yasnitsky, R. van der Veer & M. Ferrari (Eds.), *The Cambridge Handbook of Cultural–Historical Psychology* (pp. 148–173). Cambridge, UK: Cambridge University Press.

Van Geert, P. (2003). Dynamic systems approaches and modeling of developmental processes. In J. Valsiner & K. J. Connolly (Eds.), *Handbook of Developmental Psychology* (pp. 640–673). London, UK: Sage.

Zittoun, T., Valsiner, J., Vedeler, D., Salgado, J., Gonçalves, M. & Ferring, D. (2013). *Melodies of Living*. Cambridge, UK: Cambridge University Press.

Part I

Emerging representations of development

Chapter 1

Goethe and Werner

From morphology to orthogenetic principle

Ulrich Müller and Abigail Graves

Heinz Werner (1890–1964) has been considered a key figure in developmental psychology. His theory is summarized, along with those of Freud, Piaget, and Vygotsky, in a widely read textbook, *Theories of Development* (Crain, 2011), a review of his theory was included in the third edition of Carmichael's *Manual of Child Psychology* (Langer, 1970), and an article was devoted to the description of his theory in the special series on historical figures that was published in *Developmental Psychology* (Glick, 1992). Werner's empirical work focused on symbol formation (Werner & Kaplan, 1963) and perceptual development (Wapner & Werner, 1957; Werner & Wapner, 1952), with the former work still influential in contemporary research (e.g., Callaghan & Corbit, 2015; MacWhinney, 2015). From a theoretical perspective, Werner advanced the idea that the concept of development provides a useful approach for investigating phenomena in all life sciences, including biology, anthropology, psychopathology, comparative psychology, and child psychology (Werner, 1926/1948, 1957). In this vein, Werner proposed the orthogenetic principle as the key theoretical principle that unifies the study of development across different disciplines: "[T]he development of biological forms is expressed in an *increasing differentiation* of parts and an *increasing subordination, or hierarchization*" (Werner, 1926/1948, p. 41, emphasis in original). However, Werner credits the eminent German poet, politician, and scientist Johann Wolfgang von Goethe (1749–1832) as the source of the orthogenetic principle: "For him, the very essence of the development of biological forms is symbolized by the differentiation of the organic parts and their subordination to the whole of the organism" (Werner, 1926/1948, p. 41). Werner then references one of Goethe's writings on morphology to further expound on the orthogenetic principle:

> The less perfect the creation, the more its parts are alike or similar and the more they resemble the whole. The more perfect the creation the less similar its parts become. In the first instance the whole is like its parts to a degree, in the second instance the whole is unlike its parts. The more similar its parts, the less they will be subordinated to one another. Subordination of parts indicates a more perfect solution.
>
> (Goethe, 1988, p. 64)

This quote, however, is part of a much more comprehensive treatment of development in Goethe's work. In this chapter, we examine the concept of development in the context of Goethe's work, with special emphasis on his writings on plant metamorphosis and morphology. Next, we compare Goethe's and Werner's concepts of development. Finally, we discuss the relevance of Goethe's concept of development as well as the orthogenetic principle for contemporary psychology.

The concept of development in the context of Goethe's work

Nowadays, Johann Wolfgang Goethe is mostly known for his epic and lyric poetry, not for his scientific writings. However, Goethe (1988) did write several papers on scientific method and on a variety of topics in different natural sciences, including anatomy, botany, zoology, geology, meteorology, and physics. In fact, Goethe was certain that his scientific writings, and not his literary work, would later be recognized as his greatest contribution to humankind (Seamon, 1998).

In general, Goethe's scientific writings highlight the dynamic, productive side of nature (*natura naturans*) as he was searching for ways of capturing the productivity and deeper unity of nature. In this respect, Goethe stood in opposition to the dominating scientific frameworks of his time. In botany, for example, Carl Linnaeus (1707–1778) had established a static taxonomy in order to classify plants in an exhaustive fashion on the basis of their external features. Goethe was well versed in Linnaeus' system, but he thought it was taxonomically unstable because it did not reveal the inner necessity, organic wholeness, and dynamic nature of life (see Goethe, 1966, pp. 67, 75–77; Goethe, 1968, p. 15; Wellmon, 2010). This basic idea of Goethe's philosophy of nature is well expressed by Cassirer (1945):

> To put it briefly and clearly, Goethe completed the transition from the previous generic view to the modern genetic view of organic nature. The generic view of the plant world found its classic expression in Linnaeus' system of nature. It holds that we have understood nature when we have succeeded in arranging it in the pigeonholes of our concepts, dividing it into species and genera, into families, classes, and orders. But for Goethe such an enterprise was not enough. According to him, what we grasp in this way are only the products, not the process of life. And into this life process he wanted, not only as poet but also as scientist, to win an insight; in it he saw what was greatest and highest.
>
> (p. 69)

Goethe coined the term *morphology* to characterize his alternative to the taxonomic method (Breidbach, 2006; Kuhn, 1988; Mocek, 1998). Morphology deals with structured forms or Gestalts. Whereas the term Gestalt usually refers to fixed unchangeable wholes, for Goethe *organic* Gestalten are in a "flux of continual motion. This is why German frequently and fittingly makes use of the word *Bildung* [formation] to describe the end product and what is in process of production as well" (Goethe, 1988, p. 63). A Gestalt is an abstraction, an "empirical element held fast for a mere moment of time" (Goethe, 1988, p. 64). Thus, for Goethe morphology is inherently dynamic and process oriented since it includes "the principles of structured form and the formation and transformation of organic bodies" (1988, p. 57). The formation and transformation of organic bodies cannot be explained by mechanical principles:

> The central concept . . . that must form the basis for any consideration of living beings . . . is that it is consistent with itself, that its parts are in a necessary relation with each other, and nothing mechanistic can somehow be constructed or affected from the outside, even though the parts influence the outside and are, in turn, influenced from the outside. The determination of forms comes from within and everything determined arose through a process of differentiation, as a product of this process.
>
> (Goethe, 1966b, p. 60)

In a similar vein, Goethe (1988) tells us that each animal needs to be conceived "as a small world, existing for its own sake, by its own means. Every creature is its own reason to be. All its parts have a direct effect on one another, a relationship to one another, thereby constantly renewing the circle of life; thus we are justified in considering every animal physiologically perfect" (p. 121).

Goethe formulated his dynamic idea of nature in most detail in his major botanical work, *The Metamorphosis of Plants* (1790/2009), in which he replaced the classificatory approach of Linnaeus with the idea of metamorphosis: the external organs of plants go through successive changes (due to the successive refinement with which each organ processes the sap) beginning with the seed-leaf such that each organ metamorphosizes into the next increasingly complex organ—for instance, the seed-leaves metamorphosize into the plumule, calyx, stamens, nectaries, pistils, style, fruit. Therefore, the whole plant ultimately develops from the same organ: "the various plant parts developed in sequence are intrinsically identical despite their manifold differences in outer form" (Goethe, 1790/2009, p. 56). As Goethe wrote in his journal on July 31st, 1787, "While walking in the Public Gardens of Palermo, it came to me in a flash that in the organ we usually call the 'leaf' lies the true Proteus who can hide or reveal himself in all vegetal forms. From first to last, the plant is nothing but leaf, which is so inseparable from the future germ that one cannot think of one without the other" (Goethe, 1968, p. 363).

Hence, Goethe (1988, pp. 6–7) identified two driving wheels of nature: polarity and intensification (*Steigerung*), which are manifest in the development of plants. Intensification accounts for the progressive, stepwise transformation from simpler into more complex forms; it expresses "nature's desire to tend toward complexity" (Tantillo, 2002, p. 59). Intensification begins in the material, physical realm and then gradually leads the living form away from matter toward the nonphysical. For example, at first the plant is filled with crude material and born of earth and water, but exposure to light and air lead to its specialization and articulation. "Steigerung enables the plant to transcend the matter that first gave it the impetus to grow. After it begins to grow, the more material elements impede its progress, whereas air and light promote it" (Tantillo, 2002, p. 68).

The principle of polarity, however, expresses Goethe's view that opposing forces are necessary for the creation of a new product. The entire universe comprises the opposing forces of repulsion and attraction:

> The world must divide if it is to appear at all. What has been divided seeks itself again, can return to itself and reunite. This happens in a lower sense when it merely intermingles with its opposite, combines with it; here the phenomenon is nullified or at least neutralized. However, the union may occur in a higher sense if what has been divided is first intensified; then in the union the intensified halves will produce a third thing, something new, higher, unexpected.
>
> (Goethe, 1988, p. 156)

The polarity is expressed in the growth of the plant as alternation between contraction and expansion: the calyx, for example, is produced by means of contraction; the petals by expansion (Goethe, 1790/2009, p. 60). More generally, for Goethe opposing forces are necessary for creation, and polarity creates through predictable patterns (Tantillo, 2002). Intensification, by contrast, is capable of creating entirely new forms and thus represents the highest stage of creativity in nature (and in human beings): "Polarity is a state of constant attraction and repulsion, while intensification is a state of ever-striving ascent. Since, however, matter can never exist and act without spirit, nor spirit without matter, matter is also capable of undergoing intensification, and spirit cannot be denied its attraction and repulsion" (Goethe, 1988, p. 6).

Shortly before writing the *Metamorphosis of Plants*, Goethe spent an extended time in Italy, where he immersed himself in botanical studies. There, he coined the concept of an archetypal plant, a plant from which all others plants could be derived. At some point, Goethe seemed to have believed that the archetypal plant existed as a real object (Goethe, 1959, p. 607), but he soon realized that the archetypal plant was in fact an idea (see Goethe, 1988, pp. 18–22, on his conversation with Schiller). The archetype becomes a foundational idea that Goethe invokes in a variety of different contexts, using a number of different terms (Pratt & Brook, 1996). For example, Goethe (1966b, pp. 274–280; 1998, pp. 67–69) postulates an archetypal vertebrate from which the body forms of all can be derived. In the *Metamorphosis of Plants*, the *leaf* serves as an archetype; it represents a dynamic potential, a temporal form (see Brady, 1984) that, by adapting to different conditions, gives rise to different forms.

The archetype unifies the different expressions of plants (or animals) and provides the reason why a particular form is recognized as plant, despite all variations in plant forms. The archetype is intrinsically related to a *Bildungstrieb*, a formative impulse or force that drives the organism to realize its potential (Goethe, 1988, pp. 35–36). The idea of a *Bildungstrieb* (*nisus formativus*), which had previously been postulated by Caspar Friedrich Wolff (see Lenoir, 1982), refers to an activity that ensures the development of an organism is not *causally* determined by external forces but follows its own internal logic. Consequently, *Bildungstrieb* and metamorphosis constitute inseparable concepts: "When an organism manifests itself, we cannot grasp the unity and freedom of its formative impulse without the concept of metamorphosis" (Goethe, 1988, p. 36). Thus, Bildungstrieb does not exclude the possibility of development being sensitive to environmental conditions. Goethe followed Kant (who, in turn, was influenced by Wolff, Blumenbach, and Kielmeyer) in rejecting the view that the adult form is preformed at conception and gradually unfolds without anything new emerging in this process (see Lenoir, 1982), and also followed him in supporting an epigenetic position according to which forms emerge in the course of ontogenesis as a result of the interaction between organism and environment. Goethe himself (1790/2009, p. 23; 1968, pp. 14–16) had also observed that the specific form of the plant varied with environmental conditions. However, the plant does not passively adapt to environmental conditions; rather, the plant makes an active contribution to the way in which it responds to the challenges posed by its environment. In this sense: "The living organism configures itself *actively*, instead of being conditioned passively in response to the environment" (Bortoft, 2012, p. 78, emphasis in original).

Goethe's idea of archetype has been severely misunderstood (Bortoft, 1996, 2012; Brady, 1984), largely because it has been interpreted as a static archetype and as a kind of Platonic idea that exists in a state of eternal perfection separately from its individual instantiations. For example, Richard Owen's (1804–1892) notion of an archetypal vertebrate, which was supposed to capture the *essence* of the vertebrate body plan, represents a static perspective on archetype. His archetypal vertebrate is arrived at by abstracting away from the differences among vertebrate body plans and represents their *common denominator*. The archetype is then hypostasized and serves as a fixed schema that underlies and gives shape to individual members. Goethe's notion of archetype, however, is entirely different from such a static archetype. First, for Goethe (1966a), the individual and the general are not separate; rather, the general (the idea, the archetype) discloses itself in the individuals: "The general and the particular coincide: the particular is the general, appearing under different conditions" (p. 705). Thus, the archetype unifies the different forms that are its expression. For this reason, differences are not abstracted away; on the contrary, the dynamic archetype creates differences within unity. Second, the archetype refers to the temporal dimension of living beings and expresses their potential and becoming. For example, the different steps in the development of the plant are snapshots, moments frozen in time; the archetype manifests itself through the plant's becoming, or capacity to be otherwise, through a movement that links the different steps in an ordered series of transformations (Brady, 1984). Following this, the different organs of the plant are all expressions and transformations of the archetypal leaf.

Goethe's thinking is thus radically dynamic. It does not start "downstream" with finished forms (*natura naturata*), but it starts upstream, traces the differentiation of the leaf into different organs, and so brings diversity into unity. Bortoft (2012) introduces the term *self-differencing* to describe this differentiation process:

> Goethe's "one and the same organ" manifesting as different forms is a self-differencing organ producing differences of itself. *So the different organs we see are the self-differences of one organ.* What we discover here is the extraordinary idea of self-differences instead of self-sameness, the idea that something can become different from itself whilst remaining itself instead of becoming something else . . . the self-differencing *is* the unity and the unity *is* the self-differencing. . . . [S]o what we see as the diversity of organs *is* the living unity of the plant . . . . The one is not separate from the many in this way of thinking: On the contrary, what we find here is that, in the words of Gilles Deleuze: Multiplicity is the inseparable manifestation, essential transformation and constant symptom of unity. Multiplicity is the affirmation of unity; becoming is the affirmation of being.
>
> (pp. 71, 77, emphases in original)

For Goethe, then, the archetypal plant and the leaf are thus not static entities: they are movements, and, more precisely, they are a dynamic unity of self-differencing. By tracing the ordered series of transformations of the plant, the relations between its organs become intelligible and necessary. The movement becomes more vivid as we find more transitional forms that fill the gap between different developmental steps. As Brady (1984) elaborates, the movement is also the criterion by means of which we judge whether a new form belongs to the series. Presented with a series of snapshots that represent different steps in the development of a plant, we place the new form at either end of the series: if the impression of movement is strengthened, the new form is judged to be a member of the series; if the impression of movement is interrupted, the new form is rejected.

Our judgment of whether the new form belongs to the series, however, cannot be based simply on similarity. The series is extended in time, the snapshots represent changes from one time point to the next, and our judgment must take this dynamic context into account. The unifying movement is thus a distribution of similarities and differences—a differential running through the series (Brady, 1984). In the context of the movement, the way we perceive the individual members of the series changes. The forms become an arrested stage within a sequence; they no longer stand in isolation but appear as partial disclosures of the whole:

> Thus the empirical Gestalts are not, and cannot be, "parts" of the transformation. This position must be reserved for the altered forms—those produced by contexting the empirical individuals in an intended movement. But since these latter are clearly products of context, the movement must now be identified as a whole which determines its own parts.
>
> (Brady, 1984, p. 339)

Yet the movement itself, regardless of how many transitional forms we can fit into the series and how small the gaps between forms become, is not sensible itself; it is an idea, grasped only in thought and by imagination. Goethe believed that the idea of the archetypal (or primal) plant supplies some sort of necessity:

> The Primal Plant is going to be the strangest creature in the world, which Nature herself shall envy me. With this model and the key to it, it will be possible to go on for ever inventing plants and know that their existence is logical; that is to say, if they do not actually exist, they could, for they are not the shadowy phantoms of a vein imagination, but possess an inner necessity and truth. The same law will be applicable to all other living organisms.
>
> (Goethe, 1968, pp. 305–306)

Translated into the language of modern biology, one could say that the archetype provides the theoretical morphospace of plants (Riegner, 2013). According to Brady (1984), the inner necessity that Goethe refers to in the quotation above shows that archetypal movement (the differential of a series) has the status of a causal law (and not just a descriptive law). By means of the differential, we fit new forms into the series, imagine theoretically possible forms, and predict what form, given a particular stage of development, will emerge next. The differential is a generative law, "by which nature forms its productions (reminiscent of the Aristotelian formal cause). Because this idea is productive of all potential forms in the series, Goethe spoke of it in generative rather than descriptive terms" (Brady, 1984, p. 339).

In many respects, Goethe's morphology anticipated systems approaches to understanding the functioning of organisms (see von Bertalanffy, 1951, 1949/1952). For Goethe, everything is essentially related to everything else, connected by the vibrant flow of life:

> We will see the entire plant world, for example, as a vast sea which is as necessary to the existence of individual insects as the oceans and rivers are to the existence of individual fish . . . . Ultimately we will see the whole world of animals as a great element in which one species is created, or at least sustained, by and through another.
>
> (Goethe, 1988, pp. 55–56)

This is also reflected in the interdependence between different animals and between animals and their environment (Goethe, 1966b, p. 420). Furthermore, the pulsing flow of life creates a continuity among all forms of life. This assumption motivated Goethe's systematic work in comparative anatomy, which in fact resulted in the discovery of the intermaxillary bone—the upper incisors are embedded in this bone—in human embryos (Goethe, 1988).[1] At that time, the intermaxillary bone had received considerable attention because it was present in mammals but appeared to be absent in humans, and the absence of this bone in humans had been cited as evidence for the special status of humans. Goethe (1988) interpreted the finding of the intermaxillary bone as evidence for an "intermediate series of forms" (p. 116) among animals, or, in Cassirer's (1961) words, as "confirmation of the argument that no form of nature is absolutely unrelated and cut off from the others" (p. 73).

Goethe's method

What kind of method did Goethe use and advocate to study diversity and ever-changing physical forms and the underlying unity from which they emerge? Goethe (1988) tells us that he used the genetic method for this purpose:

> If I look at the created object, inquire into its creation, and follow this process back as far as I can, I will find a series of steps. Since these are not actually seen together before me, I must visualize them in my memory so that they form a certain ideal whole. At first I will tend to think in terms of steps, but nature leaves no gaps, and thus, in the end, I will have to see this progression of uninterrupted activity as a whole. I can do so by dissolving the particular without destroying the impression itself.
>
> (p. 75)

The genetic method involves the integration of sensory experience and imagination (Bortoft, 1996). First, the researcher must carefully observe the different stages in the process of growth and place the phenomena (or depictions thereof) in a serial order. In the second step, the phenomena are appropriated by the observer by being recreated inwardly through imagination. Goethe suggests that the metamorphic process of the organs of the plant should be visualized in backward and forward order. Thus, for example, a petal can be seen as a metamorphosis of a stamen equally well as a stamen can be seen as a metamorphosis of a petal (Goethe, 1790/2009, p. 102).

The second step addresses the fundamental problem that we cannot perceive organic development and uninterrupted progression; all we can see are particular Gestalten. As Simmel (1912) commented, in Goethe's writings there is the inherent tension between the continuity of the flowing movement and the singularity of the individual Gestalt. In reflecting on the Kantian argument that the ideas of reason cannot be sensibly portrayed, Goethe (1988) himself offers the following consideration:

> This difficulty in uniting idea and experience presents obstacles in all scientific research: the idea is independent of space and time while scientific research is bound by space and time. In the idea, then, simultaneous elements are closely bound up with sequential ones, but our experience always shows them to be separate; we are seemingly plunged into madness by a natural process which must be conceived of in an idea as both simultaneous and sequential. Our intellect cannot think of something as united when the senses present it as separate, and thus the conflict between what is grasped as experience and what is formed as idea remains forever unresolved.
>
> (p. 33)

Goethe thought that the solution to this problem resided in combining discursive (understanding) and intuitive thinking (reason). This comes about by reflecting on the reproduction of the various steps in the plant's development, which amounts to reflecting on phenomena that are imagined in the observer's own mind. The synthesis of understanding and reason that Goethe had in mind is well captured by Wellmon (2010): "The observer must engage in a reflective thinking of the plant's development; he can only think development by reflecting on his own discursive thought process. Because all of a plant's parts stand in a 'necessary relationship,' this process must happen with all parts at once . . . . The *Typus*, or the universal form that guides this process, then, is not a taxonomic category but a *Bild* that emerges and reemerges from the interaction of experience and ideas" (p. 164).

By moving through the different steps of the developmental sequence inwardly, we are connecting the different stages of growth, and in doing so, the mind engages in a motion that corresponds to the metamorphosis of the plant. Our thinking becomes as flexible and mobile as nature itself, and from the reflection on this thinking emerges an image that symbolizes the dynamic process (Goethe, 1988, p. 64). According to Amrine (1990), Goethe's method moves from mere looking to observation, then to reflection, and ultimately to connecting; thus each of these steps must be accompanied by "consciousness, self-knowledge, freedom . . . with irony" (p. 205). Thus, for Goethe (1988), reason is fundamental to the understanding of development:

> Reason is applied to what is developing, practical understanding to what is developed. The former does not ask, What is the purpose? and the latter does not ask, What is the source? Reason takes pleasure in development; practical understanding tries to hold things fast so that it can use them.
>
> (p. 308)[2]

One upshot of the genetic method is that it not only reveals secrets about the productivity of nature, but also engages new powers of the mind. Truly understanding developmental change is intrinsically related to a change in the observer.

Reception of Goethe's scientific work

Goethe's work must be placed within the context of the invasion of historical consciousness in the natural sciences (Schmidt, 1984) that took place in the 19th century (see Lepenies, 1976; Toulmin & Goodfield, 1965). Goethe tried to capture the dynamic unity of nature in all its manifold expressions and he developed a methodology that he deemed appropriate to the task.

There is a "passionate ambivalence" about the value of Goethe's scientific studies (Jensen, 2010). On one hand, Goethe's work has been considered that of a dilettante meddling in areas he did not understand, fueled by irrational hatred of the work of Newton (Ribe, 1985). His work has also received more favorable assessments. For example, Helmholtz (1896) believed that two of Goethe's main achievements in his scientific work were, (1) to systematize the fragmented phenomena and derive differences in the anatomy of different organisms from a common anatomical body plan [*Bauplan*] or type, and (2) to show a similar analogy between the different parts of one and the same organism (e.g., repetition of individual parts). His work of morphology and metamorphosis was later viewed as preparing the ground for and anticipating Darwin's theory of evolution, with the difference that Goethe's use of analogies and homologies relied on intuition, whereas Darwin used careful and systematic observation and provided a causal mechanism underlying the analogies and homologies. Influenced by Haeckel, Darwin (1861, p. xiv) himself mentions that Geoffroy St. Hilaire had recognized Goethe as a transmutationist. Furthermore, Darwin favorably discussed Goethe's law of compensation, although he thought that it is a manifestation of the more general principle that "natural selection is continually trying to economise in every part of the organisation" (Darwin, 1861, p. 165). The issue of whether Goethe endorsed species evolution is discussed controversially (see Engelhardt, 1984; Richards, in press). At the same time, Goethe's more poetic approach to science, his reliance on appearance and intuition, his rejection of mathematical approaches as well as the search for causal mechanisms behind the phenomena, have been severely criticized (e.g., Helmholtz, 1896).

Goethe certainly influenced a variety of philosophers, from Hegel, to Schelling, to Wittgenstein (see Breidbach, 2006; Blunden, 2010), and his work finds renewed interest among phenomenologically oriented philosophers (Bortoft, 1996, 2012; see Seamon, 1998). He also had an influence on biologists who followed a more organismic perspective (Amrine, 1987; Portmann, 1987; see also Levitt & Meister, 2004). Moreover, his dynamic typology appears to receive attention among contemporary evolutionary-developmental biologists because it is compatible with the idea that ontogenies—rather than adult stages—undergo evolutionary change, and since it provides an explanation of the origin of form (Riegner, 2013).

However, Goethe's writings are rarely cited by psychologists, not even developmental psychologists, with few exceptions. Among the exceptions are Gestalt psychologists who base their use of the term *Gestalt* on Goethe (see Ash, 1995) and use individual ideas from Goethe as inspiration for their writings (e.g., Köhler, 1947). Among contemporary psychologists we know only of Shotter (2005) who draws on Goethe's writings, using Goethe's (1988, p. 307) notion of "delicate empiricism" to explore foundational aspects of human relatedness. Another exception, as mentioned above, is Heinz Werner, to whom we now turn.

From Goethe to Werner: similarities and differences

It is difficult to gauge Goethe's influence on Werner's work. To the best of our knowledge, in all of Werner's writings, there is only one direct reference to Goethe, and it appears in his *Comparative psychology of mental development* (1926/1948), as earlier noted. Nonetheless, there are several similarities between aspects of Werner's and Goethe's writings that go beyond the orthogenetic principle, and some of these similarities, as well as some differences, we will discuss in this section. Before this, however, we would like to address the question of how Werner became aware of Goethe's work on morphology. Let us offer a few (more speculative and not mutually exclusive) possibilities. First, Werner may have been thoroughly familiar with Goethe's scientific work all along and did not refer to Goethe more often because Goethean ideas had become so deeply entrenched in his conceptual framework. This is possible, but it does not explain why Werner makes reference exclusively to Goethe's morphology, leaving aside other aspects of Goethe's work. Second, Goethe's concept of Gestalt was adopted by Gestalt psychology, and Gestalt psychologists such as Köhler (1947) drew on Goethe's ideas. However, it is unlikely that this is the route by which Goethe's work became relevant to Werner because Gestalt psychologists mostly referred to static Gestalten and not the dynamic morphology Goethe had in mind. A third alternative is related to the fact that, while at the University of Hamburg, the philosopher Ernst Cassirer had a great influence on Werner (see Kreppner, 2005). Cassirer (1932/1995, 1945) published widely on Goethe, but these papers were published only after 1926, and so it is unlikely that Cassirer drew Werner's attention to Goethe in the early 1920s. A fourth possibility is that Werner joined the "back to Goethe" movement, which supposedly was very popular among German psychologists and biologists in the 1920s (Harrington, 1996). Again, this possibility does not explain why Werner refers only to Goethe's morphology. Ultimately, the most plausible source for Werner's familiarity with Goethe's morphology is the biologist Victor Franz (see Hoßfeld & Olsson, 2003; Junker & Hoßfeld, 2002). He (Franz, 1920, 1925) discusses a variety of criteria for determining the direction of development, and settles on Goethe's suggestion to use the degree of similarity among parts and their subordination as criterion, citing the same passage from Goethe's writing on Morphology as Werner (1926/1948) does. Werner (1926, p. 37, Note 1) was familiar with Franz's work and refers to his 1920 monograph in the context of distinguishing between the pure concept of development and the concept of perfection. The reference to Franz's work has not been included in the English translation, but it can be found in the original bibliography (Werner, 1926/1948, p. 508).

In addition to the orthogenetic principle, there are further similarities between aspects of Werner's and Goethe's work. First, the concept of development takes in Werner's theory the place of Goethe's concept of development. For Werner (1926/1948, 1957), the concept of developmental psychology signifies a particular methodological approach and not a particular subject matter. Comparative (in Werner, 1926, p. 3: *allgemeine*, i.e., general) developmental psychology has the tasks to compare the results of specialized developmental psychologies (e.g., ontogeny, animal psychology, psychopathology etc.), and to arrive at general developmental laws "applicable to mental life as a whole" (Werner, 1926/1948, p. 5). Similarly, Goethe (1988, p. 57) states that "in morphology we propose to establish a science new not because of its subject matter . . . but because of its intention and method." Morphology is closely related to other sciences (e.g., chemistry, physics, physiology), deals with subject matters that are tackled by the other sciences only in passing, and establishes a new "standpoint from which things of nature may readily be observed" (Goethe, 1988, p. 59).

A second similarity consists in the holistic framework to which both Goethe and Werner subscribed. For Werner (1926/1948, Werner & Kaplan, 1963), holism is expressed in the context-dependency of the part on the whole: the meaning of a part may change, depending on the overall pattern to which it belongs. The whole is also more than the sum of its parts and has qualities and is governed by laws that cannot be derived from nor reduced to the parts. Since the whole determines its parts, the composition of the whole through its parts (creative synthesis) must take a backseat to the analysis of the whole into its parts (creative analysis). Goethe (1988, p. 63) also endorsed holism: he acknowledges that the analysis and dissection of, for example, organisms into their constituent parts contributes to our understanding of nature, but he points out that "from these parts it will be impossible to restore it [the living organism] and bring it back to life." However, Goethe's holism seems to be such that the whole is defined by its elements and their relations. Consequently, he valued both analysis and synthesis: "the sciences come to life only when the two exist side by side like exhaling and inhaling" (Goethe, 1988, p. 49). He warned against the use of only one method and claimed that "every analysis presupposes a synthesis" (Goethe, 1988, p. 49).

A further difference between Werner and Goethe consists in the way in which they anchor the orthogenetic principle. Werner (1926, p. 4; this passage has not been included in the English translation) argued that the principle of development is necessary to understand the manifold of biological forms that is graded by degrees. Werner (1926/1948) tells us that a developmental approach has two goals: (1) the delineation of structures (developmental stages) and (2) the determination of relation between stages, and thus their direction. However, he focused largely on the comparison of phenomena that belong to different disciplines and assigned them to particular stages (e.g., syncretic thought). As a result, stages appear to be rather isolated, and the "time-form" that connects them to make them part of the same movement is not discernible (Werner, 1926/1948). Furthermore, Goethe's goal was to understand the unity that underlies the manifold, and the primary movement for him was self-differencing.

A third difference is that Goethe's orthogenetic principle is part of a theory of nature that emphasizes self-organization. Werner's organismic framework is certainly compatible with a self-organization framework, and he acknowledges (Werner, 1926, p. 17; this passage has not been included in the English translation) that "life is formation [Gestaltung], development is neoformation [Neugestaltung], creative change" (our translation). Yet the idea that there is pulsing, creative unity of nature that ensures the continuity of all forms of life is absent from Werner's writings.

Finally, for Goethe the study of development had important methodological implications and required the use of imagination and the recreation of the creative movement of nature in the mind of the scientist. Ultimately, the study of change required a transformation of the scientist herself. Werner (1957), too, argued that the study of development requires particular methods, but for him these methods largely were limited to specific developmental designs and did not involve a transformation of the scientist.

Conclusion: the future of the orthogenetic principle

In this chapter, we have shown that the passage of Goethe that Werner (1926/1948) identifies as the source of the orthogenetic principle must be viewed within the context of Goethe's thoroughly dynamic view of nature. Within this view of nature, the archetype refers to a self-differencing unity, a time-form that is open to the future. Without archetype, the comparison of different forms is problematic (Brady, 1984). It is therefore likely that Goethe would have been critical of Werner's comparative developmental psychology, as the comparison is not anchored in an archetype.

As we mentioned above, Goethe's dynamic, developmental thinking has not received attention from developmental psychologists; and even Werner's orthogenetic principle is rarely cited in contemporary developmental psychology, thus slowly fading into oblivion. This is likely due to inherent problems of the orthogenetic principle. For example, the nature of the relation between integration and differentiation is underdetermined (Poddiakov, 2006; see already Franz, 1920, 1925). The role that sociocultural processes play in the differentiation and integration of children's actions, emotions, and cognition has likewise not been sufficiently clarified (but see Raeff, 2011). However, a main reason for the loss of interest in the orthogenetic principle appears to us to be due to a lack of interest in developmental sequences, which may be symptomatic of the disappearance of genuine developmental thought itself. Today, developmental phenomena are studied in isolation and often a causal (or computation–functional) explanation is provided for these phenomena without regard to the developmental sequence of which they are part (Müller & Overton, 1998). Hence, the rejuvenation of the orthogenetic principle certainly requires that its relation to sociocultural processes is clarified and the measurement of steps along the sequence is refined (Adolph, Robinson, Young, & Gill-Alvarez, 2008; Raeff, 2011). However, following Goethe, it is more important to identify the overall movement that provides the context for each individual Gestalt.

Notes

1 Unbeknownst to Goethe, the intermaxillary bone had already been described before, by the French physician Félix Vicq d'Azyr in 1780.
2 Notice in this context also that Kant (1790/2007, §80) considered but discarded the possibility of species evolution, stating that "[a]n hypothesis of this kind may be called a daring venture on the part of reason; and there are probably few, even among the most acute scientists, to whose minds it has not sometimes occurred." Goethe, by contrast, stated that "nothing prevented me from resolutely embarking on this venture of reason" (Goethe, 1962, p. 879).

References

Adolph, K. E., Robinson, S. R., Young, J. W., & Gill-Alvarez, F (2008). What is the shape of developmental change? *Psychological Review, 115, 527–543.*

Amrine, F. (1987). Goethean method in the work of Jochen Bockemühl. In F. Amrine, F. J. Zucker, & H. Wheeler (Eds.), *Goethe and the sciences: A reappraisal* (pp. 301–318). Dordrecht, Netherlands: Reidel.

Amrine, F. (1990). The metamorphosis of the scientist. *Goethe Yearbook, 5,* 187–212.

Ash, M. G. (1995). *Gestalt psychology in German culture, 1890–1967.* New York, NY: Cambridge University Press.

Bertalanffy, L. von (1951). Goethe's concept of nature. *Main Currents in Modern Thought, 8,* 78–83.

Bertalanffy, L. von (1952). *Problems of life.* New York, NY: Wiley. (Original work published 1949)

Bortoft, H. (1996). *The wholeness of nature: Goethe's way of science.* Edinburgh, Scotland: Floris Books.

Bortoft, H. (2012). *Taking appearance seriously: The dynamic way of seeing in Goethe and European thought.* Edinburgh, Scotland: Floris Books.

Blunden, A. (2010). *How Hegel put Goethe's Urphänomen to philosophical use.* Retrieved April 21, 2015 from http://home.mira.net/~andy/works/philosophical-use.htm

Brady, R. H. (1984). The causal dimension of Goethe's morphology. *Journal of Social and Biological Structures, 7,* 325–344.

Breidbach, O. (2006). *Goethes Metamorphosenlehre* [Goethe's doctrine of metamorphosis]. Paderborn, Germany: Wilhelm Fink Verlag.

Callaghan, T. & Corbit, J. (2015). The development of symbolic representation. In L. S. Liben & U. Müller (Vol. Eds.), R. M. Lerner (Series Ed.), *Handbook of child psychology and developmental science, Vol. 2: Cognitive processes* (7th ed., pp. 250–295). Hoboken, NJ: Wiley.

Cassirer, E. (1945). *Rousseau, Kant, and Goethe.* Princeton, NJ: Princeton University Press.

Cassirer, E. (1955). *The philosophy of symbolic forms* (Vol. 1). New Haven, CT: Yale University Press. (Original work published 1923)

Cassirer, E. (1961). *The logic of the humanities.* New Haven, CT: Yale University Press.

Cassirer, E. (1995). *Goethe und die geschichtliche Welt* [Goethe and the historical world]. Hamburg, Germany: Felix Meiner Verlag. (Original work published 1932)

Crain, W. (2011). *Theories of development: Concepts and applications* (7th ed.). Upper Saddle River, NJ: Pearson.

Darwin, C. (1861). *On the origin of species by means of natural selection, or the preservation of favoured races in the struggle for life* (3rd ed.). London, UK: John Murray.

Engelhardt, D. von (1984). Schellings philosophische Grundlegung der Medizin [Schelling's philosophical grounding of medicine]. In H.-J. Sandkühler (Ed.), *Natur und geschichtlicher Prozess: Studien zur Naturphilosophie F. W. J. Schellings* (pp. 305–325). Frankfurt, Germany: Suhrkamp Verlag.

Franz, V. (1920). *Die Vervollkommnung in der lebenden Natur* [Perfection in living nature]. Jena, Germany: Gustav Fischer Verlag.

Franz, V. (1925). Zur Kennzeichnung der allgemeinen Entwicklungsrichtungen des Organismenreiches [On the characterization of general developmental direction for organisms]. *Zeitschrift für induktive Abstammungs- und Vererbungslehre, 36,* 33–58.

Glick, J. A. (1992). Werner's relevance for contemporary developmental psychology. *Developmental Psychology, 28*, 558–565.

Goethe, J. W. von (1959). *Goethe, Sämtliche Werke 3.2: Italien und Weimar 1786–1790* (Münchner Ausgabe) [Goethe, Collected works, 3.2: Italy and Weimar 1786–1790, Munich edition]. Gütersloh, Germany: Bertelsmann.

Goethe, J. W. von (1962). *Goethes Briefe: Hamburger Ausgabe* [Goethe's letters: Hamburg edition] (Vol. 1). Hamburg, Germany: Christian Wegner.

Goethe, J. W. von (1966a). *Gedenkausgabe der Werke, Briefe, und Gespräche, Vol. 16: Schriften zur Farbenlehre* (2nd ed.) [Memorial edition of the work, letters and conversations, Vol. 16: Writings on color theory]. Zürich, Switzerland: Artemis.

Goethe, J. W. von (1966b). *Gedenkausgabe der Werke, Briefe, und Gespräche, Vol. 17: Naturwissenschaftliche Schriften, Zweiter Teil* (2nd ed.) [Memorial edition of the work, letters, and conversations, Vol. 17: Writings on natural science, part 2]. Zürich, Switzerland: Artemis.

Goethe, J. W. von (1968). *The Italian journey (1786–1788)*. New York, NY: Schocken Books.

Goethe, J. W. von (1988). *Goethe: Scientific studies* (Ed. and Trans. D. Miller). New York, NY: Suhrkamp.

Goethe, J. W. von (2009). *The metamorphosis of plants*. Cambridge, MA: MIT Press. (Original work published 1790)

Harrington, A. (1996). *Reenchanted science: Holism in German culture: From Wilhelm II to Hitler*. Princeton, NJ: Princeton University Press.

Helmholtz, H. von (1896). *Vorträge und Reden* (4th ed.) [Lectures and speeches]. Braunschweig, Germany: Vieweg.

Hoßfeld, U., & Olsson, L. (2003). The road from Haeckel: The Jena tradition in evolutionary morphology and the origins of "Evo-Devo". *Biology and Philosophy, 18*, 285–307.

Jensen, K. (2010). *Johann Wolfgang von Goethe (1749–1832)*. Retrieved April 21, 2015 from http://www.iep.utm.edu/goethe/

Junker, T. & Hoßfeld, U. (2002). The architects of the evolutionary synthesis in national socialist Germany: Science and politics. *Biology and Philosophy*, 17, 223–249.

Kant, I. (2007). *Critique of judgement* (translated by James Creed Meredith). Oxford, UK: Oxford University Press. (Original work published 1790)

Köhler, W. (1947). *Gestalt psychology*. New York, NY: Liveright.

Kreppner, K. (2005). Heinz Werner and the Psychological Institute in Hamburg. In J. Valsiner (Ed.), *Heinz Werner and developmental science* (pp. 55–74). New York, NY: Kluwer Academic/Plenum Publishers.

Kuhn, D. (1988). *Typus und Metamorphose* [Type and metamorphosis]. Marbach, Germany: Deutsche Schillergesellschaft.

Langer, J. (1970). Werner's comparative organismic theory. In W. Kessen (Ed.), *Handbook of child psychology, Vol. 1. History, theory, and methods* (pp. 733–771). New York, NY: Wiley.

Lenoir, T. (1982). *The strategy of life: Teleology and mechanics in nineteenth century German biology*. Dordrecht, Netherlands: Reidel.

Lepenies, W. (1976). *Das Ende der Naturgeschichte: Wandel kultureller Selbstverständlichkeiten in den Wissenschaften des 18. und 19. Jahrhunderts* [The end of natural history: The change in the cultural self-understanding of sciences in the 18th and 19th centuries]. München, Germany: Hanser Verlag.

Levitt, G. S., & Meister, K. (2004). Goethes langer Atem: Methodologische Ideologien in der Deutschen Morphologie des 20. Jahrhunderts [Goethe's staying power: Methodological ideologies in German morphology in the 20th century]. In M. Kaasch, J. Kaasch, & V. Wissemann (Eds.), Beiträge zur 13. Jahrestagung der DGGTB in Neuburg an der Donau. *Verhandlungen zur Geschichte und Theorie der Biologie*, Vol. 12, 209–232.

MacWhinney, B. (2015). Language development. In L. S. Liben & U. Müller (Vol. Eds.), R. M. Lerner (Series Ed.), *Handbook of child psychology and developmental science, Vol. 2: Cognitive processes* (7th ed., pp. 296–336). Hoboken, NJ: Wiley.

Mocek, R. (1998). *Die werdende Form: Eine Geschichte der kausalen Morphologie* [The developing form: A history of causal morphology]. Marburg, Germany: Basilisken-Presse.

Müller, U., & Overton, W. F. (1998). How to grow a baby: A reevaluation of image-schema and Piagetian action approaches to representation. *Human Development, 41*, 71–111.

Poddiakov, A. (2006). Review essay: Comparative psychology and development of comparisons. *Culture & Psychology, 12*, 352–377.

Portmann, A. (1987). Goethe and the concept of metamorphosis. In F. Amrine, F. J. Zucker, & H. Wheeler (Eds.), *Goethe and the sciences: A reappraisal* (pp. 133–145). Dordrecht, Netherlands: Reidel.

Pratt, V., & Brook, I. (1996). Goethe's archetype and the Romantic concept of the self. *Studies in History and Philosophy of Science, 27*, 351–365.

Raeff, C. (2011). Distinguishing between development and change: reviving organismic–developmental theory. *Human Development, 54*, 4–33.

Ribe, N. M. (1985). Goethe's critique of Newton: A reconsideration. *Studies in History and Philosophy of Science, 16*, 315–335.

Richards, R. J. (in press). Did Goethe and Schelling endorse species evolution? In J. Lambier & J. Faflak (Eds.), *Marking time: Romanticism and evolution.* Toronto, Canada: University of Toronto Press.

Riegner, M. F. (2013). Ancestor of the new archetypal biology: Goethe's dynamic typology as a model for contemporary evolutionary developmental biology. *Studies in the History of Biological Sciences, 44*, 735–744.

Schmidt, A. (1984). *Goethes herrlich leuchtende Natur* [Goethe's magnificently vibrant nature]. München, Germany: Carl Hanser Verlag.

Seamon, D. (1998). Goethe, nature, and phenomenology. In D. Seamon & A. Zajonc (Eds.), *Goethe's way of science: A phenomenology of nature* (pp. 1–14). Albany, NY: State University of New York Press.

Shotter, J. (2005). Goethe and the refiguring of intellectual inquiry: From "aboutness"-thinking to "withness"-thinking in everyday life. *Janus Head, 8*, 132–158.

Simmel, G. (1912). Die Stetigkeit in Goethes Weltbild [Continuity in Goethe's world picture]. *Der Tag, Moderne Illustrierte Zeitung, Vol. 515, Illustrierter Teil Nr. 237*, October 9, 1–3. Retrieved April 21, 2015 from: http://socio.ch/sim/verschiedenes/1912/goethe_weltbild.htm

Tantillo, A. (2002). *The will to create: Goethe's philosophy of nature.* Pittsburgh, PA: University of Pittsburgh Press.

Toulmin, S. & Goodfield, J. (1965). *The discovery of time.* London, UK: Hutchinson.

Wapner, S. & Werner, H. (1957). *Perceptual development: An investigation within the framework of sensory-tonic field theory.* Worcester, MA: Clark University Press.

Wellmon, C. (2010). Goethe's morphology of knowledge, or the overgrowth of nomenclature. *Goethe Yearbook, 17*, 153–177.

Werner, H. (1926). *Einführung in die Entwicklungspsychologie* [Introduction to developmental psychology]. Leipzig, Germany: Barth.

Werner, H. (1948). *Comparative psychology of mental development* (2nd ed.). Chicago, IL: Follett Publishing. (Original work published 1926)

Werner, H. (1957). The concept of development from a comparative and organismic point of view. In D. B. Harris (Ed.), *The concept of development: An issue in the study of human behavior* (pp. 125–148). Minneapolis, MN: University of Minnesota Press.

Werner, H. & Kaplan, B. (1963). *Symbol formation: An organismic–developmental approach to language and the expression of thought.* New York, NY: Wiley.

Werner, H. & Wapner, S. (1952). Toward a general theory of perception. *Psychological Review, 59*, 324–338.

Chapter 2

Making sense of self-completing wholes

Epistemological travels of Hans Driesch

Jaan Valsiner

> The logic of vitalism is a branch of the logic of *wholeness*. The logic of *wholeness*, however, is the beginning and the end of all logic—at least if it is understood that *logic* is essentially the *theory of order*.
>
> (Driesch, 1914b, p. 41)

Biological order is *developmental* order. As such it is different from the order implied by the static assumptions of classical logic. To claim that "if A then not non-A" would not fit developmental phenomena, where in every state A the potential for the next qualitative transformation (non-A) is open for emergence. While classical logic enforces a binary distinction by the "law of excluded middle"—A or non-A, nothing "in between"—, development happens always "in-between" of A (as already emerged) and some not yet emerged (non-A). Development entails movement towards horizons—creating novelty during that movement.[1]

In this vein, development is a puzzling phenomenon: it happens over irreversible time, its current forms are unfinished, and it is open-ended as to what may happen in the future. Yet that open-endedness has limits. Given the previous state of the developing organism, only some innovations are possible—but not all of them are sustainable, and many are not desired. It is here where all developmental sciences—embryology, epigenetics and psychology—converge and create new theoretical challenges.

However, even as phenomena of development defy our traditional, classical logic, its regularities keep up our suspicion that it is operating by a certain logic of its own. Still our contemporary science has failed to formalize such logic, despite substantial efforts in this exact direction (Baldwin, 1906, 1908, 1911, 1915). To construct any theory about the order of complex developing systems is a complicated intellectual task that requires breaking an existing order in the process of development of a new one. Thus, the notion of order is in itself in seeming contradiction with the notion of development. In other terms, the epistemological puzzle is to understand the order in the apparent disorder of development. This task remains unsolved up to our times; yet quite a few scholars in the past understood the challenge, and attempted to provide solutions.

Hans Driesch (1867–1941) was one of the most notable—yet forgotten—scholars who attempted the latter. He was a traveler, both in the sense of visiting very many different countries over his lifetime (Driesch, 1951), as well as transcending borders of ideas and disciplines. Having first established himself as an excellent experimental embryologist, whose work on regenerative embryogenesis in the 1890s became classic in its role as *experimentum crucis*, he turned into a philosopher of life sciences in the early 1900s. Currently he is considered the originator of theoretical biology (Meyer-Abich, 1947) along with Jakob von Uexküll (1902, 1909, 1913, 1926, 1928; also Kull, 2001 for an overview). Driesch and von Uexküll shared the understanding that biology needs to go beyond the immediate observable phenomena and see generalities behind the abundance of natural forms. Both were skeptical of the avalanche of Anglo-Saxon fascination with the notion of fight-for-survival as an explanatory principle in biology—borrowed from Malthus's population theory and fortified by Darwinian evolutionary theory. As a result, Driesch and von Uexküll remained relatively unknown—or fashionably forgotten—in the theory-phobic biological and social sciences of the 20th century. Yet biology then—as well as now—is in great need of a general theory of living systems. As our recent advances in genomic sciences show, the empirical work has outpaced theoretical advances and so it has become a blind search for simple solutions—where there can only be complex ones.

The fight for the autonomy of biology as science

Driesch saw the relevance of biology as an independent science in its own theoretical realm (Driesch, 1893) in which the specificity of living beings is not reducible to mechanical physiological processes. That claim—and its labeling as *vitalism* at the time—was far from popular among physics-fascinated fellow biologists during his time. It became clear over the 19th century that the living matter had characteristics not reducible to their non-living constituents (Toepfer, 2005a, 2005b). Yet the principles of organization of the living matter were not clear. What was clear was that biological phenomena could not be reduced to non-biological ones. This paralleled previous disputes between chemistry and physics regarding the qualitative uniqueness and non-reducibility of chemistry to physics, and within chemistry itself on the non-reducibility of organic to inorganic chemistry. In psychology we face a similar fight for the *psyche* in resisting the temptations to reduce it to physiological or neuroanatomical substrates, or defining the psychological phenomena away through reducing them to sociological processes where living human beings are barely the robot-like carriers of social voices, class consciousness, or combiners of available social representations.

Biologists' controversy about vitalism is thus an epistemological parallel to psychologists' disputes about the *psyche*—or the soul. The perspective of vitalism was oriented on the proof of the special organizational status of biological organism and its non-reducibility to physiological and physical material bases. As such, the movement of vitalism was an effort to negotiate a place for a teleological perspective on biological systems—in contrast to non-organized aggregates—within the natural sciences. This negotiation continued over the 20th century and was based on two crucial theoretical decisions, namely existence of levels of organization, and processes of emergence (Emmeche, Køppe & Stjernfeldt, 1997). Both ideas were obvious for biology—any multicellular organism can survive as a biological structure (involving levels of organization) and requires reproduction (emergence). These features have been downplayed in a psychology that has habitually reduced multi-level hierarchical systems into one level—be that called "behavioral", "cognitive" or "ecological". Efforts to elaborate multi-level systems have been rare (Gottlieb, 1999; Laubichler, 2005) even though the emergence of new qualitative levels of organization is the central issue in development.

The central issue of becoming

Development is frequently a topic of discussions, but rarely specific to the actual processes that are referenced. Partly this has been due to how slow and complex actual processes are in the case of human beings. With an extended, seemingly stable adult age, *Homo sapiens* is not the most fitting species to ask questions about *becoming* something. Development, however, is precisely about becoming, not about being. In this sense, viruses, sea urchins, nematodes (*C. elegans*), may fit better as appropriate empirical models for science looking after principles of development. All embryology started from the study of hen embryos discovered by Karl Ernst von Baer.

All developmental perspectives are thus necessarily *para-ontological*—they need to conceptualize the "being of the becoming", as in the "being" of the moment it is not yet clear what might be "becoming" out of the "being". In terms of James Mark Baldwin, developmental processes operate with non-convertible propositions. These are propositions that cannot be reversed, like "John is the son of Henry", which is of the structure "X is Y". Although the latter can be reversed into "Y is X", the resultant proposition does not fit "Henry is the father of John". Hence, Baldwin posited a general law for development, involving a number of postulates. The first (or "negative") postulate emphasized the irreversibility of time in development:

> *the logic of genesis is not expressed in convertible propositions.* Genetically, A = (that is, *becomes*, for which the sign "((" is now used) B; but it does not follow that B = (becomes, (( ) A.
>
> (Baldwin, 1906, p. 21)

This first postulate specifies the realm of possible relations that are allowable among the formulae of "genetic logic"; namely, each proposition includes a temporal directionality vector. The second (so-called "positive") postulate was given as:

> that series of events is truly genetic which cannot be constructed before it has happened, and which cannot be exhausted backwards, after it has happened.
>
> (Baldwin, 1906, p. 21)

The "positive" nature of this postulate is in its focusing of the study of development on that of the actual process of emergence. Doing that would force the acceptance of irreversible time as the core for any methodological build-up. For example, the creation of categories—"coding schemes"—would need to include the direction of extension of the "code".

The era for embryology: the 1890s

The 1890s were rich in ideas. It is precisely around that decade that the focus on irreversibility of time was brought into European philosophy and sciences. It came from two historical roots: physics (see the discussions about the Second Law of Thermodynamics), and the philosophy of Henri Bergson. Of course the disputes around reversibility versus irreversibility centered on the contrast between living and non-living phenomena: it is almost trivial to point out that a child is destined to grow up and become an adult, but the reverse growth—from adult into child—is not possible. This contrast does not apply to mechanical events—a chemist can distill salt out of seawater and put the salt back into the same water container, thus restoring the seawater to its initial state.

Yet even in the case of physical events history matters. The proverbial apple that is supposed to have fallen onto Newton's head is not expected to be able to restore its original place on the apple tree, unless some divine force rather than the law of gravity—in the reverse—is presumed. It has irreversibly changed its place—and nature—by the happening of its falling. The falling apple is a transformation of a biological object (interdependent with the tree on which it grows) to a mechanical object (an example of a falling body). For Newton this transformation is irrelevant: he extracts the apple from its falling context and treats it as one of the many in the homogeneous class of "fallen objects". In fact, abstracting from the irreversible time made it possible to arrive at the general law. Yet the other general law—that of irreversible transformations in nature—remained hidden behind the mechanical generalization. The disputes about reversibility versus irreversibility of time in the *abstract* notion of order that characterized the 1890s led into the efforts to make sense of developmental processes (genetic logic of J. M. Baldwin), the role of energy in the physical world (Ostwald), and the unique growth properties of biological systems.

Biology was on its way to becoming a science in its own right, to end up replacing physics as the center of public focus of interest, and Hans Driesch (1893) certainly played an important role in this process. Ironically, his insistence on the special quality of living systems—the relative autonomy of the whole—became dismissed along with other "vitalist" concepts (Ungerer, 1927). Considering some thinker a vitalist added an aura of mysticism to the thinker's way of developing ideas that would immediately disqualify the stigmatized thinker from "serious" natural science. As shown by the fate of vitalist thinking, stigmatization is an "effective" social method to block the consideration of an idea through declaring it to be beyond the border of social acceptability—belonging to the obscure domain of "the Other".

How could the idea of vitalism develop?

Hans Driesch entered the field of biological research at an interesting time. In the 1880s until the 1900s the gene theory of heredity had not yet been rediscovered—the name of Gregor Mendel was still hidden in a garden of a monastery. Darwinian ideas were in vogue. Embryologists enjoyed the focus of attention as being on the forefront of science. The focus was that of inductive natural science:

> It was a time when certain techniques developed in plant physiology and cytology converged into embryology to broach questions about the activities of the cleaving egg—questions, more specifically, about the role of the nucleus in heredity and development, about the formative influences exerted by some cells upon other cells or by external stimuli, and about the regenerative capacities of experimentally altered embryos. Amphibians and echinoderms were the chief martyrs in these quests, but roundworms, gastropods, even protozoa, served embryology too. There were almost as many explanations of development and heredity as experimental animals, and often the choice of the latter determined the tenets of the former.
>
> (Churchill, 1969, p. 165)

The meta-theoretical context in this fervor of activities was the opposition between materialistic *Naturwissenschaft* on the one hand, and the holistic traditions of *Naturphilosophie* on the other. The former borrowed its models from mechanics, like Wilhelm Roux's notion of "developmental mechanics" (*Entwicklungsmechanik*), introduced to embryology in 1885 (Hamburger, 1997; Roux, 1885, 1923), or August Weismann's "germ theory" in 1892. Furthermore, Ernst Haeckel's propagation of Darwinian ideas in the German context prioritized the notion of natural selection—together with Haeckel's own Biogenetic Law.

In this environment it is interesting to look at the academic life course of Hans Driesch moving in the opposite direction. Starting his academic work with Ernst Haeckel, he moved on to conduct experimental work along the *Entwicklungsmechanik* lines of Wilhelm Roux; only to develop a general theory that would counter Darwinian selection ideas and advance a notion of holistic future-oriented developmental science. It is an indicator of the ideological conflicts in science that Driesch's *Entelechie* notion became almost immediately stigmatized as a version of vitalism. Vitalism was then—and now—a word indicating some mystical component of living organisms: a whole that cannot be reduced to its components. The issue of qualitative differences between objects of investigation has remained a major divider in the history of different sciences.[2] Yet there is nothing mystical about the relative autonomy of complex biological systems operating within their teleogenetic[3] predicament, i.e. anticipating their immediate futures in an effort of pre-adaptation to constantly unpredictable environments.

To the present date, Driesch remains in the history of embryology for his regeneration experiments of the 1890s; his later move to become a philosopher has been mostly ignored or—as seen—stigmatized in biology. Nonetheless, his move into philosophy gave him the arena for generalization of basic ideas that were exemplified in his experiments.

The Naples' Zoological Station: growth environment of groundbreaking research

Driesch's life history, starting from zoology studies in Jena, to then becoming a key figure in experimental embryology in the 1890s, and ending up as a philosopher of issues of life in Heidelberg, includes a critical phase of his work in Naples in the Zoological Station established by Anton Dohrn (Müller, 1996). Aside from being Europe's leading research facility on embryology at the time, it was also a germinal environment for development of ideas, where opposite perspectives could thrive in the same social space. Wilhelm Roux's developmental mechanics (*Entwicklungsmechanik*) and Hans Driesch's opposite emerging vitalist focus—that denied the mechanical explanation of embryogenesis—could find their way within the "permanent congress of zoologists" (Müller, 1996, p. 110) that the Naples station turned out to be.

Driesch travelled over a decade, every winter and spring, to Naples to perform various experiments, all of which took the form of what could be better called *pre-generational longitudinal studies*. At an early—blastula—stage of the cell division process the experimenter introduces an intervention into the growth process, usually cutting the growing organism into a half. After that, the organism grows into some final form, which could be anything from failing to grow at all to arrival at the adult form, or even into some abnormal new form. The species-typical pattern of growth is known to the researcher, but for the particular embryo that has been experimentally manipulated there is no explicit "knowledge" on how to grow under the altered circumstances. Roux had demonstrated on frog embryos that cutting the blastula in half would result in the growth of a half-embryo that misses the cutout counterpart.

Marine biologists moved around Europe in their search for good experimental conditions. Driesch—after a stay in Plymouth—began his studies of sea urchin embryos during his field trips to Lesina in the late summer of 1890 and Trieste biological station (in 1891), followed by recurrent stays in the Naples Zoological Station on 1891, 1892 and 1894/95 (Mocek, 1998b, pp. 282–294). While attempting to replicate Roux's experiments on sea urchin embryos at gastrula stage, he failed to do so; the sea urchin embryos regenerated the missing part and developed into full final form, albeit smaller in size (Figure 2.1). Both halves of the embryo somehow "knew" how to grow into the normal bodily form. Importantly, cuts that preserved both endoderm and ectoderm in the same whole grew up to complete final form (figures 2.1 and 2.2), while larger cuts of gastrula stage, i.e. not preserving the parts of the whole, could lead to abnormal larvae. Hence there are limits on the regenerational capacities of the embryo; yet, under many conditions, damage into the cellular structure allows for regenerating the whole.

Experimental breakthroughs came in the winter of 1894/95 in Naples[4]—less than a year after Driesch had published a book trying to find new alternatives to the mechanistic ideas of Wilhelm Roux to explain previous experimental results

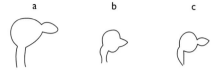

Figure 2.1 Normal growth of *Sphaerechinus granularis* (a) in comparison with relative size of embryos who were cut in half in their gastrula stage (b and c) (adapted from Driesch, 1899, p. 39)

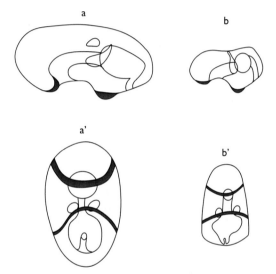

Figure 2.2 Driesch's drawings of *Asterias glacialis* (left side, normal growth; right side, cut into halves at gastrula stage) (adapted from Driesch, 1899, p. 49)

(Driesch, 1894). The theoretical innovation that grew out of it—focus on *equipotentiality* and *equifinality*, together with the notion of *regulations*—became formed between 1894 and 1899 (Driesch, 1899, 1901).

The idea of harmonious–equipotential systems

As a general principle, Driesch placed harmony over conflict. In summarizing his experimental work—already looking back at it with a philosopher's eye—he would emphasize the harmony regenerated in the whole:

> of whatever material you deprive these organs or animals, the remainder, unless it is very small, will always develop in the normal manner, though, so to speak, in miniature. That is to say: there will develop out of the part of the

embryonic organ the animal left by the operation, as might be expected, not a part of the organization but the whole, only of a smaller scale.

(Driesch, 1914a, p. 208)

How would a developing homogeneous cell structure {O-O} "know" that if either the left {Ø-O} or the right side {O-Ø} of the structure is damaged, the remainder would still differentiate into a multicellular organism of the expected form? Each cell needs to carry equal potency to develop into the expected final form, even if of different size. What is at stake here is the Parts<>Whole relationship, where emerging parts—cells in multicellular conglomerates—are given *before* the whole comes into existence. Thus, the harmonious systems for organs:

are "equipotential" because all elements (cells) quite evidently must possess same morphogenetic "potency," otherwise the experimental result would be impossible; and their components work "harmoniously" together in each single experimental case.

(Driesch, 1914a, p. 209)

Driesch's experiments with embryonic development—unfolding of structures in time under experimental conditions—indicated the move from homogeneous possibilities to heterogeneous distribution of realities. This led him to posit—in analogy with Aristotle—an *entelechy*. This is a non-mechanical agent of nature that—instead of mechanical causality—grants the functioning of the harmonious–equipotential systems. It is the movement towards the construction of a whole (holistic causality) that is operating into the future of the developing embryo. Otherwise, the question of how can a growing individual organism "know" that it has reached a version of the final form of the multicellular structure that has been "known" in the phylogeny of the species, but that is a completely new formation for *this particular* growing organism, remains unanswered.

Equipotentiality and equifinality

Driesch introduced the notion of equifinality into the biological sciences. Equifinality entails the arrival in the same end (or intermediate) developmental state through various pathways. Importantly, the notion was brought into his theory in the context of *regulations* (*Äquifinale regulationen*; Driesch, 1905, p. 213). Based on the starting point characterized by potentiality for the future, it is the hypothetical regulators that—via different trajectories—would bring the organism to its expected (equi)final form.

It is easy to see (Figure 2.3) how the notions of prospective potency (*prospective Potenz*) and equifinality are coordinated across the different time-based issues involved. If our conceptual focus is the present state and its future pathways, the terminology of prospective potentiality allows us a look at potentially branching out trajectories that are about to move towards the future. If, however, our focus

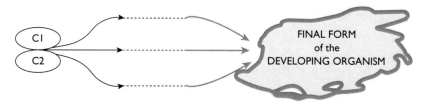

EQUIPOTENTIALITY PHASE:
The BEGINNING FORM
of the minimal DEVELOPING
ORGANISM (first differentiating
System of 2 cells) WITH
PROSPECTIVE POTENCY to move in
multiple pathways

EQUIFINALITY PHASE:
The FINAL FORM
of the DEVELOPING
ORGANISM individually varied
pathways

Figure 2.3 The corresponding notions of *equipotentiality* and *equifinality*

is on the arrival point—in the future, or in the present—it is equifinality notion that fits our discourse.

However, equifinal regulators can themselves be regulated by second-order regulators. The latter can support or override the equifinal regulation that would bring the developmental process to the expected final form. Thus, both the equi-potentiality and equifinality—and multifinality—are the results of regulatory processes.[5] Hence development of new forms becomes possible—albeit on the basis of the previously existing general forms, and in specific time periods of development (*Regulationsmoment*—Driesch, 1901, p.127). While the first-order regulations guarantee regeneration of the expected-but-blocked final form, the second-order regulators can lead to innovation in that form. Driesch solved the theoretical problem of continuity in development by positing the notion of regulator hierarchy (1901). This hierarchy guarantees innovation that is based on the in turn guaranteed production of the regular forms. Therefore, innovation takes place near the domain of continuity with the past.

The critically relevant idea stemming from Driesch's efforts towards understanding of the processes of nature is the focus on the primacy of *regulation* over that of causation. Development is regulated, not caused by its biological substrate. This is an inevitable situation in case of relative autonomy of living organisms, which is characterized by *dynamic* teleology (Driesch, 1901).

From experimental embryology to philosophy: looking for general meaning

By his own confession (Driesch, 1923, 1951) Driesch had always—from his gymnasium studies—been interested in general philosophical issues of biology. It is thus not surprising that he took the opportunity to re-qualify himself as a philosopher. At the beginning of the 20th century, the circumstances turned out to facilitate this.

The invitation to give the Gifford Lectures at University of Aberdeen in 1907 paved the way. These lectures were written by Driesch first in English as *The science and philosophy of the organism* (Driesch, 1908), and later translated (by himself) into German (Driesch, 1909), which involved a symptomatic title change. The German version, *Philosophie des Organischen*, gets rid of the distinction between "science" and "philosophy" and addresses the questions of the living, organic phenomena as a whole rather than organisms only.[6] The move to philosophy took place during his stay at the University of Heidelberg—specifically at the Third International Congress of Philosophy, held at Heidelberg in 1908. After habilitation, he first moved as a *Privatdozent* at the natural sciences and mathematics faculty (Driesch, 1951, pp. 147–148), and from 1912 he took an extraordinary professor position at the faculty of philosophy. Driesch stayed in Heidelberg through the years of World War I, becoming known for his anti-war stand at the university. He moved to the University of Cologne in 1920 for a brief period, prior to taking over the philosophy chair at the University of Leipzig in 1923, where he stayed for the rest of his university career; this ended in enforced retirement in 1933, on the Nazi takeover of most of the universities in Germany.

Logic: a tool for, and an obstacle to, developmental thinking

Driesch's move into philosophy was a result of seeking explanations to his counterintuitive findings of the regeneration experiments. Any philosopher of his time[7] needed to take a position in relation to logic; which, at that time, had not yet differentiated beyond the classical Aristotelian/Boolean. Driesch's perspective on logic was symptomatic for the search efforts of his time, and it certainly antedates his later turn into psychology:

> Pure logic, as the general theory of *order*, deals with everything that is in the most general sense of being. Being here means nothing but *being had by myself consciously* in the form of a *this*. We shall apply the word object— (Meinong's "Gegenstand")—in this most general sense. Everything then that may be "consciously had" is object—a sensation or a feeling or a reproduction of a sensation or a thought of whatever kind: and the totality of objects in this sense is to be *ordered*.
>
> (Driesch, 1914a, p. 189)

Driesch here models the processes of ordering in nature through the process of psychological ordering—through *Gegenstand* creation—applied by the human mind.

Differently from Meinong's ontological perspective (where time played no role beyond an analogy to space), Driesch (similarly to Henri Bergson) introduced the irreversibility of time:

> I possess or *have* all these *objects* which are *this* and *such* and *related* as *so many*, etc. I *have* them consciously. And I have them always in a now, in a certain moment. But in a certain moment I may also have consciously

a something that bears an indication or sign on itself that denotes the not *being*, but *having been*, or, in relation to the Ego, *having been possessed consciously*. This sort of sign or indication—quite irreducible in its immediateness—I shall call the sign of *time*. But this is only a word; for the sign is not what we are all accustomed to call time, but only a certain irreducible content of consciousness relating to the concept of time.

(Driesch, 1914b, p. 43)

Reconstructive memory—or "sign of time"—links the ongoing "present in now" objects into its history. It creates the unity of enduring and becoming. This unity is irrelevant in an ontological perspective (where something either is, or is not), but becomes central in the developmental perspective. Being in the latter becomes enduring (over time), thus presuming that what is once came into existence, and is likely to disappear from existence at some time moment. In between these time points it "is"—that is, "endures" its own being.

Being is enduring

The perspective posed by Driesch leads to re-thinking the very notion of identity (A is A), which has been one of the axioms of classical logics. This notion—taken into the context of irreversible time—becomes "A endures as A" (from time T_n to time T_{n+1}). However, how does the enduring process proceed? For Driesch that process involves a constant becoming—becoming into itself: "*It*, i.e. objectivity, is stable or enduring as *the same It* with regard to certain of its characteristics and yet changes or *becomes* with regard to certain others" (Driesch, 1914a, pp. 43–44). Driesch captures the reality of biological organisms[8] with precision—their continuous survival (enduring) depends on their creativity for changing. To stay the same is equal to striving towards being non-same, yet maintaining the existing frame of endurance. This is the basic application of the notion of *Gegenstand*: direction towards a border to change it, yet keeping the border.

Implication in the past tense

Aside from the notion of identity, the logical link of implication goes as follows: *if X then Y* (X → Y). In classical logic implication is time free, while in Driesch's developmental logic it acquires the link from past to present: *if X then Y* becomes transformed into *if Y, then X was*. This perspective is close to Charles Sanders Peirce's notion of abduction, which involves a similar move from outcome to its trigger—if a surprising fact Y happens, it would be due of course if it were preceded by X. However, the latter (*If Y, then X was*) does not allow for the move to present-to-future (*If X now, then Y will be*). Such transposition could be possible if and only if the past and the future were symmetric. Predictability of the future on the basis of the past would then be possible. Yet it is not. Predictability is only possible in generic—phenotypic—terms. In Driesch's regeneration experiments the disturbed embryos developed into qualitatively recognized phenotypic final form, albeit different in size. None of the regenerating organisms could "know" that they are developing into a phylogenetically recognizable final state. The researcher—knowing the phylogenetic form—could make that decision.

How is identity determinable at all? In Driesch's scheme of enduring, identity becomes turned into detection of similarity across time. Identity has been: "thrown outwards; enduring is identity, but it means something that is always the same in time, not merely as a concept: it is identity petrified" (Driesch, 1914b, p. 192). The notion of being "thrown outwards" entails that of irreversible time—I presume that my identity (as I "have" it from the moment past to the present) can be projected into the future (I "will have" it then in the same form as now). Yet I develop into the future, so the "outwards thrown" petrified identity (assumption of sameness) operates as a constraint upon my own development into a future moment. Therefore, identity as such has no ontological status, as it does not exist as something "I have". It is, however, an organizing tool for development into the future, a delimiter of the organism against unbounded emergence of novelty. Identity is the border, within *Gegenstand*, against which the processes of creative transformation of the self acts As such, it needs to be "thrown outwards" into the future in order to act as a functional limit to one's development.

Yet "throwing outwards" always involves direction. Driesch had to deal with two limitations that the mechanistic world-view prescribed, namely that the world can be analyzed into elements (rather than wholes), and that the wholes are not static, but dynamic. In order to overcome these tenets, it is required the adoption of an organismic perspective, where:

> the processes within the organism are not exclusively determined by the environmental variations . . . no matter how much they are codetermined by the environment, they would be utterly unintelligible, if considered from environment alone.
>
> (Goldstein, 1995, p. 295)

Driesch—like most other embryologists of his time—focused his attention on growth processes within the developing embryo. Therefore, while not denying the relevance of the environment, his main concern was to understand the *Ganzheitskausalität* that is embedded in the systemic organization of the organism.

Vitalism and Driesch's version of *entelechy*

Our contemporary scientific discourse hates vitalism. It is habitually presented as something pre-scientific and of "no credibility" (Bechtel & Richardson, 1998). However, careful re-reading of Driesch's work would lead to de-stigmatization of that frame of thought, particularly if it is considered in the context of developmental philosophy (e.g. Henri Bergson's focus on irreversible time, which led him to the "black box" notion of *elan vital*) and of the developmental logic of James

Mark Baldwin. "Vitalism", as a general standpoint, is no better—or worse—in its lack of precision than "cognitivism", for example. Both need to be elaborated in specific terms to make them viable for conceptual advancements. Contemporary science suffers from premature closing of search for solutions to complex problems by inventing labels that are attributed derogatory value.

What is at stake here is primarily the question of biological Gestalt, whether it is reducible to its physiological or genetic components, or it entails some "whole quality" that transcends these components. Quite obviously, the process of composing the biological whole—the organism—from these components is the arena where the Gestalt emerges. Given the irreversibility of time in biological formation, the newly emerged Gestalt cannot be reduced to its components; hence the *process of emergence guarantees the unique Gestalt properties of the biological organisms*. This is recognized in developmental biology—at least from embryology onwards (von Uexküll, 1926, 1928). Living systems are constantly moving towards *emergent* Gestalts—which include innovation—instead of restoration of a form once lost.[9] This is the unique general property that restores vitalism into the realm of science. There is no mystical "vital force" in the organism, but a set of future-oriented biological processes that anticipate[10] the formation of new structures in the future.

Driesch's version of vitalism was of the kind of *organizing force* (*organisierende Kraft*) and in that it differed cardinally from those of its predecessors, Aristotle and Georg Stahl (Mocek, 1998a, p. 34). Its core is in the notion of autonomy of processes of life (Driesch, 1914b, p. 202), which implies that autonomy is always constrained, yet within these limits the pathways of development can take a multitude of individual forms. Or—reversely expressed—multitudes of individual forms, potential for each organism and actual when we look at the development of a group of organisms, is possible only under the conditions of such relative autonomy. And such autonomy opens the door for epigenesis as a constrained process of negotiating the organism's development, from the lowest (genetic and cytological) levels to the highest (human cultural development). Instead of fixed predictability of the future we can observe approximate coordination of what was in the past with what is about to become, given the conditions.

The term *entelechy* has Aristotelian origins, but Driesch was careful to distance his version from its previous form. Instead, the move into the use of the term was a natural result of his focus on morphogenesis:

> Morphogenesis, we have learned, is "epigenesis" not only in the descriptive but also in the theoretical sense: manifoldness in space is produced where no manifoldness was; real "evolutio" is limited to rather insignificant topics. But was there nothing "manifold" previous to morphogenesis? Nothing certainly of an *extensive* character, but there was something else: there was entelechy, and thus we may provisionally call entelechy an "intensive manifoldness." That then is our result: not evolutio, but epigenesis—"epigenesis vitalistica."
>
> (Driesch, 1908, p. 144)

Seen through Driesch's perspective there is nothing mystical about vitalism. Or—if one wants to claim there is—then all the biological realities of emergence of new life would need to be considered as such. Rather, Driesch's focus on entelechy is best seen as an effort to create a general abstract concept that could unite other theoretical concepts that capture developmental phenomena in their manifoldness and temporary equifinality (Driesch, 1939).

The focus on the *degree of manifoldness* (*Grad der Manninfaltigkeit*; Driesch, 1923, p. 75) in the potential development of the organisms opens the door for a unification of developmental concepts where the real and the imaginary ones have an equal stance. This fits with the notion of biological processes amplifying variability (Maruyama, 1963); the degree of manifoldness can be viewed as the "reaction norm" that guides the production of variability of multiple forms. At the level of categories—a persistent concern for German philosophers whose struggle with their intellectual father figure Immanuel Kant takes many forms—Driesch introduced a complex notion of a concept, *unentwickeltenentwickelbaren Begriff* (Driesch, 1923, p. 75), which could be (inelegantly) translated as *non-developed developmentally potential category*. Not only cellular conglomerates show prospective potency for development—their conceptual counterparts in our thinking do so too. It is an example of potentially developing scientific concept—it does not exist yet (non-A) but could emerge (A) by being cultivated by a scientist. All development in any scientific theory depends on the pool of not-yet-developed general concepts.

A century later: context-based autonomy of organisms

How can we evaluate Driesch's ideas? What of them remains valuable in our 21st-century sciences? A hundred years is a long time in some sense, and a short one in another. Over the long period of a century, biology as a discipline has progressed very far, from initial claims for being general science of living organisms (Driesch, 1893) to the very forefront of all sciences dealing with issues of human survival under changing environmental conditions. Yet for development of ideas a hundred years can turn out to be a very short time. Acceptance of ideas of irreversibility of time has taken physical sciences 80 years (from the 1890s to the 1970s; Prigogine, 1978) and has not fully found its place in the biological and social sciences, where it is by far more central. In conjunction with that, any consideration of future-oriented processes—teleology, teleogenesis—has been slow and occasional.

Science includes an ideological guidance component: fights with "dualism", for "materialism", and for many other "-isms" surface from time to time as if these could guide our knowledge away from treacherous grounds. Such fights are often ephemeral—they block efforts of inquiry, rather than directing it in directions adequate to the nature of phenomena. Particularly in psychology, the advent of behaviorism is an example of how "objectivity" has kept the discipline away from the analysis of the human *psyche* at all of its levels of organization.

Vitalism is dead—as a direction of thought—a century after Driesch. Yet the questions raised by it are very much alive. The issues of genetic regulation, emergence, and anticipation of future encounters (in immunology) are critical unresolved issues in our contemporary science. The whole genetic science has moved from its mechanistic assumptions of genetic determinacy to that of epigenesis. Instead of considering genes as "causes" for phenotypic outcomes, since the 1960s we have been getting used to the notion of gene regulation in which some genes may enable—or inhibit—other genes in their activities. Given these changes in the biological sciences it is time to make sense of Hans Driesch's theoretical efforts during his time.

Equipotentiality rediscovered

Scientific concepts have curious histories. While the notion of *regulation* has found its honorable place in contemporary epigenetics (Davidson, 2006; Lux & Richter, 2014), and the concept of *equifinality* has been maintained within the general systems theory (as a defining characteristic of open systems), the third notion with which Driesch operated—*equipotentiality*—has become lost. Yet psychologists have been working with the notion of *competence*, as contrasted with *performance*, in the domain of problem solving. That contrast has features similar to Driesch's—something that could happen as becoming performed— but it retains the implication of linearity of the translation. Competence can become expressed in performance in a *unilinear* way, while equipotentiality becomes expressed in a singular outcome (performance) through a multitude of trajectories. The loss of Driesch's focus on multilinearity is symptomatic of the slow advancement of developmental science; moreover, it illustrates how "empirical science" that builds upon inductive generalization is blind to its own axiomatic premises.

However, another empirical effort—decoding of complex genomes of various species in the 21st century—has forced the biological sciences to reconsider their ways of thinking. Surprises emerge in the case of sequenced genomes. Of course these surprises are embedded in the encoding mechanisms of enormous complexity—the decoded genome of the sea urchin (*Strongylocentrotus purpuratus*) includes an 814-megabase sequence, divided into 23,300 genes (Sea Urchin Sequencing Consortium, 2006). Among that genome as a whole, 200–700 genes were discovered to be similar to those that in human beings are known to encode chemosensory, hearing, balance and visual (retinal) functions (pp. 948–949). This finding could be interpreted "backwards", in evolutionary terms, considering these as evolutionary antecedents for human neural functions; but in their species-specific ecology sea urchins have no ears or eyes to rely upon auditory and visual inputs. Hence the presence of the "human" genes is either an artifact of the recognition of their function in the human genome; or rather—in Driesch's terms—an example of pre-adaptive potentiality of the genome of one species for the emergence of many species in the far future, counting from their common ancestors. The genomic surprises here constitute a case of phylogenetic pluripotentiality of the genome. Furthermore—they indicate that the answer to generic organization of living beings is not in the description of the DNA sequences, but in the functional regulation of some parts of the sequences by others. Driesch's original idea of various regulations finds a new form in our 21st-century genetics.

Hierarchical organization

Establishing hierarchies—starting from the simplest dominance relation ($A > B$)— is the general basis for any structured unit in an organization—be it biological, psychological or social. Some of these become morphologically fixed in development; in this sense the bodily form of an organism reaches a state of recognizability of its uniqueness as still a specimen of the given species. Others may take temporarily stable or even quickly transient forms. Embryologists and developmental biologists as a whole have the advantage of their research objects developing—in ontogeny or in phylogeny—through describable structural forms. Sociologists and cultural anthropologists may be in a position to describe temporarily fixed forms like those of social institutions (which emerge, maintain themselves and become dissolved) or forms of rituals. In contrast, psychologists, focusing largely on the microgenetic and ontogenetic forms of the developing *psyche*, may have difficulties describing the hierarchical orders, and they certainly face the difficult theoretical problem of making sense of the emergence of new orders. The practical focus on "measurement" (of existing characteristics, rather than emerging ones) further muddles the scientific evidence as it becomes de facto accepted that all "measured" and mutually "correlated" indexes ("variables") operate as equal partners in the "making" of an outcome. The notion of hierarchical order is easy to by-pass under these assumptions. Inductive generalization that starts from the equality of "variables" eliminates any reconstruction of the reality of hierarchical (even stable) order.

Driesch was more fortunate in his embryological experiments. Working with embryos in the early process of cellular division he could observe how hierarchical order emerged even after violation of the existing symmetric relations within the structure of cells. His experiments were focused precisely on the structural reorganization of the disturbed cellular complexes. Their taking of the final form despite the violation of the current state created a phenomenological puzzle of development *despite* intervention. Looking for conditions that make the hierarchical order generate itself even under disturbed conditions indicated the primacy of the whole over its parts.

In the 1890s the Whole<>Parts relationship was a favorite topic in psychology, where various versions of *Gestalt* and *Ganzheitspsychologie* emerged to make the claim about the primacy of the wholes. However, the latter were already established wholes, while Driesch's phenomena included not-yet-established ones. Driesch's own look at his contemporary psychology was linked with his habilitation thesis, and first of all covered the practices of looking at thinking dynamics in the "Würzburg School" of Oswald Külpe, Karl Bühler and their colleagues (Driesch, 1913). Driesch's interest in the higher-order phenomena—those of the soul (*Seele*)—fitted squarely with his general theory of order. His critique of his contemporary behaviorism (Driesch, 1927a, 1927b) continued from his discovery of its practices back in 1903. When participating in the discussion of the crisis in psychology (Driesch, 1925, 1927c) he defined psychology within the framework of his *Ordnungslehre*:

> Psychology is psychology, and is nothing but a part of the general *theory of order*, studying the order in the sequence of that which I *consciously have*.
>
> My psychology is a real "psych"-ology. It starts from that which is immediately given to me as to a consciously having (not "doing") subject. It then enumerates, under the name of a *theory of materials* the various *somethings* which I may consciously have. This is the static part, as it were. The dynamic part that follows then studies the laws of sequence of my somethings. It is forced to break with the old association theory and to introduce limiting and directing agents. Also the concepts of subconsciousness and co-consciousness and a good many others appear upon the scene. My soul is the fundamental theoretical concept.
>
> (Driesch, 1927b, p. 12)

Driesch preserved the level of organization of the *psyche*—the *Seele*—as the arena for psychological ordering processes (1903). In this he—as a biologist—acted directly contrary to the behaviorist credo of reducing the level of complexity to the lowest possible one, namely that of behavior. Without the preservation of the levels of organization it is impossible to talk about the emergence of new quality. In a multi-level open system, the process of emergence is an inevitable concept to entertain[11] since it entails the construction of something on the basis of a qualitatively different something else.

Conclusion: vitalism in the 21st century

Hans Driesch's theoretical contributions to developmental science are notable—yet forgotten. Branding him as a "vitalist" (or—in psychology—"parapsychologist") has led to the disinterest in his *entelechy* concept, which stands for a family of ideas that has been socially stigmatized in scientific discourses. This has been undoubtedly detrimental for developmental science. The key issue of living systems—anticipation of their own growth into a final form in the future—requires theoretical construction not available in the sciences that can ignore irreversible time and levels of organization as central for existing and *becoming*.

Acknowledgments

The author is grateful to Kalevi Kull for suggestions and to David Carré for his editorial corrections. The preparation of this chapter was supported by the Niels Bohr Professorship grant from the *Danske Grundforskningsfond*.

Notes

1 This nature of development—i.e. not following the static assumptions of ontological logics—has been the major epistemological difficulty for developing theoretical models of development (Valsiner & van der Veer, 2014).

2 The science of chemistry as it emerged in the late 18th century needed to prove that its object has qualities that go beyond the principles of physics. Once chemistry established itself and differentiated into two parts, inorganic and organic, the latter had to prove to the former that its objects have a different quality that cannot be reduced to the former. Physiology, in turn, has had to prove that its phenomena cannot be reduced to biochemical principles, and psychology as not to be reducible to physiology. Inside psychology the tension about reducing complex subjective phenomena to physiological (or even genetic) "roots" continues. In that light, the question of whether the growth of multicellular organisms can be explained by mechanical principles (*Entwicklungsmechanik*) is not surprising.

3 *Teleogenetic* plainly means creating one's own future goals. This contrasts with the term *teleological*, where such goals are pre-given.

4 Driesch continued episodic returns to Naples and experimental work even after that—the latest in 1909 (Mocek, 1998a)—as he moved into the realm of philosophy. The Gifford Lectures were a key change point and then he arrived at the position of philosopher at Heidelberg University in 1911 (habilitated in 1909 on *Naturphilosophie* with Wilhelm Windelband and Oswald Külpe).

5 In the original: "*Regulation ist ein am lebenden Organismus geschehender Vorgang oder die Änderung eines solchen Vorgangs, durch welchen oder durch welche eine irgendwie gesetzte Störung seines vorher bestandenen 'normalen' Zustandes ganz oder teilweise, direkt oder indirekt, kompensiert und zu den 'normale' Zustand oder wenigstens eine Annäherung an ihn wieder herbeigeführt wird*" (Driesch, 1901, p. 92).

6 By Driesch's own admission, the Gifford Lectures (Driesch, 1908) were his most "fluid and lightly written" texts (Driesch, 1923, p. 7), which he attempted to make serious through the German translation. The 1906–1908 period was for him the time of consolidation of his bio-theoretical system where the specificity of the living matter (*entelechy*) played a central role.

7 James Mark Baldwin (1906, 1908, 1911, 1915; Valsiner, 2009) as well as Charles Sanders Peirce, struggled with the limitations of the classical logic—the former giving it up, the latter being reluctant to do so (Pizarroso & Valsiner, 2009). Bertrand Russell assumed logic as a given. The *Gegenstandstheorie* of Alexius Meinong—and the whole of "the Graz School"—was situated on the border of the ontological worldview while recognizing its paradoxicality. It is in the slowness of changes of basic axioms that developmental thought has been caught over the 20th century.

8 This point needs to be generalized (even if Driesch did not do it) to all open systems—of which biological organisms is one, yet basic, example. Their dependence on the interchange with the environment enduring (being "the same") is possible only and only if intra-systemic variability is generated in the movement towards the future—Maruyama's (1963) principle of variability amplification is fundamental for all enduring systems, including psychological, social and aesthetic systems.

9 Jean Piaget's theoretical contribution—quite aside from his "stage account" of development—includes the notions of *equilibration* (restoration of previous Gestalt) and *progressing equilibration* (*équilibration majorante*—striving towards a form that is not yet given). It is only the latter that is adequate for looking at development.

10 The area of science that has had to work out adequate solutions to this issue is immunology. The innovation happening in the changes of viruses and the ways in which the organism pre-emptively buffers itself against (many but not all) new viral invasions is the central question for immunology. In fact, Driesch used the immunology example explicitly (1908, p. 208).

11 The concept of emergence enters into scientific discourse in 1875 (Emmeche et al., 1997).

References

Baldwin, J. M. (1906). *Thought and things: A study of the development and meaning of thought, or genetic logic*: Vol. 1. *Functional logic, or genetic theory of knowledge*. London, UK: Swan Sonnenschein.

Baldwin, J. M. (1908). *Thought and things: A study of the development and meaning of thought, or genetic logic*: Vol. 2. *Experimental logic, or genetic theory of thought*. London, UK: Swan Sonnenschein.

Baldwin, J. M. (1911). *Thought and things: A study of the development and meaning of thought, or genetic logic*: Vol. 3. *Interest and art being real logic*. London, UK: Swan Sonnenschein.

Baldwin, J. M. (1915). *Genetic theory of reality*. New York, NY: Putnam.

Bechtel, W. & Richardson, R. C. (1998). Vitalism. In E. Craig (Ed.), *Routledge Encyclopedia of Philosophy*. London, UK: Routledge.

Churchill, F. (1969). From machine-theory to Entelechy: Two studies in developmental teleology. *Journal of the History of Biology*, *2*, 1, 165–185.

Davidson, E. H. (2006). The sea urchin's genome: Where will it lead us? *Science*, *314*, 929–930.

Driesch, H. (1891). *Die mathematisch-mechanische Betrachtung morphologischer Probleme der Biologie* [The mathematical–mechanical contemplation of the morphological problems of biology]. Jena, Germany: Gustav Fischer.

Driesch, H. (1893). *Die Biologie als selbständige Grundwissenschaft* [Biology as an independent basic science]. Leipzig, Germany: Verlag von Wilhelm Engelmann.

Driesch, H. (1894). *Analytische Theorie der organischen Entwicklung* [Analytic theory of organic development]. Leipzig, Germany: Verlag von Wilhelm Engelmann.

Driesch, H. (1899). Die Lokalisation morphogenetischer Vorgänge [The localization of morphogenetic operations]. *Archiv für Entwicklungsmechanik*, *8*, 35–111.

Driesch, H. (1901). *Die Organischen Regulationen* [The organic regulations]. Leipzig, Germany: Verlag von Wilhelm Engelmann.

Driesch, H. (1903). *Die "Seele" als elementarer Naturfaktor* [The "soul" as fundamental natural factor]. Leipzig, Germany: Verlag von Wilhelm Engelmann.

Driesch, H. (1905). *Der Vitalismus als Geschichte und als Lehre* [Vitalism as history and as doctrine]. Leipzig, Germany: J.A. Barth.

Driesch, H. (1908). *The science and philosophy of the organism*. London, UK: Adam and Charles Black.

Driesch, H. (1909). *Philosophie des Organischen* [Philosophy of the organic]. Leipzig, Germany: Verlag von Wilhelm Engelmann.

Driesch, H. (1913). *Die Logik als Aufgabe* [Logic as a task]. Tübingen, Germany: J. C. B. Mohr.

Driesch, H. (1914a). *The history and theory of vitalism*. London, UK: Macmillan.

Driesch, H. (1914b). *The problem of individuality*. London, UK: Macmillan.

Driesch, H. (1923). Mein system und sein Werdigung [My system and its development]. In R. Schmidt (Ed.), *Die Philosophie der Gegenwart in Selbstdarstellungen* (pp. 49–78). Leipzig, Germany: Felix Meiner.

Driesch, H. (1925). *The crisis in psychology*. Princeton, NJ: Princeton University Press.

Driesch, H. (1927a). Behaviorismus und Vitalismus [Behaviorism and Vitalism]. *Sitzungsberichte der Heidelberger Akademie der Wissenschaften: Philosophisch-historische Klasse*. Heidelberg, Germany: Carl Winters Universitätsbuchhandlung.

Driesch, H. (1927b). Critical remarks on some modern types of psychology. *Pedagogical Seminary, 34*, 1–13.

Driesch, H. (1927c). *Mind and body*. London, UK: Methuen.

Driesch, H. (1939). Entelechie und Seele [Entelechy and Soul]. *Synthese, 4*, 6, 266–279.

Driesch, H. (1951). *Lebenserinnerungen: Aufzeichnungen eines Forschers und Denkers* [Memoirs: Notes of a researcher and thinker]. Basel, Switzerland: Ernst Reinhardt Verlag.

Emmeche, C., Køppe, S. & Stjernfeldt, F. (1997). Explaining emergence: Towards the ontology of levels. *Journal for the General Theory of Science, 28*, 1, 83–119.

Goldstein, K. (1995). *The organism*. New York, NY: Zone Books.

Gottlieb, G. (1999). *Probabilistic epigenesis and evolution*. Heinz Werner Lecture No. 23. Worcester, MA: Clark University Press.

Hamburger, V. (1997). Wilhelm Roux: Visionary with a blind spot. *Journal of the History of Biology, 30*, 229–238.

Kull, K. (2001). Jakob von Uexküll: An introduction. *Semiotica, 134*, 1, 1–59.

Laubichler, M. D. (2005). Systemtheoretische Organismuskonzeptionen [System-theoretical concepts of organism]. In U. Krohs and G. Toepfer (Eds.), *Philosophie der Biologie* (pp. 109–124). Frankfurt, Germany: Suhrkamp.

Lux, V. & Richter, J. T. (Eds.) (2014). *Kulturen der Epigenetik: Vererbt, codiert, übertragen* [Cultures of Epigenetics: Inherited, encoded, transmitted]. Berlin, Germany: De Gruyter.

Maruyama, M. (1963). The second cybernetics: Deviation-amplifying mutual causal processes. *American Scientist, 51*, 164–179.

Meyer-Abich, A. (1947). Hans Driesch, der Begründer der theoretischen Biologie [Hans Driesch, the founder of theoretical biology]. *Zeitschrift für philosophische Forschung, 1*, 2/3, 356–369.

Mocek, R. (1998a). Kausale Morphologie und aktueller Evolutionskurs [Causal morphology and the current evolution course]. *MPI für Wissenschaftllehre Preprint, 92*, 1–73.

Mocek, R. (1998b). *Die werdende Form: Eine Geschichte der Kausalen Morphologie* [The emergent form: A history of causal morphology]. Marburg an der Lahn, Germany: Basilisken-Presse.

Müller, I. (1996). The impact of the Zoological Station in Naples on developmental physiology. *International Journal of Developmental Biology, 40*, 103–111.

Pizarroso, N. & Valsiner, J. (2009). Why developmental psychology is not developmental: Moving towards abductive methodology. Paper presented at the Society of Research in Child Development, April, Denver, CO.

Prigogine, I. (1978). Time, structure and fluctuations. *Science, 201*, 777–785.

Roux, W. (1885). Beiträgen zur Entwicklungsmechanik des Embryo [Contributions to the development mechanics of the embryo]. *Zeitschrift für Biologie, 21*, 411–428.

Roux, W. (1923). Prinzipielles der Entwicklungsmechanik [Principles of the development mechanism]. *Annalen der Philosophie, 3*, 3, 454–473.

Sea Urchin Sequencing Consortium (2006). The genome of the sea urchin *Strongylocentrotus purpuratus*. *Science, 314*, 941–950.

Toepfer, G. (2005a). Der Begriff des Lebens [The concept of life]. In U. Krohs and G. Toepfer (Eds.), *Philosophie der Biologie* (pp. 157–174). Frankfurt, Germany: Suhrkamp.

Toepfer, G. (2005b). Teleologie [Teleology]. In U. Krohs and G. Toepfer (Eds.), *Philosophie der Biologie* (pp. 36–52). Frankfurt, Germany: Suhrkamp.

Uexküll, J. J. (1902). *Im Kampf um der Tierseele* [In the struggle for the animal soul]. Wiesbaden, Germany: Bergmann.

Uexküll, J.J. (1909). *Umwelt und Innenwelt der Tiere* [Environment and inner world of the animal]. Berlin, Germany: Julius Springer.

Uexküll, J. J. (1913). *Bausteine zu einer biologischen Weltanschauung* [Building blocks for a biological worldview]. München, Germany: Grudman.

Uexküll, J. J. (1926). *Theoretical Biology*. New York, NY: Harcourt Brace and Co.

Uexküll, J. J. (1928). *Theoretische Biologie* [Theoretical Biology] (2nd ed.). Berlin, Germany: Julius Springer.

Ungerer, E. (1927). Der Sinn des Vitalismus und des Mechanismus in der Lebensforschung [The meaning of vitalism and mechanism in life research]. In H. Schneider & W. Schingritz (Eds.), *Hans Driesch zum 60. Geburtstag* (pp. 149–168). Leipzig, Germany: Emmanuel Reinecke.

Valsiner, J. (2009). Baldwin's quest: A universal logic of development. In J. W. Clegg (Ed.), *The observation of human systems: Lessons from the history of anti-reductionistic empirical psychology* (pp. 45–82). New Brunswick, NJ: Transaction.

Valsiner, J. & van der Veer, R. (2014). Encountering the border: Vygotsky's zona blizaishego razvitya and its implications for theory of development. In A. Yasnitsky, R. van der Veer & M. Ferrari (Eds.), *The Cambridge handbook of cultural–historical psychology* (pp. 148–173). Cambridge, UK: Cambridge University Press.

Chapter 3

The need to bridge concepts of development in the life sciences

Vanessa Lux

Development is a key concept in biology. Early on, it was used not only for organ development and the process of ontogenesis but also for phylogenetic change (Toepfer, 2011, p. 392).[1] Following the rediscovery of Mendel, the rise of genetics, and the Synthetic Theory of Evolution in the early 20th century, phylogenetic and ontogenetic development were considered separated processes; moreover, the latter was considered a result of the former. However, phylogenetic processes are studied at the population level, based on transmission of genes and random mutations, while ontogenetic processes are studied at the individual level, based on self-differentiation and induction including imprinting and learning. How both concepts of development can be integrated within a common theoretical framework and methodology has marked a key question for developmental science ever since. Today, we observe a new rise of developmental thinking in some areas of the life sciences, such as epigenetics (e.g. Fagiolini, Jensen, & Champagne, 2009) and developmental neuroscience (e.g. Munakata, Casey, & Diamond, 2004; Mason, 2009). The question of how to integrate developmental data collected at a population level and individual level remains a major challenge for these emerging research fields. This is especially the case for research concerned with psychobiological development.

In the following, I first describe the main changes of developmental thinking in biology, from the early controversy between preformationism and epigenesis to current developmental genetics. Second, I introduce Conrad H. Waddington's *developmental epigenetics* approach, which represents a forgotten attempt for a synthesis of evolutionary theory, genetics, and embryology; here I also outline Susan Oyama's approach of developmental systems theory. I use Waddington's and Oyama's ideas to point out some of the problems that arise when we try to mingle developmental concepts modeled at the population level with those modeled at the individual level. Third, I describe the use of developmental models in psychology. Early models of mental development in psychology conceptualized development at an individual level and were mainly inspired by embryology. Despite this, one of the most important approaches in developmental psychology today, the life-span perspective, was inspired by epidemiology and population statistics and thus conceptualizes development at the population level. I trace this shift and discuss the consequences for theories and studies of psychobiological development. Finally, I show how the differences between these two concepts of development, especially between their methodological implications, create a major barrier for newly arising research fields in the life sciences such as epigenetics and developmental neuroscience.

From embryology to developmental genetics

Early accounts of embryological change date back at least to Aristotle's studies of the chick embryo. Since the 17th century, those changes in the embryo were interpreted as "development". The nature of this developmental process was very differently explained by two theories: the theory of preformationism and the theory of epigenesis. Preformationists claimed that all features of an adult individual already exist in the germ cells—often illustrated with the picture of a mini-man inhabiting the ovum or the sperm—and, therefore, that development mainly means growth. In contrast, those who referred to embryological development as epigenesis (e.g. Galen, William Harvey) argued that central morphological structures of the later organism newly evolve during the growth process of the embryo. Notoriously, Caspar Friedrich Wolff (1734–1794) documented with precision a series of structural changes in the developing chick embryo, as he first published in his dissertation *Theoria Generationis* in 1759. His observations led to a major controversy with the leading preformationist at the time, Albrecht von Haller (1708–1777). Thence, Wolff's empirical and theoretical work laid ground for the overall acceptance of the theory of epigenesis and the formation of embryology as science of developmental processes.

During the 18th and most of the 19th century, embryology merely described what could be seen of the developmental process. This, however, changed with Wilhelm His (1831–1904), Wilhelm Roux (1850–1924), and Hans Driesch (1867–1941) and their systematic experiments with fertilized eggs (van Speybroeck, de Waele, & van de Vijver, 2002, pp. 31–32). Thenceforth, embryology became an experimental science dedicated to uncovering the causal mechanisms underlying biological development. Based on his experiments, Roux described a combining mechanism of self-differentiation (*Selbstdifferenzierung*), partly located in the nucleus, and induced differentiation (*abhängige Differenzierung*) through neighboring cells to be at work in organic development. He understood these mechanisms as basic principles of development upon which he built his developmental mechanics (*Entwicklungsmechanik*) (Roux, 1888). Roux also pointed out that, in contrast to a predetermined development that would have to be exactly the same in all individuals of one species and which would be highly sensitive to varying developmental conditions, the mechanism of self-regulation allows for variability in the process of development enabling stability in its outcome despite changes in the environment (Roux, 1895, p. 981). In the following years, the material basis of these mechanisms became the major focus in embryology. In the early 1920s, Hans Spemann and Hilde Mangold identified a biochemical signaling center in egg cells of *Amphibia*, later called the Spemann organizer, as well as a correspondence between the distribution of signaling proteins in those cells and the later differentiation of cell lines (Spemann & Mangold, 1924). According to Spemann, the role of the "organizer" was to induce a direction of development in otherwise totipotent tissue (Spemann & Mangold, 1924, p. 637). Any further specification of the causal mechanisms underlying induction and cell differentiation remained a major challenge for embryologists.

Due to the rise of genetics, embryology and its induction problem soon after became more or less abandoned. According to Scott F. Gilbert, "[f]rom the late 1930s to the mid-1980s the 'primary induction problem' was considered a graveyard of biologists, a problem so fraught with non-specificity, uninterpretable results, and conflicting data, that a young biologist would be foolish to enter the morass" (Gilbert, 2000, p. 556). The synthesis of population genetics and evolutionary theory and the discovery of the DNA seemed to further legitimize the growing neglect of embryonic development in biology. This situation slightly changed with the discovery of hox genes and developmental gradients in *Drosophila melanogaster* by Christiane Nüsslein-Volhard and Eric F. Wieschaus in 1979 (published Nüsslein-Volhard & Wieschaus, 1980). Although their discovery brought the question of embryonic development back to the center of biological research, it did so within a genetic framework. Following their work, the hope was to identify the genes responsible for the developmental program in other species as well.

This emphasis on the genes did not change until the early 1990s. New DNA sequencing methods in combination with cytological visualization allowed characterizing the functional role of the chromatin structure in gene expression and development. With the description of the position-effect variegation, according to which the expression of the gene for the red eye color mutation in *Drosophila melanogaster* depends on its chromosomal position, the functional role of the chromatin structure and other molecules surrounding the DNA came into focus in developmental genetics (Kreß, 2014, p. 182). However, it took another ten years before the study of mechanisms regulating gene expression, today called "epigenetics", became a major research field in molecular biology.

Waddington's forgotten synthesis and Oyama's developmental systems

The term "epigenetics" was originally coined by Conrad H. Waddington in 1942 (Waddington, 1942; see also Holliday, 2002; Jablonka & Lamb, 2002, p. 82). It is not accidental that the term is philologically and conceptually reminiscent of the term "epigenesis" (Waddington, 1942; Petronis, Gottesman, Crow, DeLisi, Klar, Macciardi et al., 2000, p. 342; van Speybroeck et al., 2002; Willer, 2010). In fact, Waddington's aim was to reconcile the new field of genetics and its experimental methodology with the earlier experimental embryology (Gilbert, 2012). According to Waddington, epigenetics was to become the biological sub-discipline to study "the causal mechanisms at work" in embryological development "by which the genes of the genotype bring about phenotypic effects" (Waddington, 1942, p. 18).

More precisely, Waddington's *developmental epigenetics* was a renewal of Roux's research program in the light of genetics (Gilbert, 2012; Huxley, 1956, p. 807; Haig, 2012, p. 14). Similar to Roux, Waddington was especially interested in the question of stability of organ development under varying developmental conditions. Taking into account the relevance of induction processes during cell differentiation, he rejected a simple genetic determinism. Instead, Waddington proposed a model of developmental pathways, *chreodes*, characterized by complex self-stabilizing mechanisms of gene–environment interaction that he illustrated with the picture of the "epigenetic landscape" (Waddington, 1957, pp. 26ff). Within this pathway model the epigenotype is understood as mediating the level between genotype and phenotype. It canalizes the developmental process according to genetic and environmental conditions of the organism. Thus, the main purpose of epigenetic variability is to guarantee organism and species stability in ontogenetic as well as phylogenetic development. In addition, the individual developmental pathways, i.e. chreodes, are characterized at the same time by stability and by developmental change. For Waddington, this stability in motion is the essence of living organisms. He characterizes it as homeorhetic equilibrium: "In 'homeorhetic equilibra' . . . the concentrations of substances do not remain constant, but change along defined time-extended trajectories" (Waddington & Thom, 1968, p. 179).

Originally adapted from cell differentiation and organ development, Waddington explicitly uses his pathway model to explain ontogenetic change at the individual level as well as phylogenetic change at the species level. To do so, he assumes that the same principles of developmental change apply at all levels of development, although the "agents" or factors of development might vary (Waddington, 1957, 1970). For example, for the species level he assumes that bigger changes such as the development of a new species can be interpreted as switch of developmental pathways, with change first occurring at an individual or ontogenetic level and then at a population or phylogenetic level. In this evolutionary perspective, the epigenotype, represented by chreodes, functions as intermediate level between the genotype and the process of selection. At this position it is able to buffer environmental changes and genetic mutations through adaptive changes of an organism's ontogenesis within the range of its developmental potental given by its genotype.

Probably due to the dominance of a genetic framework at the time, Waddington's developmental epigenetics and his pathway model had very little impact in biology. This changed in the late 1980s and early 1990s with the rise of systems biology and its turn to developmental questions. One of the most influential theories within this perspective is Susan Oyama's developmental systems theory. Oyama refers to Waddington's model of developmental pathways (e.g. Oyama, 2000, p. 36), but subsitutes them with her concept of "life cycles". In doing so, she implies a highly dynamic interplay between developmental factors at the individual level. Meanwhile, Waddington conceptualizes development as cumulative and canalizing. The need for adaptation and specialization restricts a cell's or an organism's developmental potential within a given environment. In contrast, Oyama's life cycles are much more open and flexible, as she emphasizes a constitutive role of the environment. To capture the complexity of a developmental system, Oyama argues that: "one must finally describe not only intracelluar processes but also relations among cells, as well as the ways these relations influence and are influenced by higher-level processes, including organism-environment interactions" (Oyama, 2000, pp. 30–31). Following Lewontin, Rose, and Kamin (1984), Oyama (2000) characterizes the interrelationship between organism and environment as "constructivist interaction" (p. 3). For her this means a "developmental and evolutionary interdependence of organism and environment" (p. 3), as well as the fact that the "*effective* environment for a developing organism . . . to some extent is produced, chosen, and organized by the organism" (p. 34, emphasis in the original). According to her, "[g]enes and social environments are inherited interactants, available to be used in constructing a life cycle" (p. 61). Therefore, every constellation of developmental interactants of the life cycle at a given time-point has to be interpreted within this social environmental context. In this vein:

> Whether we are speaking of DNA segments, cells, organisms, or groups, however they are individuated, we must, for coherence, consistency, and comprehensiveness, include the context in the explanatory complex, and not only as a container or a causally secondary set of modulators or materials but as constitutive of the processes and products in question.
>
> (Oyama, 2006, p. 280)

In addition, she assumes an enormous flexibility among the interactants of the developmental system within an individual life cycle and even more across generations. While the characteristics of the developmental system were explained by their current role for the development of an individual, this role can change over time. "The system changes over the life cycle and is reconstituted in successive generations in ways that are similar to, but not necessarily identical with, preceding ones" (Oyama, 2000, p. 73). Similar to Waddington, she assumes that the same processes that constitute ontogenetic development are also the foundation of phylogenetic development or evolutionary change. Therefore the unit of evolution, "[i]f one must have a 'unit' of evolution, . . . would be the interactive developmental system: life cycles of organisms in their niches. Evolution would then be change in the constitution and distribution of these systems" (Oyama, 2000, pp. 199–200). Within this process of construction by organisms in their niches, the significance of each interactant of the life cycle for the developmental process, either ontogenetic or phylogenetic, can change at any moment in development (Oyama, 2000, p. 61). According to Oyama, there is no predetermined hierarchy between different analytical levels of development, and, most importantly, no exclusive role for the genotype. "The developmental system is a mobile set of interacting influences and entities. It includes all influences on development, at all levels of analysis" (Oyama, 2000, p. 72). Especially, "[t]he developmental system includes . . . not just genes, but whatever else in the living or nonliving environment contributes to or supports development" (Oyama, 2000, p. 88). However, Oyama still argues that "[d]evelopmental systems are to some extent hierarchically organized. They can be studied on many levels, and relations among the levels are crucial" (Oyama, 2000, p. 70).

Oyama's constructivist model allows for an even more dynamic and more open process of interaction between ontogenetic and phylogenetic development than Waddington's model of developmental pathways. Throughout his life, Waddington tried to determine the mechanisms of feedback regulation and self-stabilization of the developmental pathways and their evolutionary origin by modeling interactions of genes and inductions processes (Lux, in press). In contrast, Oyama's approach focuses not so much on stabilization than on change. "One benefit of this is that it makes clear where we must look if we wish to know what the possibilities for change are, for an individual or for the species: not at some set of disembodied constraints or rules or programs, but at relations within the organism and between it and its surround" (Oyama, 2000, p. 95). In theory, both models allow bridging of the gap between ontogenetic and phylogenetic development by assuming that these are based on the same developmental mechanisms; however, methodological integration of empirical data is lacking. Distribution of developmental systems, life cycles, or (epi)genotypes, which may be studied using population statistics, and causal interactions on the individual level cannot easily be projected on each other. Waddington tried to find a solution for this problem by turning to cybernetics and the mathematics of complex systems, but ultimately he never succeeded (Lux, in press). Regarding Oyama's approach, the methodological gap turns the strength of her version of developmental systems theory, i.e. the complete openness for empirical analysis of interactions and inter-relations between the different developmental levels and interactants, into its biggest weakness. Without an integrative methodology, any attempt to empirically determine the interrelationships between ontogenetic and phylogenetic changes within a developmental system will inherit this gap. This problem of methodological integration of data collected at the population and individual level currently is one of the key issues in molecular epigenetics and developmental neuroscience. However, it does have precedents in the shift from an embryological model of development to an epidemiological model of development in psychology.

The embryological heritage in developmental psychology and the shift to an epidemiological model of development

From the 17th to the mid-19th century, the development of the mind during childhood was mostly discussed in terms of education and with focus on the question of how children, from the perspective of teachers and parents, could best be taught not only knowledge but also moral values.[2] This changed with the emergence of pedagogy and psychology as scientific disciplines around 1900, which turned the mental development of children into a field of *empirical* research. Most of the early empirical studies about the development of children were single case studies based on developmental diaries. These diaries were mainly written by developmental psychologists who observed their own children growing up and noted changes in their behavior and their mental capacities. The first widely noticed of these diaries was Wilhelm Preyer's *The Mind of the Child* (Preyer, 1882). Other accounts followed, for example, by Ernst and Gertrud Scupin, James Mark Baldwin, Clara and William Stern, and, in the 1930s and 1940s, by Jean Piaget (Montada, 1995, pp. 26–27).

The embryological concept of development in psychology

According to these early accounts, mental development was considered to start with birth and to end with adolescence. It was interpreted as a combination of an initial phase of biological maturation followed by a second phase of culturalization. The concept of biological maturation was derived from embryology and understood as biological growth process based on differentiation and induction. But the process of culturalization was also often modeled as the result of biological growth processes in interaction with the cultural environment of the child. For example, Karl Bühler in his book *Die geistige Entwicklung des Kindes* [The mental development of the child] (Bühler, 1921) conceptualized ontogenetic development of mental functions in early childhood as the result of interactions between inborn reflexes and instincts and a subsequent acquisition of neuronal connectivity due to sensations and practice.[3] His book later became one of the founding works of developmental psychology.

As Baltes, Reese, and Lipsitt point out, this biological growth model of development "implies a number of defining features for classifying behavioral change as *development*. For example, a change is classified as developmental if it is qualitative, sequential, irreversible, endstate-oriented, and universal" (1980, p. 72). Several models of mental development were proposed according to these criteria in the 1950s and 1960s. One example is Erik Erikson's "epigenetic principle": Erikson directly extrapolated the notions of biological growth and differentiation from embryology to the development of the mind. According to him, mental "growth" during childhood and adolescence was like the growth of an organism in utero: "Whenever we try to understand growth, it is well to remember the epigenetic principle which is derived from the growth of organisms in utero. Somewhat generalized, this principle states that anything that grows has a ground plan, and that out of this ground plan the parts arise, each part having its time of special ascendancy, until all parts have arisen to form a functioning whole. This, obviously, is true for fetal development where each part of the organism has its critical time of ascendance or danger of defect" (Erikson, 1959, p. 53).

Erikson identified a sequence of stages of mental development, assuming gradual change, continuous progression, and ongoing differentiation—all of which can be understood as a growing complexity. Similar to Erikson, Jean Piaget also extrapolated mechanisms of biological organ development to psychogenesis and interpreted his observational data accordingly. His model of psychobiological development implies a defined sequence of stages, progressive integration of new emerging structures, and new capabilities such as growing cognitive skills and new knowledge (see Piaget, 2003). He even tried to outline a "genetic epistemology"—a psychobiological theory of knowledge (Piaget, 1980; see Martí, Chapter 5, this volume). Nonetheless, based on his observational data, he also emphasized that the child plays an active part in its own intellectual development (Piaget, 2003, pp. 109–112)—an aspect that goes beyond biological growth processes and points to the constructive nature of mental development.

Compared with Erikson and Piaget, the founder of attachment theory, John Bowlby, focuses less on stability of development and more on critical points and crises in development. In contrast to what he called the "traditional" model of development, Bowlby proposes the possibility of different developmental pathways and outcomes. To compare both pathway models he used the metaphor of two different railway systems:

> These two, alternative, theoretical models can be likened to *two* types of railway system. The traditional model resembles a single main line on which are set a series of stations. . . . The alternative model resembles a system that starts as a direction but soon forks into a range of distinct routes. Although each of these routes diverges in some degree, initially most of them continue in a direction not very different from the original one. The further each route goes from the metropolis, however, the more branches it throws off and the greater the degree of divergence of direction that can occur. . . . In terms of this model the critical points are the junctions at which the lines fork, for once a train is on any particular line, pressures are present that keep it on that line.
> (Bowlby, 1973, p. 364)

Despite these differences, Bowlby's model stays within the embryological growth model of development. Not only does he argue for differentiation but his "critical points" resonate the embryological concept of "critical periods" introduced by Charles R. Stockard (1921).

However, the embryological concept of development is not restricted to pathway models. For example, Gilbert Gottlieb conceptualizes ontogenetic development as a multi-level dynamic system based on embryological principles. He differentiates four levels—the genetic activity level, the neural activity level, the behavioral level, and the environment—and argues for hierarchical but bidirectional and co-actional relationships within and between these levels at all time-points in development[4] (Gottlieb, 1991, 1992). From his experimental studies of the acoustic development in avian embryos, he later concluded in more general terms that, "neural (and other) structures begin to function before they are fully mature and this activity, whether intrinsically derived ('spontaneous') or extrinsically stimulated (evoked), plays a significant role in the development process"

(Gottlieb, 2007, p. 2). In addition to such bidirectionality and coaction, Gottlieb's model of psychobiological development is built on two other embryological principles: the principle of equifinality and the principle of non-linear or probabilistic causality. For the principle of equifinality Gottlieb referred to Hans Driesch and his cell separation experiments in sea urchins (see Valsiner, Chapter 2, this volume), and according to whom Gottlieb interpreted equifinality as the ability of "developing organisms of the same species [to] reach the same endpoint via different developmental pathways" (Gottlieb, 2003, p. 4; see also Driesch, 1905). The principle of probability captures the non-perfect causal relationships between different levels of development for there is always "some degree of indeterminancy" within developmental processes[5] (Gottlieb, 2003, p. 14; see also Gottlieb, 2007, p. 2).

These models of psychological development highlight different aspects of the embryological concept of development: Erikson emphasizes the idea of growth and differentiation; Piaget highlights emergence of new structures and sequence of stages; Bowlby emphasizes pathway dependency and critical points or periods; and Gottlieb adopts in a more detailed manner the principles of bidirectionality, coaction, equifinality, and indeterminancy to sensory mechanisms and psychological functions.

The shift towards an epidemiological concept of development in psychology

In the 1980s developmental psychology experienced a shift in its concept of development: the existing embryological notion got challenged by an epidemiological approach. This epidemiological concept of development is based on age cohort comparisons and population statistics, and has its roots in the 18th and 19th century, more precisely in the works of Johannes Nikolaus Tetens, F. A. Carus, and Adolphe Quetelet (Baltes, 1979, pp. 16–18). As Baltes points out, Quetelet was very much concerned with the methodological side of his studies on mental development. Quetelet suggested the study of human intellectual faculties and their development over the life-span through statistical measures. In his book *Sur l'homme et le developpement de ses facultés* [On man and the development of his faculties], published in 1835, he argued for a longitudinal approach and the study of large numbers similar to demographic accounts of mortality rates (Quetelet, 1835, p. 13). For some factors, he aggregated the data to four broader age categories, namely infancy, adolescence, adulthood, and old age, to point out differences between these proposed developmental phases (Quetelet, 1835, p. 84). Furthermore, he discussed advanced methodological issues, including the mediation of socio-cultural influences by age and social status, problems of validity and comparability of populations, as well as selection processes within the population under study (see Baltes, 1979, p. 18).

Quetelet's approach had a stronger influence on demography and sociology than on psychology. With few exceptions, such as IQ diagnostics,[6] developmental psychologists focused on general mechanisms of mental development rather than inter-individual and age group differences. In fact, most of them were merely interested in early childhood development. The first longitudinal studies were established at the end of the 1920s, notoriously the Fels Study, the Berkeley Guidance Study, the Berkeley Growth Study, the Harvard Growth Study, and the Oakland Growth Study (Montada, 1995, p. 31). Nonetheless, it is worth noting that these studies did not focus on age group differences but on the question of continuity or discontinuity of development, as well as stability of inter-individual differences during childhood (Montada, 1995, p. 31).

However, this focus changed in the late 1960s, when the participants of these early longitudinal studies in developmental psychology reached adulthood; as these new data ultimately stimulated a life-course perspective on development (Baltes et al., 1980, p. 68). Thenceforth, time-point comparisons over the life-span became an important methodological tool in developmental psychology; accordingly, the framework to interpret the longitudinal data proposed by life-span developmental psychology grew in popularity. As seen, this approach uses an epidemiological concept of development: methodologically, life-span developmental psychology builds to a great extent on age-cohort comparisons ("generations") at the population level. Thus, developmental trajectories and factors of development are modeled using statistical analysis of population data. Additionally, these data sets include personality measures, IQ diagnostics, and other psychological test results, as well as information about social and health status, educational record, general socio-cultural influences, and individual life events like marriage, childbirth, death in the family, job change, etc. Hence, based on these multiple measures, psychological development is interpreted as a demographic outcome (Baltes & Goulet, 1979, pp. 51–53). The latter has obvious advantages (see Baltes et al., 1980): it allows the systematic inclusion of general health information, biographical events, and socio-cultural change as possible developmental factors. This answers the need to include environmental factors of development as well as gene–environment interaction. Furthermore, the epidemiological concept of development is not restricted to early ontogenesis, childhood, and adolescence. Based on the longitudinal data, developmental processes can be modeled over the whole life-span. In this vein, the epidemiological concept of development neither implies a developmental end-point—a so-called "steady state"—or a turning point with subsequent decline, for example, in old age, nor the same developmental trajectory for all mental functions. Following these tenets, differences in regard to developmental factors over the life-span and differences in developmental trajectories between generations, for example due to historical events or demographic change, can be modeled. Hence, the use of epidemiological data opened the concept of development in psychology to a whole new set of possible developmental factors and related research questions.

However, with the growing knowledge in genetics, epigenetics, and neuroscience, a new question arises: how can this epidemiological data be related to developmental knowledge on the molecular (genetic or epigenetic) or neural level traditionally explained by an embryological concept of development? This question becomes especially pressing for two new arising research fields, which seem to contribute important insights about mental development: molecular epigenetics and developmental neuroscience.

A new developmental paradigm in the life sciences

The new popularity of developmental perspectives and related research fields in the life sciences is partly due to the failure of previous deterministic concepts dominated by genetics and localization theory. New technologies and methods made it possible to detect molecular epigenetic changes in body cells and physiological changes in the living brain over the life-span. In both research fields the embryological concept of development is used to interpret data at the individual level and the epidemiological concept of development is used to interpret data at the population level. With the ever-increasing amount of data available, there is a growing need to integrate both types of data as well as both conceptions of development, especially with regard to psychobiological development.

Molecular epigenetics

The new emerging field of *molecular epigenetics* focuses on molecular mechanisms regulating gene activity. Accordingly, molecular epigenetics is defined as "the study of mitotically and/or meiotically heritable changes in gene function that cannot be explained by changes in DNA sequence" (Riggs, Martienssen, & Russo, 1996, p. 1; see also Holliday, 1994; Wu & Morris, 2001). DNA methylation and acetylation, histone modification, and RNA interference are all studied given their role in gene expression, their stability during cell division, and their sensitivity to environmental clues such as nutrition or stress. Molecular epigenetics research is conducted using the whole range of "omics" technologies, including DNA sequencing methods, microarray technology, computational statistics, genetically modified model organisms, as well as epidemiological data sets. In addition, the focus on genes and gene functions emphasizes the role of epigenetics for questions of inheritance. With phenomena such as the parental imprinting of chromosomes and the transgenerational transmission of acquired changes in methylation patterns, the mechanisms studied in molecular epigenetics are interpreted as additional inheritance systems complementing and interacting with genetic inheritance (e.g. Jablonka & Lamb, 2005). However, most of the effects of epigenetic mechanisms observed by now occur in soma cells during the life-span of an individual and are not transmitted to the next generation. Some authors even argue that the criterion of mitotic or meiotic transmission is too tight to capture all epigenetic mechanisms involved in gene regulation (Bird, 2007). This is most obvious in neuronal cells as these cells usually do not undergo further mitosis. Molecular epigenetics of neuronal cells, or "neuroepigenetics", is therefore defined as the study of those mechanisms "which acutely or persistently modify transcription in cells, irrespective of their position in the cell cycle and which do not mutate the genome" (Sultan & Day, 2011, p. 158; see also Gräff, Kim, Dobbin, & Tsai, 2011).

Epigenetic mechanisms play a vital role in cell differentiation (Jaenisch & Bird, 2003). Furthermore, some of them are sensitive to environmental factors (Waterland, Travisano, Tahiliani, Rached, & Mirza, 2008; Zhang & Meaney, 2009), including psychosocial stress (Franklin & Mansuy, 2010). Studies in monozygotic twins showed a growing difference in DNA methylation patterns over the life-span (Fraga, Ballestar, Paz, Ropero, Setien, Ballestar et al., 2005). However, not all epigenetic mechanisms may have developmental functions. In regard to psychobiological developments, for example, we can differentiate between genomic, developmental, and synaptic epigenetic mechanisms (Lux, 2013). Thus, epigenetic mechanisms seem to function at the intersection between gene expression and other metabolic systems. In psychobiological development they seem to regulate the interplay between neural and genetic activity, which is crucial, for example, for sensory development. Hence, they enable and regulate interlevel activity between the molecular level and the physiological systems level.

Currently, two approaches are used to study this mediating function of epigenetic mechanisms (Vergères & Gille, 2014, pp. 5f.): the first approach focuses on individual organisms or cells with the goal of mapping all epigenetic mechanisms in relation to the entire genomic and metabolomic information. This approach is inspired by systems biology and is used in studies that try to map whole micro RNA networks (e.g. Lee, Baek, Gusev, Brackett, Nuovo, & Schmittgen, 2007) or DNA methylation patterns of specific cell types (e.g. Meissner, Mikkelsen, Gu, Wernig, Hanna, Sivachenko et al., 2008). The second approach focuses on intergroup differences of single epigenetic mechanisms, mostly DNA methylation patterns at loci of candidate genes, and matches them with epidemiological data at the population level. This approach is mostly used in studies of transgenerational transmission of epigenetic changes that try to uncover gene–environment interaction (e.g. Heijmans, Tobi, Stein, Putter, Blauw, Susser et al., 2008; Pembrey, Bygren, Kaati, Edvinsson, Northstone, Sjostrom et al., 2006). Using the first approach, researchers may uncover feedback, inter, and coaction mechanisms at the molecular level for an individual cell type. In contrast, the second approach is restricted to statistical correlations between very different forms of data (molecular, behavioral, general health data) at the population level without actually addressing the (material) mechanisms of their interaction. However, this epidemiological approach allows integration of other types of information such as the social status, life events, and further social, cultural, and biographical data. The latter is especially relevant for psychological development for which these are considered as relevant developmental factors. Therefore, to finally make sense of epigenetics with regard to psychobiological development, future research needs to address the methodological gap between both approaches and to develop a developmental framework that allows integration of both levels of data collection, the individual level and the population level.

Developmental neuroscience

A similar task seems to be pressing for developmental neuroscience. Originally, its notion of development was derived from embryology. Based on concepts such as differentiation, induction, and developmental pathways, the development of the nervous system, its tissue, and the structural characteristics of the brain were studied in humans and other species. From this perspective, developmental neuroscience was mostly interested in neural development at the cellular and tissue level with specific focus on the anatomical structure of the brain and early periods of embryonic development (Munakata, Casey, & Diamond, 2004, p. 122, Box 1). The methods used for this kind of research were mainly post-mortem tissue analysis, animal models, and in vitro studies (Zhou & Mei, 2013). Nowadays, with the new imaging techniques—especially fMRI—it has become possible to compare structure and function of a particular brain at different time points. In addition to pathological changes, fMRI enables studying "normal" changes of the brain during the life time of an individual. Thus, subsequent behavioral and psychological testing—a major limitation of post-mortem studies—as well as age cohort comparisons are now possible.

With these methods a new type of studies emerged: for instance, Oishi et al. tried to find quantitative measures for the development of individual brain parts similar to those used for body height and weight (Oishi, Faria, Yoshido, Chang, & Mori, 2013); and Cao et al. studied network efficiency in relation to age over the life-span (Cao, Wang, Daia, Cao, Jiang, Fan et al., 2014). In a research review of studies mapping connectivity in the developing brain, Dennis and Thompson (2014) highlight a growing amount of studies that relate structural or functional differences to age in normal populations and in populations with developmental pathologies. Since these studies correlate structural and functional change of the brain with age at a population level, they are based on an epidemiological concept of development, which they directly or indirectly derived from life-span developmental psychology.[7]

As in the field of developmental psychology, the shift towards an epidemiological concept of development allows the integration of new types of data sets including general information about the social and health status of the participants and different psychological measures. This is especially useful in studies that try to match structural and functional changes of the brain with psychological functions. However, in order to finally uncover the underlying biological mechanisms, these data have to be linked to causal physiological mechanisms of the brain and to neural development. In spite of this, in models of brain development, and in studies of neural cell differentiation, the embryological concept of development is still used to explain the underlying biological mechanisms. Thus, there is a growing need for an integrative framework combining both types of studies: the "traditional" physiological studies of brain and neural development, which use an embryological concept of development, and the "new" functional imaging studies, which use an epidemiological concept of development.

Conclusion

The concept of development in biology was originally derived from embryology and from there extrapolated to evolutionary theory and psychology. Such concept of development focused on changes at the individual level and was based on developmental mechanisms like differentiation and induction. With the synthesis of population genetics and evolutionary theory, a population-based, epidemiological concept of development was introduced to interpret processes of phylogenetic change. As a consequence, a theoretical gap between the individual level of development—ontogenesis—and the population level of development—phylogenesis—was established. Although we observe recurrent attempts to integrate both levels of development, such as Waddington's epigenetic landscape and chreodes, or Oyama's developmental systems theory, they have failed to bridge the specificity and context dependence of individual developmental processes with the statistical character of population data.

This epistemological gap between the embryological and the epidemiological concept of development has been present in developmental psychology for several decades. It also seems to be constitutive for the emerging field of epigenetics, which studies changes of gene expression that are not caused by changes of the DNA sequence at both individual cell level and population level. Recently, this gap has emerged anew in developmental neuroscience with the introduction of functional imaging methods, which allow comparison of structural and functional changes in living brains over the life-span and therefore correlation of them with age and other epidemiological measures.

The gap between these conceptions has consequences for methodology and data interpretation. The core issue is how epidemiological data can be projected on embryological knowledge to determine causal mechanisms. Neither the embryological nor the epidemiological concept of development is able to integrate both types of data as both are limited to either the individual or the population level. Therefore, one important step is to develop a comprehensive concept of development.

Such an integrative concept could be based on a systemic perspective of development, as in Oyama's approach of developmental systems theory. However, in order to actually use a systemic approach to bridge the individual and the population level, the specificity and context dependence of developmental processes need to be further specified. This is especially important for psychobiological development, which heavily depends on embryological mechanisms, social and cultural conditions, and individual self-regulation and agency. Thus, any integrative framework proposed needs to reconstruct in detail inter- and coaction between these levels. In order to do so, for example, longitudinal studies of psychobiological developmental in psychology, neuroepigenetics, and developmental neuroscience should focus more on individual and context data analysis and less on data analysis at a population level. Hence, an open, systemic concept of development that focuses on individual specificity and inter-level interaction is the most promising approach for those life sciences currently occupied with studying the co-developing mind and brain.

Notes

1 According to Georg Toepfer, the French term "développement" was first used at the end of the 17th century to characterize anatomic and physiological change, and the English term "development" was not used in a biological sense until the second half of the 18th century (Toepfer, 2011, pp. 391–392).
2 Most importantly John Locke's *An Essay Concerning Human Understanding* (1690).
3 For a revised version of Gottlieb's model of psychobiological development, which allows integration of epigenetic activity and further differentiates between a level of sensory/motor activity and higher mental activity, see Lux, 2013.
4 For a revised version of Gottlieb's model of psychobiological development, which allows integrating epigenetic activity and further differentiates between a level of sensory/motor activity and higher mental activity, see Lux, 2013.
5 However, as Valsiner points out: "making sense of probability is the key issue" (2007, p. 835). Valsiner argues that, while there is also a frequentist and a Bayesian notion of probability, which are widely used in statistical modeling in psychology, only the propensity notion of probability—according to which probability is determined by the analysis of the structural possibilities of a given object, its surroundings, and its possible future activities—fits Gottlieb's notion of developmental probability (Valsiner, 2007).
6 In fact, age cohort comparisons on a population level set the basis for the development of IQ tests by Alfred Binet and Théodore Simon in 1905. The combination of development and age cohort enabled differentiating between normal development, understood as the mean IQ of the age group, and deficits or "overachievements" in development. Later on, William Stern (1914) further developed this epidemiological concept of IQ development.
7 One clear sign for this link is the explicit use of the term "life-span", for example, by Cao, Wang, Daia, Cao, Jiang, Fan et al. (2014).

References

Baltes, P. B. (1979). Einleitung: Einige Beobachtungen und Überlegungne zur Verknüpfung von Geschichte und Theorie der Entwicklungspsychologie der Lebensspanne [Introduction: Observations and reflections regarding the history and the theory of lifespan developmental psychology]. In P. B. Baltes (Ed.), *Klett-CottaPsychologie: Entwicklungspsychologie der Lebensspanne* (1st ed., pp. 13–33). Stuttgart: Klett-Cotta.
Baltes, P. B. & Goulet, L. R. (1979). Ortsbestimmung und Systematisierung der Fragen einer Entwicklungspsychologie der Lebensspanne [Positioning and systematization of lifespan developmental psychology]. In P. B. Baltes (Ed.), *Klett-CottaPsychologie: Entwicklungspsychologie der Lebensspanne* (1st ed., pp. 35–53). Stuttgart: Klett-Cotta.
Baltes, P. B., Reese, H. W., & Lipsitt, L. P. (1980). Life-span developmental psychology. *Annual Review of Psychology*, *31*, 65–110.
Bird, A. (2007). Perceptions of epigenetics. *Nature*, *447*(7143), 396–398.
Bowlby, J. (1973). *Separation: Anxiety and anger. Attachment and loss: Vol. 2*. New York: Basic Books.
Bühler, K. (1921). *Die geistige Entwicklung des Kindes* [The mental development of the child]. Jena: Verlag von Gustav Fischer.
Cao, M., Wang, J.-H., Daia, Z.-J., Cao, X.-Y., Jiang, L.-L., Fan, F.-M., et al. (2014). Topological organization of the human brain functionalconnectome across the lifespan. *Developmental Cognitive Neuroscience*, *7*, 76–93.
Dennis, E. L. & Thompson, P. M. (2014). Reprint of: Mapping connectivity in the developing brain. *International Journal of Developmental Neuroscience*, *32*(7), 525–542.

Driesch, H. (1905). *Der Vitalismus als Geschichte und als Lehre* [The history and theory of vitalism]. Leipzig: Verlag von Johann Ambrosius Barth.

Erikson, E. H. (1959). *Identity and the life cycle*. Selected papers. *Psychological issues: Vol. 1, No. 1*. New York: International University Press.

Fagiolini, M., Jensen, C. L., & Champagne, F. A. (2009). Epigenetic influences on brain development and plasticity: Development. *Current Opinion in Neurobiology, 19*(2), 207–212.

Fraga, M. F., Ballestar, E., Paz, M. F., Ropero, S., Setien, F., Ballestar, M. L., et al. (2005). Epigenetic differences arise during the lifetime of monozygotic twins. *Proceedings of the National Academy of Sciences of the United States of America, 102*(30), 10604–10609, doi:10.1073/pnas.0500398102.

Franklin, T. B. & Mansuy, I. M. (2010). Epigenetic inheritance in mammals: Evidence for the impact of adverse environmental effects. *Neurobiology of Disease, 39*(1), 61–65, doi:10.1016/j.nbd.2009.11.012.

Gilbert, S. F. (2000). Paradigm shifts in neural induction. *Revue d'histoire des sciences, 53*(3–4), 555–580.

Gilbert, S. F. (2012). Commentary: "The Epigenotype" by C.H. Waddington. *International Journal of Epidemiology, 41*(1), 20–23.

Gottlieb, G. (1991). Experiential canalization of behavioral development: Theory. *Developmental Psychology, 27*(1), 4–13.

Gottlieb, G. (1992). *Individual development and evolution: The genesis of novel behavior.* New York: Oxford University Press.

Gottlieb, G. (2003). Probabilistic epigenesis of development. In J. Valsiner & K. J. Connolly (Eds.), *Handbook of developmental psychology* (pp. 3–17). London: Sage Publications.

Gottlieb, G. (2007). Probabilistic epigenesis. *Developmental Science, 10*(1), 1–11.

Gräff, J., Kim, D., Dobbin, M. M., & Tsai, L.-H. (2011). Epigenetic regulation of gene expression in physiological and pathological brain processes. *Physiological Reviews, 91*(2), 603–649.

Haig, D. (2012). Commentary: The epidemiology of epigenetics. *International Journal of Epidemiology, 41*(1), 13–16.

Heijmans, B. T., Tobi, E. W., Stein, A. D., Putter, H., Blauw, G. J., Susser, E. S., et al. (2008). Persistent epigenetic differences associated with prenatal exposure to famine in humans. *Proceedings of the National Academy of Sciences of the United States of America, 105*(44), 17046–17049, doi:10.1073/pnas.0806560105.

Holliday, R. (1994). Epigenetics: An overview. *Developmental Genetics, 15*, 453–457.

Holliday, R. (2002). Epigenetics comes of age in the twenty first century. *Journal of Genetics, 81*(1), 1–4.

Huxley, J. (1956). Epigenetics. *Nature, 177*(4514), 807–809.

Jablonka, E. & Lamb, M. J. (2002). The changing concept of epigenetics. *Annals of the New York Academy of Sciences, 981*(1), 82–96.

Jablonka, E. & Lamb, M. J. (2005). *Evolution in four dimensions: Genetic, epigenetic, behavioral, and symbolic variation in the history of life* (with illustrations by Anna Zeligowski). *A Bradford book*. Cambridge, MA: MIT Press.

Jaenisch, R. & Bird, A. (2003). Epigenetic regulation of gene expression: How the genome integrates intrinsic and environmental signals. *Nature Genetics, 31*, 245–254.

Kreß, H. (2014). Epigenetische Mechanismen embryonaler Induktion und sozialer Prägungsprozesse [Epigenetic mechanisms of embryonic induction and social imprinting].

In V. Lux & J. T. Richter (Eds.), *Kulturen der Epigenetik: Vererbt, codiert, übertragen* (pp. 179–192). Berlin: De Gruyter.

Lee, E. J., Baek, M., Gusev, Y., Brackett, D. J., Nuovo, G. J., & Schmittgen, T. D. (2007). Systematic evaluation of microRNA processing patterns in tissues, cell lines, and tumors. *RNA, 14*(1), 35–42.

Lewontin, R. C., Rose, S., & Kamin, L. J. (1984). *Not in our genes: Biology, ideology, and human nature*. New York: Pantheon Books.

Locke, J. (1690). *An essay concerning human understanding*. London: Scholar Press.

Lux, V. (2013). With Gottlieb beyond Gottlieb: The role of epigenetics in psychobiological development. *International Journal of Developmental Science, 7*(2), 69–78.

Lux, V. (in press). Waddingtons Chreode [Waddington's chreode]. In T. Petzer & S. Steiner (Eds.), *Synergie: Kultur- und Wissensgeschichte einer Denkfigur*. Paderborn: Wilhelm Fink.

Mason, C. (2009). The development of developmental neuroscience. *The Journal of Neuroscience, 29*(41), 12735–12747, doi: 10.1523/JNEUROSCI.4648-09.2009.

Meissner, A., Mikkelsen, T. S., Gu, H., Wernig, M., Hanna, J., Sivachenko, A., et al. (2008). Genome-scale DNA methylation maps of pluripotent and differentiated cells. *Nature, 454*(7205), 766–770, doi:10.1038/nature07107.

Montada, L. (1995). Fragen, Konzepte, Perspektiven [Questions, concepts, perspectives]. In R. Oerter & L. Montada (Eds.), *Entwicklungspsychologie: Ein Lehrbuch* (3rd ed., pp. 1–83). Weinheim: Psychologie Verlags Union.

Munakata, Y., Casey, B. J., & Diamond, A. (2004). Developmental cognitive neuroscience: Progress and potential. *TRENDS in Cognitive Sciences, 8*(3), 122–128.

Nüsslein-Volhard, C. & Wieschaus, E. (1980). Mutations affecting segment number and polarity in Drosophila. *Nature, 287*(5785), 795–801, doi:10.1038/287795a0.

Oishi, K., Faria, A. V., Yoshido, S., Chang, L., & Mori, S. (2013). Quantitative evaluation of brain development using anatomical MRI and diffusion tensor imaging. *International Journal of Developmental Neuroscience, 31*, 512–524.

Oyama, S. (2000). *Evolution's eye: A systems view of the biology–culture divide. Science and cultural theory*. Durham, NC: Duke University Press.

Oyama, S. (2006). Boundaries and (constructive) interaction. In E. M. Neumann-Held & C. Rehmann-Sutter (Eds.), *Science and cultural theory: Genes in development. Re-reading the molecular paradigm* (pp. 272–289). Durham, NC: Duke University Press.

Pembrey, M. E., Bygren, L. O., Kaati, G., Edvinsson, S., Northstone, K., Sjostrom, M., et al. (2006). Sex-specific, male-line transgenerational responses in humans. *European Journal of Human Genetics: EJHG, 14*(2), 159–166, doi:10.1038/sj.ejhg.5201538.

Petronis, A., Gottesman, I. I., Crow, T. J., DeLisi, L. E., Klar, A. J., Macciardi, F., et al. (2000). Psychiatric epigenetics: A new focus for the new century. *Molecular Psychiatry, 5*(4), 342–346.

Piaget, J. (1980). *Abriß der genetischen Epistemologie* [Genetic epistemology: An outline]. Olten, Switzerland: Walter.

Piaget, J. (2003). *Meine Theorie der geistigen Entwicklung* [My theory of cognitive development]. Edited by Reinhard Fatke (engl. Org. Ausg. 1970). *Beltz-TaschenbuchPsychologie: Vol. 142*. Weinheim: Beltz.

Preyer, W. (1882). *The mind of the child*. In Four Books. London.

Quetelet, A. (1835). *Sur l'homme et le developpement de ses facultés: ou, Essai de physique sociale* [A treatise on man and the development of his faculties: or, Essay concerning social materiality]. Paris: Bachelier.

Riggs, A. D., Martienssen, R. A., & Russo, V. E. A. (1996). Introduction. In V. E. A. Russo, A. D. Riggs, & R. A. Martienssen (Eds.), *Cold Spring Harbor monograph series: Vol. 32. Epigenetic mechanisms of gene regulation* (pp. 1–4). Plainview, NY: Cold Spring Harbor Laboratory Press.

Roux, W. (1888). Beiträge zur Entwickelungsmechanik des Embryo [Contributions to the development mechanics of the embryo]. *Virchows Archiv, 114*(2), 246–291, doi:10.1007/BF01882630.

Roux, W. (1895). *Gesammelte Abhandlungen über Entwicklungsmechanik der Organismen: Bd. II: Abhandlungen XIII–XXXIII, über Entwicklungsmechanik des Embryo* [The developmental mechanics of the organism: Collected writings II: On the developmental mechanics of the Embryo]. Leipzig: Verlag von Wilhelm Engelmann.

Spemann, H., & Mangold, H. (1924). Über Induktion von Embryonalanlagen durch Implantation artfremder Organisatoren [On the induction of embryonic primordia by implantation of organizers of different species]. *Archiv für mikroskopische Anatomie und Entwicklungsmechanik, 100*(3–4), 599–638.

Stern, W. (1914). *The psychological methods of testing intelligence.* Baltimore, MD: Warwick & York.

Stockard, C. R. (1921). Developmental rate and structural expression: An experimental study of twins, "double monsters" and single deformities, and the interaction among embryonic organs during their origin and development. *American Journal of Anatomy, 28*(2), 115–277, doi:10.1002/aja.1000280202.

Sultan, F. A. & Day, J. J. (2011). Epigenetic mechanisms in memory and synaptic function. *Epigenomics, 3*(2), 157–181.

Toepfer, G. (2011). *Historisches Wörterbuch der Biologie: Geschichte und Theorie der biologischen Grundbegriffe* [Encyclopedia of history and theory of basic concepts in biology]. Stuttgart: Metzler.

Valsiner, J. (2007). Gilbert Gottlieb's theory of probabilistic epigenesis: Probabilites and realities in development. *Developmental Psychobiology, 49*, 832–840.

van Speybroeck, L., Waele, D. de, & van de Vijver, G. (2002). Theories in early embryology: Close connections between epigenesis, preformationism, and self-organization. *Annals of the New York Academy of Sciences, 981*(1), 7–49.

Vergères, G. & Gille, D. (2014). Nutri(epi)genomik [Nutri(epi)genomics]. In V. Lux & J. T. Richter (eds.), *Kulturen der Epigenetik: Vererbt, codiert, übertragen* (pp. 1–9). Berlin: De Gruyter.

Waddington, C. H. (1942). The epigenotype. *Endeavour, 1*, 18–20.

Waddington, C. H. (1957). *The strategy of the genes: A discussion of some aspects of theoretical biology.* London: George Allen & Unwin.

Waddington, C. H. (1970). Der gegenwärtige Stand der Evolutionstheorie [Evolutionary theory: The state of the art]. In A. Koestler & J. R. Smythies (Eds.), *Das neue Menschenbild: Die Revolutionierung der Wissenschaft vom Leben. Ein internationales Symposium* (pp. 342–373). Wien, München, Zürich: Verlag Fritz Molden.

Waddington, C. H. & Thom, R. (1968). Correspondence between Waddington and Thom. In C. H. Waddington (Ed.), *Towards a theoretical biology. 1. Prolegomena: An IUBS symposium* (pp. 166–179). Edinburgh: Edinburgh University Press.

Waterland, R. A., Travisano, M., Tahiliani, K. G., Rached, M. T., & Mirza, S. (2008). Methyl donor supplementation prevents transgenerational amplification of obesity. *International Journal of Obesity, 32*(9), 1373–1379, doi:10.1038/ijo.2008.100.

Willer, S. (2010). "Epigenesis" in epigentics: Scientific knowledge, concepts, and words. In A. Barahona, E. Suarez-Díaz, & H.-J. Rheinberger (Eds.), *Max-Planck-Institut für Wissenschaftsgeschichte: Preprint; 392. Hereditary hourglass: genetics and epigenetics 1868–2000* (pp. 13–21). Berlin: Max-Planck-Institut für Wissenschaftsgeschichte.

Wu, C. T. & Morris, J. R. (2001). Genes, genetics, and epigenetics: A correspondence. *Science, 293*(5532), 1103–1105.

Zhang, T.-Y. & Meaney, M. J. (2009). Epigenetics and the environmental regulation of the genome and its function. *Annual Review of Psychology, 61*(1), 439–466.

Zhou, R. & Mei, L. (Eds.) (2013). *Neural development: Methods and protocols.* New York: Humana Press.

Part II

Study of development in its move to the twenty-first century

Chapter 4

The passion of Bob Cairns

Creating developmental science

Jaan Valsiner

Development is a very difficult concept to handle by science. It is a process of sustained transformation that occurs everywhere. Galaxies and planetary systems develop—so do viruses and immune systems. Life has emerged—developed—out of non-organic materials; human beings have invented various tools to enhance and stop development—ranging from fertility amulets and kindergartens, to condoms and guillotines. We invent new devices—and reflect upon our creations in terms of the notion of *development*.

Development is an ideologically contested process—be it in nature (the loss of the ozone layer) or in society (emergent adulthood and emerging markets). It is a social utopia—presented as "something good"—while at the same time it entails the destruction of the previous state of affairs. In this sense, talking about development can bring about irrevocable transformations—some desired, others feared. There exist many courses in universities for how to raise a child, or create companies—but none on how to make a revolution or organize a military *coup d'état*. Development can look dangerous.

The social ambivalence towards development is paralleled by the lack of conceptual readiness to handle developing phenomena. It requires conceptualizing the relationship across the timeline of the present, in between the future and the past, in the ever-moving structure of PAST–PRESENT–FUTURE along the lines of irreversible time (Valsiner, 2014). This structure is invariant over time—yet each and every concrete content of it is completely unique. There is no repetition of the here-and-now event as "the same"—irreversibility of time makes recognition of continuities in development possible only in terms of similarity, not "sameness". In the world view of irreversible time, an event A that occurs now, and will be followed sometime later by another one that we recognize as if it is the "second coming" of A, is actually that of relation of similarity, not sameness. A *coming after* another A is not the same, but similar. It is an indicator of continuity in development indeed—while the crucial issue in development actually is the discontinuity in its different forms. The latter entail breakdowns, regressions (i.e., recognition of forms now that look similar to some earlier stages in development), small novelties within similarity ($A_1 \rightarrow A_2$), and—most importantly—emergence ($A \rightarrow B$ where B is not similar to any form observed before). Emergence is the creation of new properties regardless of the substances involved (Emmeche, Køppe, and Stjernfeldt, 1997, p. 88) and so is a question of the scientists' meta-theoretical perspectives in their field—whether it is astrophysics, biology, or psychology.

Epistemologically, the basic distinction within sciences is this between non-developmental and developmental science perspectives (Shanahan, Valsiner, and Gottlieb, 1997). The former are based on ontological postulate (A is A), while the latter presume an ontology on becoming (A becomes A or B or vanishes into non-existence). What is ontological in the developmental science is the *process of becoming*, not any states of being. States of being are transitory—they create the background at which the processes of becoming can be discerned. Furthermore, analyzing becoming entails conceptualizing what is not yet observable—i.e., the potential, which is not yet actual. Developmental sciences necessarily include some teleological conceptual component (see the struggles around vitalism in developmental biology—Valsiner, Chapter 2 in this volume).

What becomes obvious from this juxtaposition of state and process ontologies is that these are not reducible into each other. They are complementary—thus, there can exist (in principle) specific sciences like developmental astrophysics, developmental sociology, developmental anthropology, yet such disciplines do not exist. In psychology there is the branch of developmental psychology, which is often reduced to the sequential ontologies of children (and sometimes adults) over the life course (Cairns, 1998; Cairns & Cairns, 2006).

Psychology is a deeply ideological discipline (Valsiner, 2012) in which issues of child and adolescent development have been of practical discursive value. Hence, the discursive—but not actual—notion of development has been used in the description of child, adolescent, and (at times) elder ways of being. As is shown in our recent development of life-course analyses (Zittoun et al., 2013), the problems are theoretical and meta-theoretical. Even the most celebrated developmental psychologist of the 20th century—Jean Piaget—was in the final analysis mostly non-developmental in his work (Valsiner, 2001).

Yet there was an active proponent of the developmental orientation in psychology—Robert B. Cairns (1933–1999). While quintessentially a thinker of North American background of the venerable traditions of William James, John Dewey, and Burrhus Skinner, Bob Cairns would compare favorably with all of the best scholars from the New World who integrated worldwide knowledge into their incessant and unbounded quest to find new solutions to basic problems in science. The result—by the 1990s—was the creation of the movement of Developmental Science around the institutional unit (Center for Developmental Science) that Bob Cairns managed to establish in Chapel Hill, North Carolina, at its old university—University of North Carolina at Chapel Hill. As of now—15 years after his death at the time of writing—the Center still stands under the same name, but the theoretical innovations attempted by Bob at the time have vanished. The present chapter is written with the aim of making Bob Cairns' quest manifest, and maintaining his ideas for the readers who might develop these further.

The making of developmental science

One of the most productive and visible initiatives to put development in the foreground of psychological research was the Carolina Consortium on Human Development—currently the Center for Developmental Science—that was established in 1994 by Bob Cairns after a long local struggle with fellow psychologists and university administrators for the need to establish a top-of-the-line think-tank on advancing developmental ideas. As any university administration around the world is limited in its view to the immediate teaching tasks, so was the leadership of the University of North Carolina at Chapel Hill. However, if you get a grant (better a big one, and from a U.S. Federal source with a high "overhead" coming to the administration), you might put your plans into practice. Bob Cairns did—and the granting success made possible the innovation in developmental ideas in North Carolina during the 1980s and 1990s.

The resulting synthesis was deeply interdisciplinary. By integrating ideas from developmental biology and psychology while bringing colleagues from sociology and anthropology to discuss developmental ideas, Cairns managed to synthetize a framework aimed at understanding *and* explaining human development in its multiple levels—thus addressing ontogenetic to cross-generational processes. The need to learn from the history of developmental ideas in conjunction with longitudinal empirical investigations was the root for his intellectual success.

The most important aspect of Cairns' contributions to developmental science was the way in which he managed to weave the ideas from history of the biological and behavioral sciences[1] with the development of new research methodologies. Even as developmental science has been brought to the public view since then (Cairns, Elder, & Costello, 1996), the question of what development is and how it can be studied continues to puzzle developmental psychologists.

Inherent ambivalence in developmental thinking

Thinking of developmental psychologists is ambivalent. On the one hand, the phenomena of development set severe constraints upon how they can be studied. These constraints point to the uniqueness of any developmental phenomenon, as well as to the need for conceptualizing emergence of new phenomena. The question of generalized knowledge about development is a difficult one here—how can we arrive at general knowledge based on unique and emergent phenomena? New methodology is needed for that.

On the other hand, tenets of contemporary psychology are solidly based on non-developmental premises. Instead of focusing on uniqueness and emergence, psychology—including its developmental branch—regularly eliminates the latter and overlooks the former. Hence the need for independent developmental science, which unifies research issues based on axioms of development across biology, psychology, sociology, and anthropology. When developmental research proceeds within psychology, it struggles either with loss of its phenomena (as amply described in Cairns, 1986b), or with inconsistencies between those phenomena and normative methodology (cf. Magnusson & Cairns, 1996).

It is in the context of uncertainties about developmental science that the uses of history of developmental thought may guide our future inquiries. Bob Cairns understood this point very well, and used his knowledge of history for these purposes. By narrating specific episodes from the history of developmental ideas, he created a dialogue with the contemporary field of developmental thought. The latter, however, is fragmented by different implicit models of development assumed by the researchers.

Retrospective and prospective models of development

The concept of development is a difficult idea to handle for people who look for stability. On the one extreme it leads to proliferation of plasticity and "anything-may-happen" orientation. That may seem in line with the "post-modernist" intellectual disease of accepting the context-specificity of knowledge and its fragmentation as a given, thus refraining from any generalization efforts. What a heaven this is for blind empiricism: if any context of human existence is unique, a science of the study of that (narrow) context can be put on the map of science, and diligently studied as long as any of the research participants is still at least remotely cooperating.

On the other side, the notion of development is habitually eliminated from scientific discourse, and replaced by one or another form of stability as captured by concepts that exclude any emergence of "developmental surprises". This may take different forms. For example, the reduction of the variability of developmental phenomena to accounts of stages (i.e., to fixed sequences of stable states) amounts to treating development not as a constructive but as a pre-determined process. Piaget's claim that his stage sequence of cognitive development is invariant across societies and history may be true; yet it has made a way to elimination of a focus upon the developmental process. Even the analyses of developmental trajectories—depicted as non-linear or linear curves superimposed upon the data of development (up to the present moment)—replace the uncertainty of the ongoing developmental process by a static, *post factum* (yet time-inclusive) account of the *results* of development. In this respect, stage accounts and descriptions of developmental trajectories are examples of *retrospective models* of development. These models idealize that side of the development that has taken place, and leave out of consideration the set of possibilities that existed at each moment of development—but were not actualized.

In contrast, theoretical models that operate with the notion of restricted open-endedness of the *next* developmental moment (in relation to the present) would allow access to the "surprises" that development brings with it. Such perspectives—let us call them *progressive models* of development—can operate with the notion of complex of psychological functions (such as Vygotsky's notion of the "zone of proximal development"; see Valsiner & van der Veer, 1993, 2014) or on the basis of a generalized notion of probabilism (Gottlieb, 1999). The focus in these approaches is in capturing the emergence of novelty. This focus is shared by researchers in other areas—such as cognitive problem solving (e.g., Karl Duncker, Max Wertheimer), which is not noted to belong to the category of developmental perspectives. Yet the interest of these researchers in *how new solutions* to problems *emerge* makes them developmental in the process-oriented way.

It is the tension between different kinds of conceptual models that makes the progress in developmental science slow and torturous. The move from considering development via retrospective models (where the highly valued notions of "control" and "prediction" may be—in *post factum* analyses—possible) to that in terms of prospective models is a major step. It entails acceptance of the unpredictability of the future, and of the notion of structural synthesis in irreversible time. Basic natural sciences have only recently arrived at this theoretical platform (Prigogine, 1973), essentially building upon the achievements of developmental science of the end of the 19th century.

Models of development of ideas

Histories of ideas are narrated as meta-level stories in relation of the target ideas. Thus, any history of the developmental perspectives is a meta-narrative about the ideas used to understand development per se. As such, it can also be of different kinds—different models of history of psychology parallel those of development. For example, a *retrospective* (stage) model involves focusing on the sequence of popular ideas over time (e.g., how "mentalism" in psychology was succeeded by "behaviorism", then "behaviorism" by "cognitivism", etc.). Alternatively, a *prospective transitions* model would lead to a scrutiny of the ideas that made it possible for one tradition to be replaced by another. Different history-makers use different models to write about history of the discipline.

The initial bond: Bob Cairns' affiliations and transcendence

In some ways, the primary social contexts of one's academic development matter. Bob Cairns grew out of the social learning traditions—particularly those of Robert Sears and Albert Bandura. His first scientific work was firmly fitted within the social learning perspectives, dealing with the role that established dependency *inhibition* in adolescent boys in a juvenile institution played in disabling the efforts of social reinforcement (Cairns, 1961). No traces of interest in wider issues of development (nor of the history of developmental ideas) are visible in that early work. Such interests show their emergence in later work on dependency (and attachment, see Cairns, 1972, p. 30; see also Cairns, 1973, p. 60), and certainly flourish by the second half of the 1970s. Later on, brief excursions into selected aspects of history became a regular feature in Bob Cairns' writings—usually when he needed to make some critical point about issues of development or its study methodology.

While remaining true to the positive input that the early rearing environment of social learning provided for him, Bob himself performed the task of critical analysis of the social learning traditions (Cairns, 1977, pp. 18–19; 1979, chapter 19). Social learning perspectives emerged from international roots, but proceeded in a fully North America-centered fashion—thus mediated by the overwhelming focus on learning of American psychology. Cognitive features are slow and tentative emerging characteristics within the social learning perspectives ("social–cognitive reinterpretation"). This historical overview of the ways in which the social learning perspectives constituted efforts at synthesis of all psychological processes in North America represents the general post-World War II move of the center of research from the Old to the New World. With it came its adaptation to new socio-moral (and religious) conditions, and to the mass (democratic) society's dealing with social problems. In the context of post-1945 psychology, mostly advanced in the U.S., the ideas of development (and, more generally, focus on psychological *processes*) have been constantly diminished in researchers' thinking in favor of description of psychological functions (and even development) in terms of outcomes (i.e., test scores, "diagnoses" of children's "developmental stages", and the like). The emphases on development as a process have been kept alive by few scholars of the caliber of Z.-Y. Kuo, T. C. Schneirla, G. Gottlieb, the legacy of Heinz Werner's students— largely in opposition to the "mainstream" of psychology. Bob Cairns joins in that effort of preserving and advancing ideas of development in his selection of empirical work topics, as well as in his narrating of history of developmental ideas.

In his own transcending of the confines of his social learning background, Bob Cairns pointed to the limitations of thought in the latter. First, a shortcoming common to all generations of social learning is that they only pay lip-service to the concept of the child as a developing, changing organism. A correlated oversight is to ignore the maturation-paced changes that are woven into virtually all features of the child's social adaptation. The second unfinished task for the social learning views concerns the job of building an adequate theory of how interchanges are learned and organized, changed and generalized. Finally, the harshest criticism that can be leveled at social learning theories is that they offer a convincing explanation—for everything. A large stockpile of learning concepts has accumulated in three generations of theory building (including some nebulous and tautological ones), and few have been discarded. If one set of concepts fails to explain a given finding, another set can be called into action. Although such flexibility is admirable, the theory becomes virtually impossible to falsify. And if a theory cannot be shown to be wrong, one must have questions about whether its explanations are accurate or merely plausible (Cairns, 1979, p. 344). Study of development needed a different start, one that would be relatively free from the confines of learning theories, and built upon the history of developmental ideas in other sciences— especially in developmental biology.

History of developmental ideas, as narrated by Bob Cairns: a continuing dialogue

Why are histories written at all? Being supposedly about the past of the given science, their making (and re-making) is an indicator of efforts to construct the future of the science. The interest in history of developmental psychology that Bob Cairns took over all his life was part of his construction of the new developmental science.[2] Furthermore, I would like to suggest that the main function for Bob Cairns' uses of history of developmental ideas was to create a scholarly pool of ideas that are relevant for our intellectual efforts at the present time. Thus, through telling stories of the ideas of Wilhelm Preyer, Karl Ernst von Baer, James Mark Baldwin, G. Stanley Hall, Alfred Binet, and others, Bob brought these historical figures into the sphere of our contemporary inquiries as our equal (or sometimes superior) interlocutors.

Furthermore, that writing of history as a message participating in our contemporary discussions entailed for Bob a clear anchoring in the contribution to human welfare in the sense of betterment of human condition. Although being pan-human, and appreciative of variation across societies, his primary focus was that of the historical development of the U.S. society in its whole complexity. While most of Bob's research on psychobiological and interactive development was based on the work with lambs (Cairns, 1966) and mice (e.g., Cairns & Scholtz, 1973, out of the earlier work), ever since his graduate years he was deeply interested in the human development. This interest stems from his own development within the framework of social learning theories of Robert Sears and Albert Bandura, and from his early clinical work. It is somewhere through these formative years—perhaps best described as Bob Cairns' "academic adolescence"—that the focus on synthesis across different levels of organization of developmental issues took shape. Thus, his ideas resonated with cognitive developmental psychology as well as with developmental aspects of sociology.

Two general themes constituted the intellectual playground for Bob Cairns to move skillfully across different levels of developmental organization. First, the notion of *relationships* in its various versions—attachment, dyadic interchange, and social networks—has been central for his thinking. Second, the focus on *development across generations*—be that over many generations of mice, or of humans in the Carolina Longitudinal Study—was his relevant thematic ground. Overriding both, however, was his basic humanistic attitude to life and society, which showed itself in the compassion for the consensually stigmatized "outsiders"— the aggressive mice (or adolescents), the urban poor, and the developmental thinkers who had been pushed out of academia (e.g., Baldwin). The unity of basic developmental science knows no boundaries between disciplines, or countries. The applied efforts to make the social world better for the development of individuals is bound to a particular social system—the society Bob Cairns knew best, the U.S.—and for developmental scientists worldwide,[3] this was the crucial feature of Bob Cairns' synthesis of his life-work.

Main sources

Bob Cairns' uses of history of psychology provide us with a continuing narrative—the function of which can be seen in his effort to build up a consistent developmental science (The Carolina Consortium of Human Development, 1996; Magnusson & Cairns, 1996). Although there are glimpses of the role of historical accounts in his writings before 1979 (Cairns, 1970), the major sources of a continuing narrative of the history of developmental psychology are three: Hearst's chapter of 1979 (Cairns & Ornstein, 1979), the Mussen Handbook chapter of 1983 (Cairns, 1983), and the Damon Handbook chapter of 1998 (Cairns, 1998). These three sources are partially overlapping, hence one can document how specific ideas expressed within them—on the basis of stories about history—have transformed over two decades.

Summary of the authors and topics covered in the three sources can be found in Table 4.1 and Table 4.2 respectively.

There are some interesting changes evident over the two decades covered by these three sources. While some of the historical figures in Bob's narrative—such as Wilhelm Preyer, James Mark Baldwin, G. S. Hall, Alfred Binet, Jean Piaget, Sigmund Freud, Kurt Lewin, Zing-Yang Kuo—remain constantly in focus over the three texts, others show changes over time. Thus, William Stern is briefly mentioned in 1979 (as the originator of the IQ ratio, see Cairns & Ornstein, 1979, p. 485), gets similar treatment in the second presentation (Cairns, 1983, p. 60), and becomes expanded to a two-page exposition in the third (Cairns, 1998, pp. 54–55). In the third rendering, Stern is presented as a major theoretician of person–environment relations; and no longer merely the inventor of IQ. His fate in the history of developmental psychology was likened to that of James Mark Baldwin (Cairns, 1998, p. 55).

Table 4.1 Authors covered in Cairns' three major history-oriented publications

Author	Pages in		
	Cairns & Ornstein, 1979	*Cairns, 1983*	*Cairns, 1998*
G. S. Hall	462–463, 468–470	51–54, 86	32, 40–43
K. E. von Baer	464–465	42 (brief mention)	28–30
W. Preyer	466–468	43–45	32–35
J. M. Baldwin	470–476	54–58	43–51
W. Stern	485 (brief mention)	60	54–55
J. Sully		61	
A. Binet	476–481	46–50	35–40
S. Freud	481–482	59–60	51–54
J. Bowlby	504	83–84	80–82
Z.-Y. Kuo	501–502	81	78
A. Gesell	467 (brief mention), 501	66, 72–74	68–71
J. Dewey			55–56
C. L. Morgan			57
C. B. Hillis	486–488		61
H. Werner	489–490		
J. Piaget	491, 499	78	74–77
L. Vygotsky		79–80	74–77
K. Lewin	491–492	84–85	82–83

Table 4.2 Topics covered in Cairns' three major history-oriented publications

Topic	Pages in		
	Cairns & Ornstein, 1979	Cairns, 1983	Cairns, 1998
Concept of Development	460–466	501–503	26–27
Science of Behavioral Development		90	
Interdisciplinary Science			92
Behaviorism	483–485	69–71, 82	66–68, 80
Cognitive Development	498–500		
Mental Testing	485–486	67–68	62–64
Learning Theory	490–91, 493–496	87–89	85–88
Learning in Children	496–498		
Life-span Development	488, 500–501		59, 91
Longitudinal Studies			64–66
Knowledge & Consciousness		62	90–91
Morality & Perfectibility		62	59, 91–92
Volition & Intentionality		62	
Ontogeny & Phylogeny		62	58–59, 91
Heredity & Environment		62	
Maturation & Growth		72–74	
Social & Personality Development		74–76	71–73
Attachment			88–90
Moral Development		76–77	73–74
Language & Thought		77–79	
Cognition			74–77, 91
Organismic Theory	488–490	80	
Evolution, Ethology	503–504	80–82	30–31
Developmental Psychobiology			77–79
Application, Policy, & Institutionalization		64–66	61–62, 92

The increasing focus on Stern parallels the advancement of the "person-oriented" and "variables-oriented" contrast of perspectives in the unfolding of developmental science in the 1990s (Cairns, 2000; Magnusson & Cairns, 1996).

The role of Arnold Gesell received minimal coverage in 1979 (Cairns & Ornstein, 1979, p. 467 and p. 501), but in both handbook chapters it was elaborated as a counter-figure to Watson's behaviorism (Cairns, 1983, pp. 72–74; 1998, pp. 68–71). The latter coverage repeats the earlier one verbatim, except for two paragraphs (pp. 70–71). Where it had been customary to see a maturationist emphasis on human infancy, Bob pointed to Gesell's transactionist core of the developmental viewpoint, thus finding in it parallels with the ideas of Baldwin.

The alter ego: James Mark Baldwin

The developmental perspective of James Mark Baldwin was of special relevance for Bob Cairns. As Baldwin was consistent in his developmental orientation, his closeness in mind to Bob would be natural. Yet there are other reasons too—for instance, Baldwin's focus on the self as a dynamic process was the root of Bob Cairns' treatment of that complex issue (Cairns, 1986a; Cairns, Cairns, & Neckerman, 1989). The most usual Baldwin source were his *"Mental development in the child and the race"* (Baldwin, 1895) and *"Social and ethical interpretations in mental development"* (Baldwin, 1897).[4] The unity of the development of the person and of the field of social suggestions in which the developing person is embedded was appealing, and Baldwin was one of the most remarkable champions of that idea (for others, see Valsiner & van der Veer, 2000). The social suggestions are carried through interaction with real "social others"—that is, parents, teachers, peers, etc.—hence the relevance of studying social networks for understanding how the socialization system works (Cairns, Neckerman, & Cairns, 1989). Furthermore, the centrality of the SELF <> OTHER comparisons for the development of the person was the axiom Cairns took from Baldwin.

Bob Cairns has been one of the very few analysts of the history of developmental ideas who has pointed to the substantive continuity between the theorizing of James Mark Baldwin (with his "genetic logic") and the empirical research program of Jean Piaget (Cairns, 1998, pp. 49–50). It is indeed the case that Piaget's early work (up to the mid-1930s, see Martí, Chapter 5, this volume) was an effort to put into empirical practice the logic of developmental transformations that Baldwin (1906, 1908, 1911, 1915; Valsiner, 2009) had developed. Yet Cairns took Baldwin's writing with a grain of salt:

> Baldwin's style may have been more than an inconvenience for readers. It permitted him to reform explanations and concepts so that one and the same term could take on fresh nuances or alternative meanings, depending on its context. *Imprecision in presentation thereby promotes projection in interpretation.*
>
> (Cairns, 1998, p. 48, added emphasis)

The latter "snippet" can be an example of a dialogue with the language use by psychologists. Clarity of use of terms has not been the highest, from Freud and Jung to the fixation of ideas in DSM-V and its possible sequels. Here we get a glimpse of a stylistic feature of Bob Cairns' writing style—the use of seemingly peripheral innocuous side comments.

The relevance of subtlety: allusional dialogues with the present

In reading Bob Cairns' rendering of the history of developmental psychology, one comes across his small inserted personal comments upon the issues he was writing about. I would argue that these comments represent Bob Cairns' personal push to shape the discipline of developmental science, as well as use selected aspects of the figures of the past to evaluate the state of affairs in the discipline in the present. He took great delight in inserting these little comments into the text, often repeating the inserts or using the same material repeatedly. Such little nuances of evaluation that are scattered around Bob's writing are implicit dialogues with selected features of our contemporary scientific enterprise. For example, he wrote about the work of Preyer: "Though not unflawed, his observations were carefully recorded and *sanely written*" (Cairns, 1998, p. 35, added emphasis). The notion of "sanely written" is a little step into the dialogue with the contemporary writing style of psychologists, which often is incomplete (see Cairns, 1986b). Contemporary psychology is indeed filled with unwarranted statements not linkable with the empirical evidence, or "pseudo-empirical" (Smedslund, 1995), as they reiterate known beliefs *as if* those came from the evidence.

Of course some historical figures captured Bob's interest more than others in making such little dialogues possible. And he expanded his knowhow of history in conjunction with presenting and re-presenting such dialogues. His narratives on the role of Alfred Binet are particularly interesting in that respect.[5]

Going beyond IQ: expositions of Alfred Binet

Already concentrating on the *full* contribution of Alfred Binet to developmental psychology can be viewed as an example of a dialogue with the historical myopia of contemporary psychology. Binet, of course, has been considered relevant for his famous—or infamous, depending upon the perspective taken—intelligence tests. Binet's contributions certainly were by far wider than this small applied aspect, and for Bob the overlook of Binet's work created a good possibility to chart out the values of person-oriented, multi-level analyses examples. He was fascinated by the intellectual brilliance of many relevant contributors to the history of developmental psychology.[6] Among them, Alfred Binet came to occupy a special place.

Binet's prolific research reports allowed Bob to introduce a commentary upon our contemporary writings in psychology:

> Prolificacy can be embarrassing *if one hasn't much to write about*. This seems not to have been a problem for Binet, due in large measure to his "very open, curious and searching" mind.
>
> (Cairns, 1983 p. 47 and 1998,
> p. 37, added emphasis)

Binet was a good example of a phenomena-oriented researcher who prioritized empirical investigations in relation to theory building. Both directions were relevant, of course, yet comparing Baldwin and Binet led Bob to make a statement about the distinction between THEORY and RESEARCH:

During the period from 1894 to 1910, Baldwin was almost as prolific in creating and writing on developmental *theory* as Alfred Binet was in creating and
writing on developmental *research*.

(Cairns, 1983, p. 54, added emphasis)

It can be claimed that the use of this contrast is another example of creating a
bridge from the history of French thought (where theory and empirical work would
not be separated) to that of our contemporary North America. Bob's appreciation
of both Binet and Baldwin—which runs though all of his historical writing (see
Table 4.1)—certainly indicates his adherence to the basic natural-scientific look
at development (evident in developmental science as proclaimed, see Magnusson
& Cairns, 1996). Yet at the same time he seems to have himself operated with two
different models of linking theory and empirical work

Bob was overtly critical of mindless empiricism—or "pseudoempiricism", as
Smedslund (1995) has emphasized. Furthermore he appreciated thoughtful attitude towards methods—rather than using a habitually normative approach. Again,
letting Alfred Binet speak for himself, he created a crucial message for our time:

Nor was Binet impressed by the large-scale studies of Hall and his students who
used the questionnaire methodology. On the latter he wrote: "The American
authors, who love to do things big, often publish experiments made on
hundreds or even thousands of persons; they believe that the conclusive value of
a study is proportional to the number of observations. That is only an illusion."
(1904, p. 299) (Cairns, 1983, p. 47)

Bob Cairns repeatedly returned to quoting Binet on the issue of American pre-
ponderance towards large sample research (e.g., Cairns, 1984, p. 7; Cairns, 1986b,
p. 100; Cairns, 1998b, p. 37). The immediate target of this characterization was the
large-sample questionnaire research sponsored by G. Stanley Hall. Yet the focus
on the large samples has been the trademark of psychology in the U.S. over the last
century, and, if anything, has grown in its normative role rather than declined.

Bob Cairns took particular momentary pleasure from pointing out our present
world of discourse about research that uncritically looks for large numbers of subjects as if the security of scientific facts is in those numbers. Furthermore, he used
Binet as an example for another suggestive criticism of our contemporary habits:

Binet thoroughly dissected *behavioral* phenomena. To explore memory, for
instance, he varied the nature of the stimuli (memory for figures and for linguistic material; memory for meaningful sentences vs. individual words), the
subjects tested (chess masters and superior "calculators" who performed on the
stage; normal children and retarded children), measures employed (free recall,
recognition, physiological measures of blood pressure and electrical activity),
type of design (large group samples, individual analysis over longer-term periods), and statistics employed. Through it all, Binet selected designs, procedures,

and subjects with a purpose, *not merely because they were available*. To investigate imagination and creativity, he studied gifted playwrights and explored new techniques (inkblots, word association, and case-history information).

(Cairns, 1983, p. 48, added emphases)

Two relevant features are worth noticing here. First, the reference to Binet as studying "behavioral phenomena" is certainly a translation of the French focus on psychological phenomena into the language of North American psychology. The second emphasis (on purposefulness rather than availability) can be interpreted as another "commentary by allusion" on the research enterprise of our contemporary psychology. Instead of carefully designing which studies, how, and with whom, are likely to answer our questions, psychology usually conducts those that are ready at hand. Binet's focus on addressing relevant questions at multiple levels of their complexity (and with level-appropriate methods) fits well with the goals of developmental science, among which, "recognizing the complexity of development is the first step toward understanding its coherence and simplicity" (The Carolina Consortium on Human Development, 1996, p. 1). Different levels of organization of the developing system require different kinds of methods for analysis. Binet operated simultaneously at different levels of analysis, and provided an example for a multi-method research orientation towards complex developing systems.

Progressive social movement

In Bob Cairns' writings on history, the issue of the betterment of society—in this case the U.S. society—emerged in multiple ways. First of all, in the context of writing about the developmental thought in the U.S. at the beginning of the 20th century (mostly about the "child study" movement led by G. S. Hall), and again in the form of an embedded commentary, Bob captured the ethos of application:

> Persons concerned with the science tended to act as child advocates, lending their prestige to the passage of child labor laws, the revision of elementary and secondary school curricula, and the promulgation of child-centered rearing and control practices. The *discipline may not have directly benefited* from these efforts, *but the welfare of children did.* Happily, the field moved ahead to consolidate its claim to be an empirical science *as well as* a progressive social movement.

(Cairns, 1983, p. 64, added emphases)

The ambivalence of basic and applied efforts of developmental psychologists of that time matches that of ours. Then, the reliance on Haeckel's biogenetic law on the one hand, and religious sentiments on the other, made G. Stanley Hall one of the controversial developmentalists—the theme Cairns emphasized in all of his history writings. Yet the concern for improvement of children's health and welfare would find its positive appreciation in Bob Cairns' narrating of the paedology story.

In a similar vein, the focus on the improvement of childhood development found its sub-text in the story of Cora Bussey Hillis. Borrowing the information from Sears (1975), the story was told already in the first history paper (see Cairns & Ornstein, 1979, p. 486). In the second presentation of the same information, we can observe an elaboration:

> The child study movement led by G. Stanley Hall in the 1880s and 1890s came to maturity some 20 years later. Child study associations had been established in one form or another in all regions of *the country*. Collectively, they formed a potent movement for child advocacy. In 1906, an Iowa house-wife and mother, Cora Bussey Hillis, proposed that a research station be established for the study of improvement of child rearing (Sears, 1975). Her argument was *simple but compelling*: If research could improve corn and hogs, why could it not improve the rearing of children? The campaign to establish a Child Welfare Research Station at the University of Iowa was eventually successful.
> (Cairns, 1983, p. 65, also Cairns, 1998, p. 61; added emphases)

The comparison of children with corn and hogs in this quote comes directly from Sears (1975, p. 19), but Cairns added the marking of it as being "simple and compelling".

The theoretical ambivalence in relation to G. S. Hall that Bob Cairns had—appreciating the focus on development yet rejecting the reliance on Haeckel and Hall's ways of doing empirical work—is replaced by appreciation of the effects of the grass-roots social movement for child welfare (for "the country", read the U.S.A.), stemming from Hall's organizational bases. So, the recognition of the scientific limitations of G. S. Hall's enterprise was paired with the positive fascination for the social intervention efforts that emerged from the "child study". The benefits for the children stemming from the various practical implementations of the "child study" movement outweighed the ambivalences of theoretical kind.

Belief in the future

Bob Cairns was filled with serious and careful concerns about the future of developmental science. The lack of historical knowledge among developmentalists was a concern for him from the viewpoint of the future. Discussing our contemporary theoretical habits in psychology, as representing the state of affairs of "the lowest common denominator", he showed his interest in time-honored ideas that have re-emerged based on the history of ideas (e.g., the "person-centered analysis").

He believed in the making of the future—with the help of the "correlated constraints" of the realities of the present, and tried-out ideas of the past. The plasticity of development of organisms needed to be complemented by the plasticity of the developmental science facing the future. This optimism had its own development. The assuredness in the future was somewhat hypothetical in 1983:

Developmental psychologists have not been especially mindful of the persons and ideas in their past. *It is mildly ironic* that an area that is committed to the study of the origins of behavior and consciousness should have shown so little interest in its own origins. Yet it is understandable. If progress is to be made in empirical research, it will *probably* be won by those who look forward, not backward.

(Cairns, 1983, p. 42, added emphases)

The advancement of developmental science reduced that tentativeness by 1998, in a re-write of the same paragraph:

It is mildly ironic that an area committed to the study of the origins and development of behavior and consciousness traditionally has shown little interest in its own origins and development . . . . The earlier reluctance to look at our past, though regrettable, is understandable. If substantive progress is to be made in new empirical research, *it will be won* by those who look ahead rather than backward. There are also institutional and economic limits on scholarship where journal space is precious, and historical reviews and comments are afforded low priority. The upshot is that contemporaneous research articles tend to bypass the work and insights of earlier investigators. *This neglect of the past has been correlated with a more general tendency to give short shrift to competing findings, concepts, and interpretations.* Such shortcomings in scholarship, if unchecked, can undermine real progress in the discipline.

(Cairns, 1998, p. 26, added emphases)

The expression "it is *mildly ironic* that [X]" is one of the favorite textual markers that Bob Cairns used to indicate—subtly, and usually on the basis of a historical narrative—his advanced criticism of the particular state of affairs [X]. The critique of contemporary literature's social myopia for history is not an issue of mere oversight of the past. It encodes his worry about the state of affairs in the discipline in its present, and in its future. In an arena of developmental research where ideas become separated from phenomena, and methods dominate over rationale of the study of development, it is dangerous for the future of the discipline.

The holistic (person-centered) approach: self and culture

In order to understand Bob's interest in the context dependency of basic ontogeny, one has to understand the lives of youngsters in the United States inner cities. As the story goes:

In the summer of 1974, a research team at the University of North Carolina observed a young boy, Peter, who was 5 years old when he was placed in school.

Along with 25 other children of the same age, Peter had been enrolled in a special summer preschool program before entering kindergarten in the fall. . . . A team of researchers observed Peter and several of his classmates throughout the summer to obtain an overview of how they got along with the other children and with adults. . . . Peter had originally been selected because he had been one of the most passive, withdrawn children on the first day of the program when he was brought to class by his mother. By the third week of school, his behavior had changed dramatically. He was no longer withdrawn, as he had been during the first week; rather he had become one of the leaders of one of the most influential groups of boys, and was the most popular boy in class.

(Cairns, 1979, p. 6)

This story of transformation—from a withdrawn child to the leader in a group—was only a first approximation of the reality in Peter's case. Careful observations revealed a distinction between the preschool setting, where Peter was marginally participating in teacher-led activities yet did not "get into trouble", and outside of the classroom, where he played the leadership role in his group. At the same time, many aspects of Peter's conduct transcended the expectations of the context:

Peter infrequently sought other children's company, but they sought his. During the entire observation period, he was sometimes provoked by other boys, but he rarely fought back. Instead, he merely terminated the relationship and went on to some other activity. On some occasions, other boys were observed to take up his cause, and as he walked away, they would become involved in scuffles in his defense. Moreover, Peter showed the same good-natured tolerance in his relationships with girls as with boys. The teasing in which he became involved rarely escalated to more hostile forms of behavior, as did teasing among other children.

(Cairns, 1979, p. 7)

The basic mechanisms for granting avoidance of conflict—non-escalation of assertive encounters, and tolerance of others—were the constant core for Peter's intra-individual variability in his friendship relations:

Although friendships that Peter established were generally stable, specific associations would last only 2–3 days—that is, Peter typically selected his friends from a group of 4 boys, but at any given time in the summer he would have one friend with whom he spent more time than the others . . . . Activity preferences seemed to play a significant role. Peter liked to ride his bike, play ball, and splash out in the water tank, but these activities were enjoyed to different extents by others. Hence the context and Peter's choice of activity helped to determine whether he was to be found with a given peer at a particular day. The researchers were sometimes able to identify a specific incident that precipitated the beginning or ending of a cycle. For example, *a friend was overheard yelling a racial slur* at Peter. This particular association was terminated for a few days, and *then was resumed.*

(Cairns, 1979, p. 7, added emphases)

We can see the unity of context specificity and trans-context continuity in the description of Peter's realities of living in that summer. The plasticity of conduct—intra-personal variability of observable behavior in different contexts—is the basis for the development of the person.

The focus on social interdependence continued to interest over the following twenty years. In July 1994, a group of anthropologists and developmental psychologists at the Center of Developmental Science began to observe a group of inner-city children in their ordinary habitats over the summer. The observations continued through the following school-year and ended in August 1995.

The basic development of Bob Cairns: from social learning theories to developmental science

Let me try to integrate the different threads of the preceding story into one by considering Bob Cairns' lifetime quest to be that for societally responsive developmental science. As such, it is an example of a humanist tradition that grew out from the context of social learning perspectives into that of developmental science. The society to which that science is primarily responsive is that of the United States. Yet science knows no country boundaries. Hence Bob's main interlocutors were timeless and country-less—Alfred Binet, James Mark Baldwin, Kurt Lewin, and David Magnusson could have happily drank beer together with him at the *Top of the Hill* in the 1990s, had they been alive.

Yet the social learning background of Bob Cairns' thinking should not be underestimated. It seems to have contributed three major features towards the making of developmental science. First, it led to the consideration of *social interaction*—in the form of dyadic relations, and group interrelations. The role of Robert Sears in that has been notable. Second, the phenomena of complex social settings that social learning perspectives necessarily dealt with opened the road for development of a *multi-level systemic account of development*. This was possible in Bob Cairns' uniting the ideas coming from his social learning background with those of developmental biology. As a result, Bob may have well become a cognitivist, yet one with a focus on dynamic processes of mental development (and not with a focus on fixed mental schemata, or "knowledge base" in abstract). The cognitive level of the whole of developmental processes is a natural part of a holistic developmental science.

Finally, the social learning basis gave Bob Cairns a clear focus on the *dynamic processes* that are involved in development. Staying close to his phenomena—ranging from attachment in sheep to handling of friendship relations by Peter, to (later) the ontogeny of group dynamics as revealed in the Carolina Longitudinal

Study—made it very clear for him that the developmental system is simulta-neously in two states. There is the organized "steady state" core of the system that is carried—by the individual organism—from one setting to another. Yet in each of these settings the "steady state" is brought under challenges for change. Development can occur in the middle of such challenges—or not:

> An additional element is a concern with indeterminacy and development. The system should not become so rigid that it is not open to modification, if the appropriate rules were spelled out. It is not a capitulation to fate so much as it is challenge to understand the principles of modification and change.
>
> (Cairns, 2000, p. 61)

Bob Cairns, with all of his intellectual power and capacity for synthesis of evidence from different species, and ideas from very diverse thinkers from the history of human sciences, created a powerful basis for the developmental ideas to stay alive in our contemporary psychology. He could not force them to gain dominance in the research enterprise of psychology, where, as he often mentioned, research questions are based on the thinking of the "lowest common denominator" kind. Yet he made sure that both phenomena and serious consideration of development as a basic process be in the center of science—of the *developmental* science.

Acknowledgments

A preliminary version of this chapter was presented at the Robert B. Cairns Memorial Conference at Chapel Hill, NC, on October 14, 2000. My gratitude in the writing of this chapter goes back to the many afternoons of drinking beer with Bob Cairns in Chapel Hill (earlier at *Papagayo's*, later at the *Top of the Hill*). We had the rule of not wasting our mental energies on issues of local academic politics (which were many, and which we both vehemently detested), but to concentrate on our recent basic thoughts about how to make sense of development. Recalling the days of the actual writing of this chapter, I would like to thank Debra Skinner for her memories of the anthropological fieldwork in the Center for Developmental Science. Peter Ornstein and Gilbert Gottlieb kindly illuminated my mind about some missing links of Bob Cairns' linkages with the history of psychology. The final finishing of this manuscript—15 years later—was supported by the Niels Bohr Professorship Grant from the *Danske Grundforskningsfond*. Editorial sug-gestions by David Carré helped out in the finalization of this chapter.

Notes

1 In fact, he was the author of the major chapter on history in the fifth (1998) and sixth (2006) edition of *Carmichael's Handbook of Child Psychology*.
2 Prior to coming to vogue in the context of the Carolina Consortium of Human Development in the 1980s, and in the Center for Developmental Science, the term itself was introduced in 1970 (Cairns, 1970) and can also be found in Cairns & Ornstein (1979, p. 466).

3 Here I want to emphasize the active participation by Bob and Beverly Cairns in different summer schools—in Czechoslovakia and Estonia—intended for younger-generation researchers interested in development.
4 Interestingly, Bob Cairns did not develop a liking for Baldwin's opus magnum—the three-volume monograph *Thought and things* (Baldwin, 1906, 1908, 1911) and its sequel *Genetic theory of reality* (Baldwin, 1915), as he considered those too wordy and a movement away from empirical science.
5 Bob developed extended focus on Binet in the process of writing the first consistent overview of the history of developmental psychology, together with Peter Ornstein (Cairns & Ornstein, 1979), and largely on the basis of the background on memory research that Peter Ornstein brought into their collaboration (Ornstein, personal communication, September 18, 2000)
6 See, for instance, the following quote: "The emergence of modern developmental psychology in the late nineteenth and early twentieth centuries was hardly a coherent, systematic enterprise. But it was vigorous, contentious, fresh, and, in some instances, brilliant" (Cairns, 1983, p. 62).

References

Baldwin, J. M. (1895). *Mental development of the child and the race.* New York, NY: Macmillan.

Baldwin, J. M. (1897). *Social and ethical interpretations in mental development.* New York, NY: Macmillan.

Baldwin, J. M. (1906). *Thought and things: A study of the development and meaning of thought, or genetic logic: Vol. 1. Functional logic, or genetic theory of knowledge.* London, UK: Swan Sonnenschein.

Baldwin, J. M. (1908). *Thought and things: A study of the development and meaning of thought, or genetic logic: Vol. 2. Experimental logic, or genetic theory of thought.* London, UK: Swan Sonnenschein.

Baldwin, J. M. (1911). *Thought and things: A study of the development and meaning of thought, or genetic logic: Vol. 3. Interest and art being real logic.* London, UK: Swan Sonnenschein.

Baldwin, J. M. (1915). *Genetic theory of reality.* New York, NY: Putnam.

Cairns, R. B. (1961). The influence of dependency inhibition on the effectiveness of social reinforcement. *Journal of Personality, 29,* 466–488.

Cairns, R. B. (1966). Development, maintenance, and extinction of social attachment behavior in sheep. *Journal of Comparative & Physiological Psychology, 62,* 298–306.

Cairns, R. B. (1970). Towards a unified science of development. *Contemporary Psychology, 15,* 214–215.

Cairns, R. B. (1972). Attachment and dependency: A psychobiological and social learning synthesis. In J. L. Gewirtz (Ed.), *Attachment and dependency* (pp. 29–80). New York, NY: Winston.

Cairns, R. B. (1973). Fighting and punishment from a developmental perspective. In J. Cole & D. Jensen (Eds.), *Nebraska symposium on motivation* (Vol. 20, pp. 59–124). Lincoln, NE: University of Nebraska Press.

Cairns, R. B. (1977). Beyond social attachment: the dynamics of interactional development. In T. Alloway, P. Pliner, & L. Krames (Eds.), *Attachment behavior* (pp. 1–24). New York, NY: Plenum.

Cairns, R. B. (1979). *Social development: The origins and plasticity of interchanges.* San Francisco, CA: W.H. Freeman

Cairns, R. B. (1983). The emergence of developmental psychology. In W. Kessen (Ed.), *Handbook of Child Psychology* (4th ed.): *Vol. 1. History, theory, and methods* (pp. 41–102). New York, NY: Wiley.

Cairns, R. B. (1984). *Alfred Binet and the concept of development.* Paper presented at the meeting of the Society for Research on Child Development, March.

Cairns, R. B. (1986a). A contemporary perspective on social development. In P. S. Strain, M. J. Guralnick, & H. M. Walker (Eds.), *Children's social behavior* (pp. 3–47). Orlando, FL: Academic Press.

Cairns, R. B. (1986b). Phenomena lost. In J. Valsiner (Ed.), *The individual subject and scientific psychology* (pp. 97–111). New York, NY: Plenum.

Cairns, R. B. (1998). The making of developmental psychology In W. Damon & R. Lerner (Eds.), *Handbook of child psychology* (5th ed.): *Vol. 1. Theoretical models of human development* (pp. 25–105). New York, NY: Wiley.

Cairns, R. B. (2000). Developmental science: Three audacious implications. In L. R. Bergman, R. B. Cairns, L.-G. Nilsson, & L. Nystedt (Eds.), *Developmental science and the holistic approach* (pp. 49–62). Mahwah, NJ: Erlbaum.

Cairns, R. B. & Cairns, B. D. (2006). The making of developmental psychology. In R. M. Lerner (Ed.), *Handbook of child psychology: Vol. 1. Theoretical models of human development* (6th ed., pp. 89–165). Hoboken, NJ: Wiley.

Cairns, R. B. & Ornstein, P. A. (1979). Developmental psychology. In E. Hearst (Ed.), *The first century of experimental psychology* (pp. 459–510). Hillsdale, NJ: Erlbaum.

Cairns, R. B. & Scholz, S. D. (1973). On fighting in mice: Dyadic escalation and what is learned. *Journal of Comparative & Physiological Psychology, 85,* 540–550.

Cairns, R. B., Cairns, B. D., & Neckerman, H. J. (1989). Early school dropout: Configurations and determinants. *Child Development, 60*(6), 1437–1452. DOI: 10.2307/1130933.

Cairns, R. B., Elder, G. H., & Costello, E. J. (Eds.) (1996). *Developmental science.* New York: Cambridge University Press.

Emmeche, C., Køppe, S., & Stjernfeldt, F. (1997). Explaining emergence: Towards an ontology of levels. *Journal for General Philosophy of Science, 28,* 1, 83–119.

Gottlieb, G. (1999). *Probabilistic epigenesis and evolution.* Heinz Werner Lecture No. 23. Worcester, MA: Clark University Press.

Magnusson, D. & Cairns, R. B. (1996). Developmental science: Toward a unified framework. In R. B. Cairns, G. H. Elder, & E. J. Costello (Eds.), *Developmental science* (pp. 7–30). New York, NY: Cambridge University Press.

Prigogine, I. (1973). Irreversibility as a symmetry-breaking process. *Nature, 246,* 67–71.

Sears, R. (1975). Your ancients revisited: A history of child development. In E. M. Hetherington (Ed.), *Review of child development research.* Vol. 5 (pp. 1–73). Chicago, IL: University of Chicago Press.

Shanahan, M., Valsiner, J., & Gottlieb, G. (1997). Developmental concepts across disciplines. In J. Tudge, M. Shanahan, & J. Valsiner (Eds.), *Comparisons in human development: Understanding time and context* (pp. 13–71). New York, NY: Cambridge University Press.

Smedslund, J. (1995). Psychologic: Common sense and the pseudoempirical. In J. A. Smith, R. Harré, & L. van Langenhove (Eds.), *Rethinking psychology* (pp. 196–206). London, UK: Sage.

The Carolina Consortium on Human Development (1996). Developmental science: A collaborative statement. In R. B. Cairns, G. H. Elder, & E. J. Costello (Eds.), *Developmental science* (pp. 1–6). New York, NY: Cambridge University Press.

Valsiner, J. (2001). Constructive curiosity of the human mind: Participating in Piaget. Introduction in Piaget, J., *The child's conception of physical causality* (pp. ix–xxii). New Brunswick, NJ: Transaction Publishers.

Valsiner, J. (2009). Baldwin's quest: A universal logic of development. In J. W. Clegg (Ed.), *The observation of human systems: Lessons from the history of anti-reductionistic empirical psychology* (pp. 45–82). New Brunswick, NJ: Transaction.

Valsiner, J. (2012). *A guided science: History of psychology in the mirror of its making.* New Brunswick, NJ: Transaction.

Valsiner, J. (2014). *An invitation to cultural psychology.* London, UK: Sage.

Valsiner, J. & van der Veer, R. (1993). The encoding of distance: The concept of the zone of proximal development and its interpretations. In R. R. Cocking & K. A. Renninger (Eds.), *The development and meaning of psychological distance* (pp. 35–62). Hillsdale, NJ: Erlbaum.

Valsiner, J. & van der Veer, R. (2014). Encountering the border: Vygotsky's zona blizaishego razvitya and its implications for theory of development. In A. Yasnitsky, R. van der Veer, & M. Ferrari (eds.), *The Cambridge handbook of cultural–historical psychology* (pp. 148–173). Cambridge: Cambridge University Press.

Zittoun, T., Valsiner, J., Vedeler, D., Salgado, J., Gonçalves, M., & Ferring, D. (2013). *Melodies of living.* Cambridge: Cambridge University Press.

Chapter 5

The loss of Piaget as a symptom

The issue of development in contemporary cognitive psychology

Eduardo Martí

Piaget has been a key figure of 20th century psychology. Along with Freud, Baldwin, and Vygotsky, he developed an ambitious, creative, and decisive developmental psychology that illuminated facets of the human mind. Following his death in 1980, his theories barely advanced and instead lost significance. This was not only due to limitations of his theories, his personality, and the theoretical context, but it also reflects the decline of the developmental perspective in psychology at the dawn of the 21st century. The objective of this chapter is to examine both Piaget's proposal and the reasons behind its loss of relevance in order to better understand the decline of the developmental perspective in contemporary cognitive psychology.

Young Piaget in context: the richness of the developmental perspective during the first half of the 20th century

Piaget's intellectual journey (1896–1980) is very peculiar. A curious child with an early interest in mechanics, birds, fossils, and, above all, mollusks, the young Piaget experienced a series of crises between the ages of fifteen and twenty that led him to read, reflect on, and develop a passion for philosophical questions (Piaget, 1952). His exposure to Bergson's *Creative Evolution* was decisive in that it oriented Piaget toward what would become the *leitmotiv* of his work: biological explanations for knowledge. However, due to its speculative nature and limited scientific basis, philosophical inquiry did not ultimately capture his attention, which is understandable for a youth with such a passion for the natural sciences (Piaget, 1965). Thus, Piaget found in psychology a way of empirically addressing questions regarding knowledge. However, what psychological perspectives formed his theoretical sources, and how did he elaborate his psychological and epistemological theoretical approach?

Piaget first came to know the discipline of psychology at the University of Zurich in 1915. He worked in a psychology laboratory, where his exposure to studies by Eugen Bleuler introduced him to psychoanalytic theory—mainly, to the works of Freud, Jung, and Adler. It is interesting to question the degree to which the "genetic" approach of psychoanalysis, which attempts to make sense of adult behavior based on childhood experiences, affected Piaget. He appears to have been directly influenced by psychoanalysis in his way of conceiving of cognitive development as a progression from a subjective, "autistic" mode of thinking toward a more rational and socialized one (Piaget, 1923, 1932). It is also undeniable that the clinical–critical method for examining children's ideas (Bond & Tryphon, 2009) was inspired by clinical psychoanalytic methods.

Piaget's two-year stay in Paris (1919–1921) was influential, judging by important interactions he made with other psychologists during this time. His work using Cyril Burt's intelligence tests of Alfred Binet at Theodore Simon's lab allowed him to delve into child reasoning theories. He soon realized that what interested him most was understanding children's mistakes by examining their problem-solving processes rather than focusing on correct answers or on diagnosing intelligence levels. Moreover, Piaget adopted the definition of intelligence defended by Binet: an adaptive organ whose components (memory, attention, judgment, etc.) interact with as much complexity as the cells of any other bodily organ (Binet & Simon, 1909). He also adopted the functional dimension of intelligence defended by Binet that considered thinking as a form of action (Bennour & Vonèche, 2009). These two components played a critical role in his subsequent theorizing.

The influence of the psychiatrist Pierre Janet was also critical during Piaget's stay in Paris. The notion that thinking involves an internal discussion, that affectivity forms the source of action and thinking, and, above all, that thinking is rooted in sensorimotor actions, are ideas that he shared with Janet. Janet was also indirectly instrumental in helping Piaget discover the theories of Baldwin, who was living in exile in France at that time. While Piaget never met Baldwin personally, his work interested him considerably. In fact, he adopted some of Baldwin's concepts and approaches (e.g. genetic explanation, adualism, circular reactions, and phenocopy) and learned of advances in social psychology (Piaget, 1982).

Upon returning to Geneva, Piaget worked at the *Maison des Petits*, an institution created by Pierre Bovet and Edouard Claparède of the *Institut Jean-Jacques Rousseau*. There, he deepened his study of child cognition and became familiar with the pedagogical theories of Decroly and Claparède regarding children's *centers of interest*, an idea also developed by Dewey in the United States. Thus, Piaget adopted Claparède's functionalist perspective, allowing him to draw parallels between the need for food (biological level), the need for understanding (psychological level), and the need to reach the truth via explanation (at the epistemological level), representing the three different forms of vital adaptation.

However, being aware of the specificity of intelligence, Piaget took one step further in identifying a structural discontinuity in its development despite the presence of functional continuity between levels. Consequently, he conceived cognitive development as a self-organized change that gives rise to increasingly complex logical structures; this would later spur his studies on the development of logical operations in different states as well as his interest in the logical structure of thought.

Claparède was also decisive in causing Piaget to favor a perspective on learning and intelligence that spanned beyond stimulus–response explanations, which were prevalent during the first half of the 20th century in psychology due to the popularity of behaviorism and reflexology at the time. For Piaget, the fundamental unit of action lies neither in the relationship between stimuli and responses nor in the associations between stimuli, but rather in the existence of action schemes that allow meaning to be ascribed to stimuli via assimilation. Thus, the progressive coordination of different schemata creates more organized wholes along development (Piaget, 1947).

It is also worth noting young Piaget's relationship with another two psychologists, Henri Wallon and Lev Vygotsky, who defended different perspectives from his but with whom he shared ideas that definitely affected his early works. Early on, during his work at the *Institut Jean-Jacques Rousseau* at the beginning of the 1920s, Piaget sought a language-based explanation for the development of intelligence and logic. While influenced by Janet and Baldwin, Piaget considered language not as an external factor that affects intelligence but as a mean of communication. He focused on the study of conversations between children of different ages while interacting in schoolyards and formulated what he called the *collective monologue* (Piaget, 1923). The basic function of this type of language, according to Piaget, is to accompany actions rather than directing others; and thus, he considered this form of language to be egocentric in nature. Based on this interpretation, Piaget conceived development as a process through which a baby's solipsism (or "autism") evolves into the egocentrism of a small child and is finally decentered in an older child and adult. In his earlier work, socialization and exchanges between peers were key aspects of cognitive development (Piaget, 1923, 1924, 1932). However, his perspective differed in critical ways from those of Wallon and Vygotsky, who also considered social interaction to form one of the main axis of development.

While Piaget and Wallon agreed on the importance of the socialization factor in explaining cognitive development, to Wallon (1928) babies are social organisms from birth to the extent that they need adults to ascribe meaning to their surroundings. For Piaget, however, children are truly capable of socializing to the extent that they develop the ability to decenter and understand another person's point of view. In this sense, Piaget (1962) replied years later to the critiques made by Vygotsky in his *Thought and Language* on egocentric language (Vygotsky, 1934/1962). Piaget insisted that egocentrism exists as an intermediate stage between the extreme isolation of the baby and the full socialization of the older child and adult. By so doing, he argues against Vygotsky's notion that the child is a social being from birth and that egocentrism serves as the first sign of the internalization of speech as a regulator of thought. These opposing positions became even more distinct as Piaget deviated from studies on early development in order to advance his cognitive development theory based on stages, wherein structural characteristics of development dominate functional aspects.

This brief summary of Piaget's early theory, which he developed in close collaboration with other psychologists, shows that, in the discipline of psychology during the first third of the 20th century in Europe, the developmental perspective acted as a central axis of psychological theories. The study of development was considered necessary for understanding human thought. Moreover, biology, psychology, sociology, and logic were considered to form interconnected features that affect cognitive development. Finally, psychological approaches were inspired through epistemological questioning that acted as a general frame of reference. These three ideas ultimately led Piaget to develop his own new perspective, known as genetic epistemology.

Genetic epistemology: a multidisciplinary and developmental understanding of knowledge

The adjective "genetic" used by Piaget in naming his epistemological (genetic epistemology) and psychological theories (genetic psychology) is not related to the study of genes. It is rather derived from the word "genesis" and is thus related to development. In fact, Baldwin and Vygotsky also used this term to show that their theoretical perspectives considered development in explaining human behavior.[1]

For Piaget, child psychology must not be confused with genetic psychology. According to Piaget, child psychology examines how children's behaviors change as a function of age; its objective is thus to study only the child. Genetic psychology, however, goes beyond this since it involves the study of all cognitive processes (intelligence, reasoning, perception, etc.) through analyses of their development (Piaget & Inhelder, 1966). Studies of development are thus used by Piaget to understand cognitive processes.

However, genetic psychology stands only as a critical and necessary component of Piaget's theory that serves a broader goal: an empirically based theory of knowledge that Piaget named *genetic epistemology*. Epistemology and psychology are, for Piaget, intrinsically linked for two reasons. The first one is easy to understand based on Piaget's logic: psychology is necessary for understanding characteristics of human knowledge, and this scientific understanding is necessary for any epistemological approach that is based on facts and not on speculation (Piaget, 1965). The second reason may serve as one of the keys for understanding numerous studies in contemporary psychology. For Piaget, it is not possible to understand cognitive development without making epistemological assumptions on the nature of what one is studying; such as, for example, the relationship between mind and environment, or how biological and psychological functions are related (Piaget, 1970). These assumptions shape the questions to be explored, the methodological decisions, and certainly the interpretation of results. Therefore, following Piaget, epistemology cannot exist without psychology and vice versa.

However, psychology is not the only discipline that can offer empirical data on genetic epistemology. Piaget proposed that it is also necessary to examine the development of scientific knowledge from a historical perspective via *sociogenesis* (Piaget, 1967b, p. 65). This historical perspective complements the psychogenetic perspective in that it allows comparison of two different but analogous forms of development very closely. Although different in nature, these two perspectives (developmental and historical) are analogous in that they pose the same epistemological questions regarding ways through which knowledge is organized over time, how different stages in the construction of knowledge are connected, and which explanatory mechanisms drive these changes (Piaget & García, 1983).

In addition to psychology and history, Piaget was also interested in logic. While less central than the former, the need to integrate logic into genetic epistemology is essential to understanding Piaget's perspective. According to him, the issue of validity is central for anyone interested in the formation of knowledge. However, as Piaget highlights, psychology does not draw conclusions on the internal validity of knowledge but rather explains its appearance in factual terms. On the other hand, logic examines the validity of knowledge and the conditions of truth based on certain axioms (Piaget, 1947/1963). Therefore, logic and psychology need each other, and the relationship between the two is expressed through the statement, "logic is the mirror of thought" (Piaget, 1947, p. 34). Hence, for Piaget, psychological questions refer to analogous questions of logic (and vice versa) even though the methods and solutions that each proposes differ.

Hence, we can understand Piaget's interest in studying *normative facts*: that is, judgments that include a sense of obligation or need on behalf of the subject expressing them, independent of their validity according to the observer. These facts are a common occurrence in moral thought (Piaget, 1932) and are also present in situations where logical conclusions are asserted out of necessity, such as principles of object permanence, conservation, transitive property, or class inclusion hierarchy, among numerous others. Thus, it is possible to understand the complementarity between logic and psychology from the Piagetian perspective: while the former is concerned with the formal validity of a norm, psychology empirically studies how this norm is generated from the subject's perspective.

In addition to psychology, history, and logic, epistemology as conceived of by Piaget must also consider biology (Messerly, 2009). How does Piaget conceive of the relationship between the biological and the psychological? This has little to do with deterministic solutions: biology does not determine behavior (neo-Darwinian perspective), and behavior does not determine biology (neo-Lamarckian perspective). As he did with numerous other questions structured as dualities (Bennour & Vonèche, 2009), Piaget opted for a third way (*tertium quid*) of describing his views on the relationship between psychology and biology. For him, cognitive processes are the result of organic regulations but also constitute differentiated systems (organs) that regulate interactions between the individual and his or her environment (Piaget, 1967a, p. 38). This reveals one of Piaget's significant theses: there is a functional continuity at all levels of life, where the same self-regulating systems appear—as well as structural discontinuity— where the organs created are distinct. This led him to propose that ultimately all behaviors are based on organic life, not because they are contained within it (as innatists claim) but because their development is based in the same self-regulating mechanisms.[2]

As seen, Piaget's approach is necessarily interdisciplinary. Psychology, history, logic, and biology all served his epistemology as well as other scientific disciplines such as sociology, linguistics, physics, and mathematics. Such an interdisciplinary approach, which was also practiced in close collaboration with scientists of different disciplines, was decisive in developing his epistemological program (Ducret, 1990; Martí & Rodríguez, 2012).

The progressive decline of Piaget's influence

Piaget had enormous theoretical influence through the mid and late 20th century, especially in the fields of psychology and education. Even so, this influence was partial: some of his concepts, such as the concept of *stages*, were considerably more popular than others; and at times even biased—Piaget himself spoke ironically about the fact that he had been called everything, from an empiricist to an innatist, and even a neo-behaviorist.

During the second half of the 20th century, Piaget's constructivist perspective became a major perspective for explaining cognitive development in the field of psychology, as an alternative to the existing innatism and empiricism. It was considered an influential theoretical framework in education (Smith, 2009), both in Europe and in the United States, though Piaget's ideas spread later in the US, coinciding with the cognitive revolution (Hsueh, 2009).

Following his death in 1980, this situation started to change; and today, genetic epistemology no longer serves as the point of reference that it once was decades ago. While Piaget's quotes still appear in numerous psychological studies and in influential manuals,[3] Piaget's work is referenced more as a perspective of the past that must be overcome than as a relevant perspective that will guide new studies. How can we explain this loss of influence? As in all complex phenomena, there are several explanations. I focus here on three that appear to be the more influential.

The Geneva School without Piaget

Piaget's personality and theoretical convictions were decisive in the development of a specific approach to work where interpersonal relationships were essential in the construction of genetic epistemology. The scientific environment of the Geneva School was not characterized by sophisticated laboratories or material resources,[4] but by a complex collaborative network of scientists of different backgrounds. From the beginning, Piaget surrounded himself with collaborators, such as Alina Szeminska and Bärbel Inhelder (and also Piaget's spouse, Valentine), who played a key role in his scientific work. Later on, at the International Centre of Genetic Epistemology (ICGE), he brought together a large team of collaborators (psychologists, mathematicians, linguists, logicians, sociologists, biologists, etc.) who formed fundamental aspects of his work. Piaget always believed in the value of the discussion of ideas and in collaboration, especially between experts of different disciplines (Bringuier, 1980). He thus upheld two values of his own theory: the importance of discussion for promoting cognitive development, and the need to address epistemological questions through an interdisciplinary approach. However, this network of diverse exchange came second to Piaget's epistemological program; in spite of his respect and continual interest in the perspectives of his collaborators, he had always the temptation to assimilate others' points of view to his own.

Following Piaget's death, the human and institutional structure needed to continue his project dissolved. In fact, Piaget was never concerned with preparing his own legacy and did not want (or know how) to find a close collaborator to continue his studies. As a consequence, the ICGE disappeared, and the liveliness of Piagetian thought also lost strength in one of the institutions where it had become most vivid: the University of Geneva. Though it can be said that the Geneva School did not continue with the Piagetian project, it would be incorrect to claim that Piaget's contributions were forgotten entirely. Rather, his ideas were disseminated throughout the world through its supporters, thus transforming them but without losing some original traces of Piagetian identity (Martí & Rodríguez, 2012).

Internal contradictions

The popularity of genetic epistemology in Geneva also declined due to certain features of Piaget's later ideas, which exhibited internal theoretical tensions. After a long period of studying the development of cognitive notions and structures (space, number, speed, time, physical quantities, etc.), Piaget focused on cognitive functions and mechanisms (abstraction, generalization, contradiction, and, above all, equilibration) that might explain their development in order to determine the internal logic of these structures at each stage (Piaget, 1980).

This shift in direction was in part a response to challenges of Piaget's theory that arose during the 1960s and 1970s. In this vein, ICGE studies on causality showed that the application of logical operations to reality depended considerably on the resistance of this reality to operational structuring. Moreover, "horizontal décalages" were studied with greater attention[5]—this was a phenomenon that questioned the existence of stages in the first place. These novel findings drew more attention to the importance of the physical properties of objects in their interactions with subject structures and, in general, drew more attention to the particularities of cognition rather than to its general characteristics.

Furthermore, studies on learning by Inhelder, Sinclair, and Bovet (1974) showed that, under some conditions, it is possible to speed up the acquisition of certain logical operations. This drove an interest in determining the mechanisms responsible for this advance (confrontation between conflicting schemes, generalization of schemes to new situations, becoming aware of mistakes, etc.), creating a tension between general and structural aspects of cognition (the *epistemic subject*) and particular and dynamic aspects of cognition (the *psychological subject*).

It is thus not surprising that in this context, and also due to a push from problem-solving studies framed in the information-processing perspective that grew more prevalent in the U.S., studies on cognitive functions in particular situations were developed by a group of Piaget's collaborators led by Inhelder (Inhelder et al., 1992). These studies inspired a renewed interest in microgenesis and in the study of the contextual specificity of cognitive functioning. By closely studying the ways in which subjects use knowledge when solving problems, these studies highlighted limitations of Piaget's structuralist and generalist perspective.

External challenges

Piaget had enemies. Far from being a problem, having a *scapegoat* was essential to spark his creativity (Bringuier, 1980). Though he rivaled several perspectives, the most prominent was that of empiricism. Throughout his life, he placed himself against any position that would defend an empiricist epistemology. However, he also critiqued apriorism and any form of reductionism. Piaget's theoretical work was sufficiently complex and coherent to resist criticisms that he received throughout his life. His ability to slightly modify the critiques he received, reinterpret them, and then use them as he wished is widely recognized. In fact, Piaget was a great assimilator of ideas, as he himself confessed (Bringuier, 1980). His obsession with pursuing his epistemological project did not allow room to consider other perspectives. It is revealing, for example, that few external references appear in his works and that the majority are self-references.

However, after the 1970s, in addition to the internal contradictions of his theory that we discussed above, a series of criticisms was raised by a number of his own collaborators at the Geneva School (Rodríguez & Martí, 2012). On the one hand, due to pressures from the innatist perspective that gained traction in psychology at the time, Pierre Monoud's team questioned Piaget's description of newborn abilities as well as his views on newborn development (Mounoud, 1987; Rochat, 2012). Progressively, it was argued that Piaget had underestimated infant abilities as well as other stages and traits of developing subjects, including, for example, egocentrism or the acquisition of the principle of conservation (Vuyk, 1981).

On the other hand, and partly due to the recovery of Vygotsky's ideas, the low value placed on social interaction and language in Piaget's theory was questioned in Geneva both through studies on socio-cognitive conflict (Doise, Mugny, & Perret-Clermont, 1975; Perret-Clermont, 2012) and on language acquisition and learning (Bronckart, 2012). All in all, these critiques weakened the popularity of Piaget's theory by re-marking the limits of a developmental theory based entirely on internal mechanisms.

The decline of the developmental perspective in contemporary psychology

Piaget's loss of popularity by the end of the 20th century has not been redeemed through the creation of a broad theoretical perspective on cognitive development. It may appear strange to refer to a decline in the developmental perspective given that several current studies focus on children and development (see Kuhn & Siegler, 2006). However, many of these studies, while focusing on child behavior, do not adopt a developmental perspective. As Piaget noted, one must not confuse *child psychology* with *developmental psychology* (or *genetic psychology*, in his terms); studying children does not entail adopting a dynamic perspective based on change processes (Karmiloff-Smith, 2012). Instead, contemporary studies are often limited to comparative descriptions of behaviors across different ages without providing evidence or explanations for observed change processes.

To effectively address development, it is necessary to explain change and the appearance of novelty (i.e. behaviors not reducible to earlier behaviors) using a model that addresses the irreversible nature of time (Valsiner, 2011). Furthermore, it is not necessary to exclusively study children to understand development, as Piaget highlighted. One can study changes in adult behavior from a developmental perspective (microgenesis) and, of course, changes throughout history (sociogenesis). How, then, may we explain this retreat from studies on development that dominated psychology at the start of the 20th century? A series of indicators, many of which revolve around the decline of certain Piagetian ideas, help us reveal five causes of this trend.

"If you want to get ahead, get a theory"

This expression is the title of a study by Karmiloff-Smith and Inhelder (1975) that analyzed how children develop problem-solving skills based on the construction and generalization of *action theories*. However, factors shaping the scientific development of children also affect adults. An explicit elaboration of a theory is necessary to select what one will study, and how a topic will be studied and interpreted. Nevertheless, current trends in psychology have exhibited a considerable increase in empirical studies that has not been accompanied by theoretical efforts. This implies an emphasis on the use of particular methodological tools that guaranteed the study validity over its theoretical grounding.

This tendency is especially problematic when applied to the psychology of cognitive development. As Piaget noted (1965), studying knowledge necessarily implies the adoption of epistemological perspectives regarding the nature and origin of knowledge, the importance of the subject and object to knowledge, and other matters that affect how studies results are presented and interpreted. The fact that many psychological studies on cognitive development are atheoretical leads one to suspect that these studies are guided by a commonsense epistemology that reflects empiricist positions claiming that knowledge is a reproduction of reality. From this perspective, development is deemed the result of the accumulation of experience and thus does not require specific study.

Almost everything lies in the origins

Likewise, an a priori epistemological position trivializes the development process by defending the idea that knowledge is totally or partially determined. Mainly thanks to Chomsky's work on the nature of language (which resulted in part from a reaction to the behaviorist thesis on the acquisition of language), the innatist–modularist position (e.g. Chomsky, 1972) used to explain cognitive development has become standard (Hirschfeld & Gelman, 1994). This position, which cannot be reconciled with Piaget's constructivism (Piatelli-Palmarini, 1979), claims that a child's actions have little to do with cognitive development to the extent that cognition is organized from birth and already includes *core, a priori knowledge* that must be released over time. According to this perspective, essential numerical, spatial, object, biological, and even psychological knowledge (theory of the mind) is present at birth. Indeed, these authors rely on determined processes to explain changes appearing after birth, but the crux is that organization and units of cognition are innately determined (Gómez, 2010). Thus, the innatist perspective leaves little room to examine processes of change and subject activity and instead seeks to determine the origins of cognition (Carey, 2009).

Partial theories

It is undeniable that fruitful interactions between disciplines are present in contemporary psychology. We noted above how for many developmental psychologists it is essential to study the origins of knowledge, which often involves referring to neuroscientific disciplines (Rodrigo, 2010). We could indeed find other interactions between psychology and sociology or between psychology and history.

However, contrary to the propositions of early 20th century development theories, Piaget's included, it is difficult to find broad, interdisciplinary theoretical perspectives illustrating the relationship between ontogenetic and socio-historical development, between cognitive development and logic, or between ontogenetic development, phylogeny, and biology. This has led to a proliferation of fragmentary theoretical explanations centered on specific and specialized objects of study. Moreover, the innatist–modularist perspective also leads to the identification of very specific mechanisms of change that only apply to particular cognitive domains (e.g. in the domain of number, see Carey, 2009, Chapter 4). In turn, studies on relations between specific cognitive contents and general mechanisms of change have been mostly neglected (Karmiloff-Smith, 1992).

Methodological shift: from a diversity of methods to experimentation

Choosing a methodological strategy should be subordinated to theoretical approaches and to research objectives. This view, which is shared by many researchers, is not always applied. It is clear that contemporary psychology (including developmental psychology) is mostly centered in studies supported by experimental logic: definition of operational variables, hypothesis, and statistical control.

Piaget, along with other theoreticians interested in development at the beginning of the former century, used a broad range of methods to obtain and analyze data. In particular, Piaget's methods served as a logical extension of his theoretical and epistemological approach. His clinical–critical and longitudinal studies, paired with stage and logical analyzes, were fully consistent with his theoretical approach. The same could be said, for example, about the double stimulation method used by Vygotsky (1934).

The current dominance of experimental methods in developmental psychology is highly problematic. For one, it promotes a particular understanding of scientific knowledge reflecting an empiricist epistemology that does not clearly differentiate human sciences from natural sciences (Gillièron, 1985). In fact, as Piaget (1970) emphasized, in psychological studies it is necessary to make explicit epistemological assumptions. Frequently, experimental studies do not do that and are, in fact, guided by an empiricist epistemology. From this perspective, the particularities of human sciences due to the coincidence between the object of study (human beings) and the scientist (also a human being) (Martí, 1987; Piaget, 1972) are not taken into account. Additionally, experimental methods are often associated with the "age-related development" paradigm and are limited to comparisons of observed behavioral differences at different ages rather than inquiries concerning dynamic processes of change. Finally, they exclude other approaches (such as microgenetic analysis, longitudinal analysis, or case studies) that are needed to identify change processes and their variations (van Dijk & van Geert, 2011; Puche & Martí, 2011).

When development and learning are conflated

Despite their numerous agreements, Piaget and Vygotsky held very different views on developmental psychology (Martí, 1996). Vygotsky has been considerably influential in the field of developmental psychology from the 1960s, with the publication and distribution of his works throughout the U.S. and Europe. Many studies that adopt a Vygotskian approach have focused on the effect of social and cultural practices on development, following the conceptual constructs of *internalization* and of the *zone of proximal development* (Vygotsky, 1995/1931).

Despite the many novel findings inspired by Vygotsky, these have brought to contemporary psychology a simplification of Vygotsky's original concepts (van der Veer & Valsiner, 1991) and have focused on interactions between children and adults without clearly determining whether identified changes result from learning processes or from more lasting processes of reorganization that could be identified as development. This confusion is mainly due to the absence of explanatory principles for the relationships between learning and development.[6] Moreover, an exclusive emphasis placed on the study of social interactions has discredited studies that are focused on changes in individual behavior, which are considered by many Vygotskians to be erroneous, or superfluous, because they do not consider social and interactive factors. Both factors have contributed to a noticeable decrease in truly developmental studies aimed at illustrating dynamics of change and the participation of subjects in the appearance of new behaviors.

Conclusions

An examination of psychological studies of the early 20th century shows that the developmental perspective has become less influential over time. To us, the decline of Piaget's theories is a symptom of a paradigm change in contemporary cognitive psychology. The solution to this problem does not necessarily lie in recovering and extending Piaget's ideas, but rather it is in seriously considering some of his theses as tenets for the study of cognition: the need for an interdisciplinary approach, an epistemological foundation for the study of development, a rejection of reductionist explanations, a revival of epigenesist concepts, methodological diversity in service of theory, and the importance of subject actions as an organizing aspect of development, among others. In this sense, we believe that some of Piaget's axioms for studying development could be used to develop an approach to cognitive psychology that takes development seriously.

Notes

1 This term was widely used at the start of the 20th century by psychologists and, according to Piaget, was introduced during the second half of the 19th century by psychologists before biologists used the term to refer to genes (Piaget & Inhelder, 1966). Currently, this use of the word is very infrequent, and it is more common to use the term *developmental psychology*, although terms such as *ontogenesis* and *epigenesis* continue to be used.

2 Piaget's solution regarding the relationship between psychology and biology is inseparable from the concept of *epigenesis*, which supports a dynamic and double-meaning relationship between the genetic system and the environment. For Piaget, cognitive development refers to a form of *epigenesis* in which increasingly complex cognitive constructions are not determined by elemental structures present from birth but are the consequence of a reciprocal relationship between these structures and the environment that is guided by self-regulating mechanisms.

3 In the sixth edition of the influential *Handbook of Child Psychology* dedicated to cognition, perception, and language (Kuhn & Siegler, 2006), for example, Piaget is still the most frequently cited author. However, no chapter is dedicated to his perspective, and he is generally cited to illustrate an approach that is no longer relevant.

4 Piaget was characterized by his lack of ostentation, and this is likely rooted in his somewhat severe protestant upbringing (Piaget, 1952; Vidal, 1994). Two anecdotes serve as an illustration of this fact. Piaget tended to commute to the Institut Jean-Jacques Rousseau via bicycle. He never owned a car, and after his meetings at the International Centre of Genetic Epistemology (ICGE) on Mondays, he would look for a friendly driver to drop him off close to his residence. The ICGE did not have any assigned buildings or offices. Weekly meetings were held in available university rooms, and others were held as informal gatherings, occasionally at Piaget's home office. It was difficult to convince ICGE visitors to University of Geneva that the "Centre" existed at all.

5 *Horizontal décalage* refers to the temporal difference through which different content (for example, substance, weight, and volume) is organized via logical operations.

6 Vygotsky conceived of the relationship between learning and development when defining the concept of the *proximal zone of development*. Given that he does not carefully define individual mechanisms that allow learning to become development, many studies inspired by his theories do not clearly define the relationship between both processes.

References

Bennour, M. & Vonèche, J. (2009). The historical context of Piaget's ideas. In U. Müller, J. I. M. Carpendale & L. Smith (Eds.), *The Cambridge companion to Piaget* (pp. 45–63). New York, NY: Cambridge University Press.

Binet, A. & Simon, T. (1909). L'intelligence des imbéciles [The intelligence of idiots]. *Année Psychologique, 15*, 1–47.

Bond, T. & Tryphon, A. (2009). Piaget and method. In U. Müller, J. I. M. Carpendale, & L. Smith (Eds.), *The Cambridge companion to Piaget* (pp. 171–199). New York, NY: Cambridge University Press.

Bringuier, J. P. (1980). *Conversations with Jean Piaget*. Chicago, IL: The University of Chicago Press.

Bronckart, J. P. (2012). Contributions on Piagetian constructivism to social interaction. In E. Martí & C. Rodríguez (Eds.), *After Piaget* (pp. 43–58). London, UK: Transaction.

Carey, S. (2009). *The origin of concepts*. Oxford, UK: Oxford University Press.

Chomsky, N. (1972). *Language and mind*. New York, NY: Harcourt Brace Jovanovich.

van Dijk, M. & van Geert, P. (2011). Heuristic techniques for the analysis of variability as a dynamic aspect of change. *Infancia y Aprendizaje, 34*(2), 151–167.

Doise, W., Mugny, G., & Perret-Clermont, A. N. (1975). Social interaction and cognitive development: Further evidence. *European Journal of Social Psychology, 6*(2), 245–247.

Ducret, J. J. (1990). *Jean Piaget: Biographie et parcours intellectual* [Jean Piaget: Biography and intellectual pathway]. Neuchâtel, Switzerland: Delachaux et Niestlé.

Gillièron, C. (1985). *La construction du réel chez le psychologue: Épistémologie et méthodes en sciences humaines* [Construction of reality by the psychologist: Epistemology and methods in human sciences]. Berne, Switzerland: Peter Lang.

Gómez, J. C. (2010). Shadows of the living dead: Potential dangers of unsafe encounters between developmental psychology and neuroscience. *Infancia y Aprendizaje, 33*(1), 19–24.

Hirschfeld, L. A. & Gelman, S. A. (1994). *Mapping the mind: Domain specificity in cognition and culture*. Cambridge, UK: Cambridge University Press.

Hsueh, Y. (2009). Piaget in the United States: 1925–1971. In U. Müller, J. I. M. Carpendale, & L. Smith (Eds.), *The Cambridge companion to Piaget* (pp. 344–370). New York, NY: Cambridge University Press.

Inhelder, B., Sinclair, H., & Bovet, M. (1974). *Apprentissage et structures de la connaissance* [Learning and development of cognition]. Paris: Presses Universitaires de France.

Inhelder, B., Cellérier, G., Ackermann, E., Blanchet, A., Boder, A., de Caprona, D., Ducret, J. J., & Saada-Robert, M. (1992). *Le cheminement des découvertes chez l'enfant: Recherches sur les microgenèses cognitives* [The pathway of discoveries by the child: Research on cognitive microgenesis]. Neuchâtel, Switzerland: Delachaux et Niestlé.

Karmiloff-Smith, A. (1992). *Beyond modularity: A developmental approach to cognitive science*. Cambridge, MA: MIT Press.

Karmiloff-Smith, A. (2012). From constructivism to neuroconstructivism: The activity-dependent structuring of the human brain. In E. Martí & C. Rodríguez (Eds.), *After Piaget* (pp. 1–14). London, UK: Transaction.

Karmiloff-Smith, A. & Inhelder, B. (1975). If you want to get ahead, get a theory. *Cognition, 3*(3), 195–212.

Kuhn, D. & Siegler, R. S. (2006). *Handbook of child psychology: Volume 2. Cognition, perception and language*. Hoboken, NJ: Wiley.

Martí, E. (1987). Estudi objectiu de la subjectivitat [Objective study of subjectivity]. *Publicacions de la Fundació Jaume Bofill*. Barcelona: Fundació Jaume Bofill.

Martí, E. (1996). Mechanisms of internalization and externalization of knowledge in Piaget's and Vygotsky's theories. In A. Tryphon & J. Vonèche (Eds.), *Piaget–Vygotsky: The social genesis of thought* (pp. 57–83). Hove, UK: Psychology Press.

Martí, E., & Rodríguez, C. (2012). *After Piaget*. London, UK: Transaction.

Messerly, J. G. (2009). Piaget's biology. In U. Müller, J. I. M. Carpendale, & L. Smith (Eds.), *The Cambridge companion to Piaget* (pp. 94–109). New York, NY: Cambridge University Press.

Mounoud, P. (1987). L'utilisation du milieu et du corps propre par le bebé [The utilization of the environment and the own body by the infant]. In J. Piaget, P. Mounoud, & J. P. Bronckart (Eds.), *Psychologie* (pp. 563–601). Paris, France: Gallimard.

Perret-Clermont, A. N. (2012). "Choose two or three scapegoats and make your point." Should I? Critical thoughts on a fabulous experience and its heritage. In E. Martí & C. Rodríguez, C (Eds.), *After Piaget* (pp. 207–225). London, UK: Transaction.

Piaget, J. (1923). *Le langage et la pensée chez l'enfant* [The language and thought of the child]. Neuchâtel, Switzerland: Delachaux et Niestlé.

Piaget, J. (1924). *Le jugement et le raisonnement chez l'enfant* [Judgment and reasoning in the child]. Neuchâtel, Switzerland: Delachux et Niestlé.

Piaget, J. (1932). *Le jugement moral chez l'enfant* [The moral judgment of the child]. Paris, France: F. Alcan.

Piaget, J. (1947/1963). *La psychologie de l'intelligence* (3rd ed.) [The psychology of intelligence]. Paris, France: Armand Collin.

Piaget, J. (1952). Autobiography. In E. G. Boring, H. S. Langfled, H. Werner, & R. M. Yerkes (Eds.), *A history of psychology in autobiography*: Vol. 4 (pp. 237–256). New York, NY: Russell & Russell.

Piaget, J. (1962). *Comments on Vygotsky's critical remarks concerning "The language and thought of the child" and "Judgements and reasoning in the child"*. Cambridge, MA: MIT Press.

Piaget, J. (1965). *Sagesses et illusions de la philosophie* [Insights and illusions in philosophy]. Paris, France: Presses Universitaires de France.

Piaget, J. (1967a). *Biologie et connaissance* [Biology and knowledge]. Paris, France: Gallimard.

Piaget, J. (1967b). *Logique et connaissance scientifique* [Logic and scientific knowledge]. Paris, France: Gallimard.

Piaget, J. (1970). Piaget's theory. In P. Mussen (Ed.), *Handbook of child psychology* (pp. 703–732). Hoboken, NJ: Wiley.

Piaget, J. (1972). *Épistémologie des sciences de l'homme* [The epistemology of human sciences]. Paris, France: Gallimard.

Piaget, J. (1980). Recent studies in genetic epistemology. *Cahiers de la Fondation Archives Jean Piaget*, *1*, 3–7.

Piaget, J. (1982). Reflections on Baldwin, an interview conducted and presented by J. Vonèche. In J. M. Broughton & D. J. Freeman-Moir (Eds.), *The cognitive-developmental psychology of James Mark Baldwin: Current theory and research in genetic epistemology* (pp. 80–86). Englewood Cliffs, NJ: Ablex.

Piaget, J. & García, R. (1983). *Psychogenèse et histoire des sciences* [Psychogenesis and the history of science]. Paris, France: Flammarion.

Piaget, J. & Inhelder, B. (1966). *La psychologie de l'enfant* [The psychology of the child]. Paris, France: Presses Universitaires de France.

Piatelli-Palmarini, M. (1979). *Théories de langage, theories de l'apprentissage: Le débat entre Jean Piaget et Noam Chomsky* [Language and learning: The debate between Jean Piaget and Noam Chomsky]. Paris, France: Éditions du Seuil.

Puche, R. & Martí, E. (2011). Metodologías del cambio [Methodologies of change]. *Infancia y Aprendizaje, 34*(2), 131–139.

Rochat, P. (2012). Baby assault on Piaget. In E. Martí & C. Rodríguez (Eds.), *After Piaget* (pp. 71–82). London, UK: Transaction.

Rodrigo, M. J. (2010). Where developmental and neuroscience meet: A threatening or a felicitous encounter? *Infancia y Aprendizaje, 33*(1), 3–17.

Rodríguez, C. & Martí, E. (2012). The fertility of Piaget's legacy. In E. Martí & C. Rodríguez (Eds.), *After Piaget* (pp. xix–xxxviii). London, UK: Transaction.

Smith, L. (2009). Piaget's pedagogy. In U. Müller, J. I. M. Carpendale, & L. Smith (Eds.), *The Cambridge companion to Piaget* (pp. 324–343). New York, NY: Cambridge University Press.

Valsiner, J. (2011). Constructing the vanishing present between the future and the past. *Infancia y Aprendizaje, 34*(2), 141–150.

van der Veer, R. & Valsiner, J. (1991). *Understanding Vygotsky: A quest for synthesis.* Cambridge, MA: Blackwell Publishers.

Vidal, F. (1994). *Piaget before Piaget.* Cambridge, MA: Harvard University Press.

Vuyk, R. (1981). *Overview and critique of Piaget's Genetic Epistemology: 1965–1980. Volume I and II.* London, UK: Academic Press.

Vygotsky, L. S. (1962/1934). *Thought and language.* Cambridge, MA: MIT Press.

Vygotsky, L. S. (1995/1931). Historia del desarrollo de las funciones psíquicas superiores. In L. S. Vygotsky, *Obras escogidas III* (pp. 11–325). Madrid, Spain: Aprendizaje/Visor.

Wallon. H. (1928). L'autisme du malade et l'égocentrisme enfantin: intervention aux discussions de la thèse de Piaget [The autism of the patient and the child's egocentrism: Intervention on discussions about Piaget's thesis]. *Bulletin de la Société Française de Philosophie, 28*, 131–136.

Chapter 6

Neuroscience

Can it become developmental?

Aaro Toomela

Neuroscience today has many branches, some of them related to the study of the psyche directly, and others indirectly. Most of the studies in neurosciences, however, do not contribute to understanding the psyche because they have not been developmental. Developmental studies, mostly under the name developmental cognitive neuroscience, have not contributed because they are not developmental either. At the same time, without understanding the biotic structures and processes that are necessary for the emergence of the psyche, the latter cannot be fully understood. Hence, on the one hand, developmental neuroscience is necessary for understanding the psyche, but, on the other hand, this science seems not to exist today.

Perhaps this first paragraph has introduced several statements many scholars would disagree with. First I suggested that the psyche can be understood only through the studies of development.[1] Second I suggested that even studies in the so-called developmental cognitive neuroscience are actually not developmental. And third I claimed that, without understanding the nervous system, the psyche cannot be understood either. In the rest of the chapter I provide arguments supporting these three claims. Additionally, I propose a possible reason as to why development is not studied by cognitive neurosciences—or by contemporary mainstream psychology[2] at all. Finally, I suggest ways in which neurosciences could actually become relevant for psychology.

Where we are in studies of nervous system–psyche relationships

I have a series of problems to solve in the following discussion. After all, I have claimed that something—study of development—is (almost) non-existing in contemporary ("developmental") neuroscience. As a scientist I am well aware that non-existence cannot be proven scientifically. I am even more aware that I have read only a fraction of thousands of neuroscientific studies published every year. Thus I can be wrong about the non-existence of the neuroscientific studies required for understanding the psyche. Yet this is not a particularly important question to consider. I have no doubt whatsoever that there is a huge amount of studies in cognitive neurosciences that, not being developmental, do not provide much to understanding the psyche—despite the opposite claims by scholars who conduct such studies. These studies can be valuable for something, but it is not psychology; thus my aim is to understand better, what kind of neuroscientific studies would be necessary, and why.

Why study development?

The first question to answer is, why study development at all? The answer to that question is not as obvious, or straightforward, as it may seem. I suggest that in order to understand the psyche—or indeed anything we would like to under-stand—we must study the development of what we want to understand. The prob-lem, of course, is that the three central concepts in this statement—understanding, the psyche, and development—could be defined in many different ways. Whether my suggestion can be accepted or rejected depends on the definitions chosen. This is actually the reason why nowadays neither psychology nor cognitive neurosci-ence cares much about studying development—these sciences are based on epis-temology and ontology, which do not require developmental studies for achieving understanding or scientific knowledge, according to the way these notions are understood in mainstream psychology.

The absolute minimum requirement for studying development, in order to understand anything, follows from defining what (scientific) understanding is. In fact, the definition of development itself also depends on how understanding is defined. So I define here these two; the psyche will be defined later. These issues have been discussed in detail elsewhere (Toomela, 2009, 2010e, 2012), so here I just provide the essential ideas. In short, I propose that scientific knowledge— or understanding—is *knowledge of causes*. In contemporary psychology, three approaches to science can be distinguished: process oriented, cause–effect, and structural–systemic. Each of them defines differently what causality is. According to the process-oriented view, which characterizes so-called modern qualitative science, the content of scientific understanding is obscure. In this view of science, the world is characterized by constant change in continuous unity, where some things may change into their opposites, and in other cases opposites may form a harmonious unity. Things are relative and events are determined by many sources of change. According to this view, scientific understanding is reducible to impres-sions, subjective descriptions, and personally determined meanings. Cause–effect science, however, is grounded on more organized epistemology. According to this view—shared by the majority of psychologists today, especially by those relying on quantitative methodology—causes are understood as events that make effects happen. Thus to understand an effect would mean to identify the cause that made such effect to become into being. Finally, according to the structural–systemic approach, a thing[3] is understood when it is known, first, from what elements or parts it is composed; second, in which specific relationships those parts are; and third, which novel qualities characterize the whole that emerged. It is assumed that every whole has emergent qualities that do not characterize its parts. It also follows that parts, after they have been synthesized into a higher-order whole, acquire qualities of the whole as they begin to relate to the rest of the world as parts of the whole, not independently.

The definition of scientific understanding is therefore directly related to how development is conceptualized. For the process-oriented approach, the world is continuously changing and there are no universal principles underlying these changes. Thus, studies within this approach can reveal only endlessly many particulars and nothing can be really understood—including change itself. For cause–effect science, development is related to cause–effect relations: development is the cause that makes the effect happen. Accordingly, development becomes an emergence of an effect, which is explained when its cause is identified; and the explanation ends here. For the structural–systemic approach, however, inquiries begin by observing relationships between events in time. Development in this approach is thus defined as hierarchical synthesis of elements into a whole with novel qualities. Hence, contrariwise to cause–effect science, this approach explicitly looks for the way in which novelty emerges; that is, what processes exactly underlie the emergence of novelty.

Depending on how causality and development is understood, the role of developmental science is differently conceptualized. First, in process-oriented science there are no developmental studies because the aim is just description of a continuously changing world. There is no organizing principle, no directionality in such changes, and therefore no phenomenon that could be called development could be defined. Cause–effect science, in turn, may study what it calls development, but it also manages to proceed without it as well. The identification of causes of effects does not require further questioning. Development may still be conceptualized as a special subject; in that case, study of development would be a description of sequences of cause–effect relationships. Nevertheless, there is no essential difference whether the whole sequence is studied or just one cause–effect segment of it. The studied events would be understood in the same way.

The situation is different for structural–systemic science, where a thing can be understood only when development is studied. As mentioned, the aim of these studies is to discover what are the parts of a whole from which it is synthesized from, and how these parts are related to one another. When the part is already included into a whole, its qualities have changed and are not distinguishable from the qualities of the whole. Thus if we want to know what are the parts of a whole, we need to study them before they form relationships with other parts—that is, before the whole emerges. We also should know whether the hypothetical part is truly a part of the whole. Thus we need to study how that part becomes an element of a whole. Studying the elements and processes of their inclusion into a higher-order whole is the study of development. There is no other way to discover qualities of elements and distinguish them from the qualities of a whole.

One final note on this subject is in order here. All three ways of science I have described may claim that development is studied in them. We should be aware that in each case development is being defined differently; what is development for one is not development for another. When I suggest that there are (almost) no developmental cognitive neuroscientific studies, I do it following the structural–systemic definition of development. For this approach, if development is not studied, no scientific understanding can be achieved. For the other two approaches, there is no need to study development, and from their perspective my critique is probably irrelevant. Thus we understand why development became an unimportant branch of studies of the psyche—the less-developed epistemology[4] of both process-oriented and cause-effect sciences have no need for studying it.

How developmental cognitive neuroscience is not developmental

Developmental cognitive neuroscience today is not developmental because, as noted earlier, it is based on a cause–effect epistemology. Thus all the questions asked in these studies[5] inquire whether or not certain behaviors or mental processes are related to certain events in the nervous system. Knowing such relationships, regrettably, adds nothing substantially important to understanding the psyche. On the one hand, the results of such studies are trivial: as life is continuous to the physical world, and the psyche, in turn, to life, all distinguishable psychic events must also be distinguishable in the biotic and physical world. Thus we already know that different psychic states are biotically and physically distinguishable as well. On the other hand, the particulars—the specific physical and biotic aspects that are related to the specific aspects of the psychic world—must be discovered empirically. But just finding those relationships does not bring us any closer to understanding the psyche. The problem here can be understood only from the structural–systemic perspective. Every psychic process emerges on the basis of a holistic structure, on the basis of a whole. Brain studies can reveal or at least suggest that this whole is distinguished into components. Yet there is no way to understand what particular role the part has in the whole unless the study is developmental. When the parts are already operating as parts of the psychic whole, their functioning is determined by the qualities of the whole as well. Without developmental studies, it is not possible to distinguish the qualities of the whole from the qualities of its parts.

Furthermore, the psyche emerges on the basis of its own principles, which are not reducible to biotic or physical principles. Thus, more specifically, without developmental studies it is not possible to distinguish biotic and psychic principles that underlie the functioning of the whole, to understand in which way one, and in which way another, determine the processes of the parts as well as the whole of mind. As a rule, in developmental cognitive neuroscience it is assumed that the functioning of the nervous system follows the principles of life alone. This assumption is wrong: when the nervous system is organized according to the principles of the psyche, the functioning of it becomes determined *also* by the principles of the psyche—within the constraints of principles of life, of course.

In order to distinguish one from another, the emergence and development of life should be understood together with the understanding of emergence and development of the psyche.

Developmental cognitive science today is unable to distinguish qualities of parts from the qualities of the psyche as a whole. Thus neither the parts nor the whole can be understood. I think that the reason for this is partly related to ignoring one of the fundamental problems that faces cognitive neuroscience—yes, not only developmental but the whole of cognitive neuroscience—, namely, it does not define what is life and what is the psyche. Without distinguishing qualities of life from qualities of the psyche, we cannot understand which aspects of human behaviour are determined by biotic principles and which are determined by psychic ones. Only then can we also understand why and how understanding the biotic principles that underlie the functioning of the nervous system is crucial for understanding the psyche.

Why understanding the nervous system is essential for understanding the psyche

The psyche is developmentally continuous to life, and life in turn is developmentally continuous to matter. Let us see which specific theoretical consequences follow from that principle. First, the psyche as a higher-order whole must emerge as a synthesis of some lower-order elements. These elements must be physical and biotic; the psychic qualities characterize the whole that emerges in the synthesis of physical and biotic elements.

For structural–systemic science, scientific explanation consists in identification and qualitative description of the elements, the specific relationships between the elements, and the qualities of the whole that emerge in the synthesis of elements. As elements can be understood only before they become parts of the higher-order whole, the psyche can be understood when its elements are studied before they became parts of the psyche. In other words, we must know the biotic and physical parts that become elements of the psychic whole. Indeed, understanding the nervous system as a biotic basis for the psyche is absolutely essential for understanding the psyche.

At the general level, we see now why without understanding the nervous system the psyche cannot be understood. But we can go further. We can define life and psyche. This allows us to understand exactly where life principles end and principles of the psyche emerge. Supported in these definitions, we can formulate questions about the functioning of the nervous system that are relevant for understanding the psyche and we can formulate questions about the functioning of the nervous system determined by psychic principles.

Both definitions we need I have justified elsewhere; thus here I only give the definitions. Following and elaborating Anokhin's ideas (cf. Anokhin, 1978a; Konstantinov, Lomov, & Shvyrkov, 1978; see also Toomela, 2010a),

> Life is a form of organization of matter that is able on the basis of the antici-
> patory reflection of the reality to prevent the destructive effects of the envi-
> ronment by purposefully changing either itself or its environment and thereby
> preserve its holistic qualities.
>
> (Toomela, in press)

Thus, first, life is a form of organization—it characterizes certain forms of matter. Second, these living forms of matter preserve their holistic qualities even when their environment changes beyond a tolerable level at any given moment. But how is it possible to survive when the environment changes over the tolerable limit of the organism? There are, third, two possibilities—living organisms actively change themselves or they actively change their environment. As a rule, when the environment changes over limit, then it is too late to change anything. Living bodies must act before the environment changes—this is done on the basis of what Anokhin called anticipatory reflection of the reality. Each and every living organism is thus able to "foresee" (some) future changes of the environment (for discussion of this issue see Toomela, 2010a).

The psyche is a specific form of life, which relates to the environment in a novel way, not attainable for all living organisms: "Psyche is a form of organiza-tion of living matter, whose purposeful behaviour aimed at preventing destructive effects of the environment is based on individual experiences" (Toomela, in press, modified from Toomela, 2010d, p. 10; see also Hobhouse, 1901; Toomela, 2010e, 2011). The most important quality that emerges along with the emergence of the psyche is a potential of an organism to develop its ways to relate to the environ-ment on the basis of *individual experiences*.

In order to make the psyche possible, certain biotically determined neural mechanisms must exist—albeit these do not determine the relationship to the environment. Rather, these mechanisms underlie the potential to construct indi-vidual experiences and to keep them over time. First of all, there must be a system that supports the existence of experiences, and these are the senses, the only sys-tem through which the psyche connects to the world. Sensory systems are made of thousands or millions of receptors, each responding to a fraction of the physi-cal event that is sensed. By their structure, sensory systems organize sensations according to their own principles, not according to the principles of the external world. Patterns of sensory activation must be interpreted in order to be useful for the organism. Thus there must be a system responsible for organizing individual experiences; namely, thinking. But the content of thought is psychic. Individual experiences are useful, however, only when they can be used later in time. Thus there must be memory that is responsible for storing experiences—but, again, all the content of memory is psychic. Furthermore, there must be a system respon-sible for creating plans, for finding novel ways to act in accordance with novel individual experiences. The content of such plans is psychic as well.

Altogether, when an organism becomes psychic, the subsystems of the nervous system that are responsible for the emergence of the potential for the psyche become functioning according to the principles of the psyche when the world is experienced and stored, and plans are made on the basis of the experiences. Neurosciences today, to the best of my knowledge, totally fail here as the psychic principles determining the functioning of the nervous system are not distinguished—and are not distinguishable in principle from biotic in a-developmental studies. Unfortunately this also means that we are not able to fully understand the psyche because the functioning of the psyche is constrained by biotic principles. Without knowing those constraints, we lack an important knowledge that would help to separate biotically untenable theories of the psyche from those that are biotically possible.

To avoid the possibility of incorrect interpretation of my discussion so far, here is a summary: I am proposing that understanding the neural basis of the psyche is necessary for understanding the psyche, but I am not saying that it would be sufficient. On the contrary, we should also understand what is the environment, how the environment has evolved in behavioral evolution and cultural history, how the environment develops for an individual in ontogenesis, how the environment and the individual are related to one another biotically and psychically, and how the psyche develops in the individual–environment relationship. Therefore, to understand the psyche, we need a unifying theory (Toomela, 2007).

Where could we proceed in studies of nervous system–psyche relationships?

I am not going to propose where cognitive neurosciences should proceed. It is not up to me to tell other scholars what to do. Thus here I just set out where cognitive neuroscience could proceed, if the understanding of the psyche were to become its aim.

Good answers to scientific questions are absolutely necessary for science to proceed further, and yet they are not the most important element. The most important, in fact, is having questions worth answering. As we saw above, for cause–effect science, the questions asked by process-oriented science are not worth answering (and vice versa); whereas from the structural–systemic perspective, neither process-oriented nor cause–effect science questions are scientifically relevant. Thus, it is the "right" questions that determine the future of any science: if the questions are right, the answers will be found sooner or later. Accordingly, in the following I posit a number of questions for the neurosciences that can be taken as examples of questions that, when answered, would help to understand the psyche. I organize the questions into two groups: one group concerns the biotic basis of the psyche, and the other addresses the reflection of psychic principles in neural functioning.

Biotic grounds for the possibility of the psyche

As previously stated, the psyche is not possible without a nervous system, the organ that can be reorganized when interacting with the external world through the senses. It does not follow, however, that every organism with a nervous system is psychic. It is more likely that the nervous system first evolved for supporting the integration of multicellular organisms into a living whole. The nervous system became necessary when the multicellular organisms differentiated into overly complex wholes. If it is so, then it must be possible to find out, through developmental studies of evolution, what had to be introduced into the nervous system in evolution such that it became an organ for processing and storing individual experiences.

Second, psychology established a long time ago that there must be at least two different ways in which memories emerge in the brain (e.g., Köhler, 1927). Lower animals memorize their experiences through repeated exposure to them. At some point in evolution, it became possible to memorize after having an experience only once. Following the discovery of so-called long-term potentiation (cf. Lømo, 2003), the slow and repeated mechanisms of memory formation are increasingly understood. Yet, to the very best of my knowledge, there seems to be no understanding of the mechanisms underlying memory formation after a single experience. Thus, the relevant aspects of biotic mechanisms underlying the emergence of advanced forms of psyche are not yet known.

The biotic mechanisms of thinking so as to organize individual experiences are not well understood either. Understanding slow mechanisms of memory formation might also explain what guides simple associative learning—it is repeated experience of the regularity of the sensed environment. Yet many animals are able to organize their experiences internally—like apes, when solving for the first time the task in Köhler's experiments. Thus there is another mechanism of thinking, guided by internal processes. Interestingly, it seems that these mechanisms are also related to the emergence of the instant memory. However, we do not know yet how the brain has to change in order to make that internal purposeful organization of experiences possible.

Additionally, there is a fundamentally important question asked by Anokhin many years ago that remains unanswered despite its relevance—namely, how do the neurons integrate patterns of incoming synaptic excitations and inhibitions (cf. Anokhin, 1975a, 1975b, 1978b)? The main issue here is that neurons do not just summarize quantitatively the excitation, but they respond qualitatively. For instance, multimodal neurons must react only when input is received from different sensory modalities. But how do neurons distinguish between a high quantity of input from one modality and medium-level inputs from different modalities—which, when summarized, would be equal in the amount of high input from one modality—and respond only in the latter case? There seems to be no doubt that memories emerge as neural networks, but in such networks every neuron must also respond qualitatively, not only quantitatively. Therefore, memory formation has to be related also to intra-neuronal processes by which each of them may respond to a certain quality of the input.

One further question is also puzzling. Human psychic development can clearly be distinguished by stages, with each stage characterized by different psychic principles according to which units of thought are organized (cf. Toomela, 2000, 2003a, 2003b, for cultural–historical theory of stages). These stages are related to age—each stage is related to a minimum-age limit, before which higher-order thought cannot develop even when environmental organization would support such a development. The ages when a new stage becomes possible are related to brain maturation: different brain regions mature at different ages and the speed of maturation also varies (for a short review see Toomela, 2000). It is more or less known, which regions and when mature in line with ontogenesis. Yet none of the maturing regions seems to be completely silent or not functioning at all during the early ages. Thus it remains unclear why the late-maturing regions cannot support the development of higher-order thought before maturation, even though the same regions seem to participate in psychic processes also at earlier ages.

I am sure there are many more questions relevant for psychology that may be asked by neuroscientists. I have provided just some examples of unanswered questions that have bothered me for many years. These and similar questions should be asked and answered for us to develop a coherent theory of psyche. Fortunately, psychology can proceed without the answers as well. But it would miss solid ground to distinguish biotically viable theories from biotically implausible or even impossible ones.[6]

The psychic brain

The psyche is based on individual experiences. Individual experiences cannot be biotically determined; they are determined by particulars of the environment that the individual is experiencing. Thus, through processing individual experiences, the nervous system realizes its potential to become psychic. With the emergence of psychically organized experiences, however, the functioning of the nervous system must be determined by psychic principles.

Very little is known about the psychic brain. There have been, for example, a few studies where illiterate adults are compared with literate adults. It has been found that different brain regions are involved in solving the same tasks depending on whether a person is illiterate or not (e.g., Ardila et al., 2010; Carreiras et al., 2009; Castro-Caldas, 2004; Castro-Caldas et al., 2009; Castro-Caldas, Petersson, Reis, Stone-Elander, & Ingvar, 1998; Castro-Caldas & Reis, 2003; Ostrosky-Solis, Garcia, & Perez, 2004; Petersson, Reis, & Ingvar, 2001; Petersson, Silva, Castro-Caldas, Ingvar, & Reis, 2007). Thus there is seminal yet indirect evidence that the organization and functioning of the brain actually depends on the kinds of individual experiences persons have.

Theoretically, as I mentioned previously, the human psyche develops over stages. Each of the stages is characterized by a specific kind of relations according to which thought is organized. Solving some tasks becomes possible only at a higher stage of development, whereas other tasks can be solved at lower levels as well. Those simpler tasks can also be solved with higher-order thought operations. Say, for instance, adding small numbers can be performed in different ways.

Younger children can count their fingers, whereas older children learn formal arithmetic and solve the same task differently. These different ways of solving the same task must also have different brain organization. What is also important is that such differences in neural organization are determined by psychic, not biotic, principles. If there is no possibility of learning formal arithmetic, the brain will not reorganize on the basis of its internal biotic mechanisms; no arithmetic emerges in the brain without interaction with the culturally organized environment. This example would be a special case of a principle formulated long ago by Vygotsky—namely, the cerebral organization of psychic processes is determined by environmental extracerebral connections (Vygotsky, 1982; see also Toomela, 2014d).

This is enough to formulate some general questions that could be asked by cognitive neuroscientists. First, there should be a psychological developmental theory about how the structure of cognitive operations changes with changing experiences. Armed with such a theory—a theory of stages of psychic development—"developmental" cognitive neuroscience could become truly developmental and study the reorganization of cognitive structures alongside ontogenetic development. Two different sets of questions could be asked here. On the one hand, it would become possible to discover how externally the same behavior emerges from different psychic processes—these different psychic processes must also be differently related to the functioning of the brain. On the other hand, it would become possible to understand what structures and corresponding psychic processes are necessarily involved to organize late appearing forms of behavior and why these forms of behavior appear late.

The search for dynamic reorganization of the structure of psychic processes does not have to be exploratory from the beginning. There is already a well-grounded theory to guide this quest. First, there is Vygotsky's theory of systemic dynamic localization of psychic functions (Vygotsky, 1982), developed further and filled with numerous facts by Luria (1969, 1973, 1979). Luria's work concerned mainly systemic organization. His theory extended to dynamics of reorganization, but only in his theory and application of the neuropsychological rehabilitation of adults with localized brain damage (Luria, 1947, 1948; Tsvetkova, 1985). Yet it was Polyakov who founded the necessary ground for organizing knowledge about development of psychic functions as related to the reorganization of the brain (Polyakov, 1969; for a short description of his theory see Toomela, 2014d). These theories would form a solid base for studies in developmental cognitive neurosciences, but all the particulars of the developmental reorganization of psychic functioning are still in need of discovery. These particulars, in turn, would help to elaborate the psychological theory of development. Whatever would be discovered in such studies, I am sure that one pervasive principle would be constantly supported by them: we would find far fewer biotic elements in the functioning of the brain than it is thought today. The brain would become what it is for all of us, humans, in the first place—a living organ that is transformed through individual experiences into the psyche.

Acknowledgments

This work was supported by Estonian Research Council Grant No IUT03-03 (Academic and Personal Development of an Individual in the System of Formal Education).

Notes

1 In fact, I am suggesting that nothing can be understood without studying the development of the thing that one is attempting to understand.
2 "Mainstream psychology is an approach to the science of mind accepted by majority of psychologists and defined by ontological and epistemological qualities questioned by representatives of non-mainstream psychology" (see *Mainstream Psychology* in Toomela, 2014a, for definition and discussion).
3 According to the structural–systemic view, novel qualities emerge with the synthesis of a hierarchically higher-order whole. Thus, the world is understood as developmentally continuous: each lower-level whole can become a part of a higher-order whole, and higher-order wholes can be disorganized into independent elements of lower order. In our universe, three large continuous classes of qualitatively different things can be distinguished. First, there is a physical world. Part of it becomes the biotic world: the world where physical things became alive. Thus every living being is a physical thing with additional qualities that characterize only the living but not the physical world. Similarly, part of the living world has developed the psyche. The psyche must be developmentally continuous to life; otherwise we would have to posit a dualist world where matter and mind can exist independently from one another. If the psyche is a developmentally differentiated form of life, and life in turn a developmentally differentiated form of matter, both life and the psyche—as material—must in a certain sense be things, things that are organized according to specific principles that distinguish life from matter and the psyche from life. In brief, we either admit that the psyche is a form of matter, a thing, or we accept a dualist worldview. In the latter case, psychology as science would become impossible; we would have either philosophy or religion instead.
4 I am not judgmental here. The three sciences are clearly ordered in the complexity of understanding that can be achieved by each of them (cf. Toomela, 2008, 2009, 2010b, 2010c, 2011, 2012, 2014a, 2014b, 2014c; Toomela & Valsiner, 2010). The criterion I take here is the possibility to change the world according to our needs and purposes. Process-oriented science provides descriptions that actually do not ground the predictable changes of our actions. Cause–effect science grounds probabilistic prediction but fails to cope with situations where the expected cause does not bring the expected effect. The structural–systemic science, in turn, can make non-probabilistic predictions—if all the theoretically necessary parts are put into theoretically defined relationships, the whole with expected qualities must emerge. If it does not emerge, then there is a clear way to discover why the prediction failed—either some element or their relationship was wrong or missing. Just to bring one example, all machines created by humans are created on the basis of structural–systemic description. To bring it into the realm of the science of the psyche, the most efficient forms of neuropsychological rehabilitation are also structural–systemic (cf. Luria, 1947, 1948; Tsvetkova, 1985).
5 It is also interesting to look at what questions are *not* asked in so-called developmental cognitive science. As a rule, it is not asked, what do we learn about the functioning of the developed mind when we study the development of it? Instead the questions are asked about development, often defined in the cause–effect framework as "learning"; so the focus of the studies is development itself. For structural–systemic science, studying

development is the only possible way towards understanding formed wholes. Thus, metaphorically, if development were a window, the cause–effect scientists would see and study the glass and the structural–systemic scientists would look through it to see the world.

6 I note here just one quite trivial example. We may have a theory that we can directly see distinct things in the world around us. Numerous undisputable facts about how the eye works, however, would refute that theory. The pattern of retinal neural activity emerging as a response to light is not sufficient for the direct sensation of things distinguished from their background. These patterns must be internally organized before figures can be distinguished from ground and also one from another. Thus, things are distinguished by psychic processes, not by senses.

References

Anokhin, P. K. (1975a). Sistemnyi analiz integrativnoi dejatel'nosti neirona [Systemic analysis of the integrative activity of a neuron]. In P. K. Anokhin (Ed.), *Ocherki po fiziologii funktsional'nyks sistem* (pp. 347–440). Moscow, Russia: Medicina.

Anokhin, P. K. (1975b). Uzlovyje voprosy v izuchenii vyshei nervnoi dejatel'nosti [Central issues in the study of the higher nervous activity]. In P. K. Anokhin (Ed.), *Ocherki po fiziologii funktsional'nyks sistem* (pp. 108–226). Moscow, Russia: Medicina.

Anokhin, P. K. (1978a). Filosofskii smysl problemy jestestvennogo i iskusstvennogo intellekta [Philosophical meaning of the problem of natural and artificial intellect]. In F. V. Konstantinov, B. F. Lomov, & V. B. Schvyrkov (Eds.), *P. K. Anokhin. Izbrannyje trudy. Filosofskije aspekty teorii funktsional'noi sistemy* (pp. 107–124). Moscow, Russia: Nauka.

Anokhin, P. K. (1978b). Printsipial'nyje voprosy obschei teorii funktsional'nykh sistem [Fundamental questions of the general theory of functional systems]. In F. V. Konstantinov, B. F. Lomov, & V. B. Schvyrkov (Eds.), *P. K. Anokhin. Izbrannyje trudy. Filosofskije aspekty teorii funktsional'noi sistemy* (pp. 49–106). Moscow, Russia: Nauka.

Ardila, A., Bertolucci, P. H., Braga, L. W., Castro-Caldas, A., Judd, T., Kosmidis, M. H., . . . Rosselli, M. (2010). Illiteracy: The neuropsychology of cognition without reading. *Archives of Clinical Neuropsychology, 25,* 689–712.

Carreiras, M., Seghier, M. L., Baquero, S., Estevez, A., Lozano, A., Devlin, J. T., & Price, C. J. (2009). An anatomical signature for literacy. *Nature, 461,* 983–986.

Castro-Caldas, A. (2004). Targeting regions of interest for the study of the illiterate brain. *International Journal of Psychology, 39*(1), 5–17.

Castro-Caldas, A., Nunes, M. V., Maestu, F., Ortiz, T., Simoes, R., Fernandes, R., . . . Goncalves, M. (2009). Learning ortography in adulthood: A magnetoencephalographic study. *Journal of Neuropsychology, 3,* 17–30.

Castro-Caldas, A., Petersson, K. M., Reis, A., Stone-Elander, S., & Ingvar, M. (1998). The illiterate brain: Learning to read and write during childhood influences the functional organization of the adult brain. *Brain, 121,* 1053–1063.

Castro-Caldas, A., & Reis, A. (2003). The knowledge of orthography is a revolution in the brain. *Reading and Writing: An Interdisciplinary Journal, 16,* 81–97.

Hobhouse, L. T. (1901). *Mind in evolution.* London, UK: Macmillan.

Köhler, W. (1927). *The mentality of apes.* London, UK: Routledge & Kegan Paul.

Konstantinov, F. K., Lomov, B. F., & Shvyrkov, B. V. (Eds.). (1978). *P. K. Anokhin. Izbrannyje trudy. Filosofskije aspekty teorii funktsional'noi sistemy.* Moscow, Russia: Nauka.

Lømo, T. (2003). The discovery of long-term potentiation. *Philosophical Transactions of the Royal Society of London. B: Biological Sciences*, *358*, 617–620.

Luria, A. R. (1947). *Travmaticheskaja afasia. Klinika, semiotika i vosstanovitel'naya terapiya* [Traumatic aphasia: Clinic, semiotics, and rehabilitation]. Moscow, Russia: Izdatel'stvo Akademii Meditsinskikh Nauk SSSR.

Luria, A. R. (1948). *Vosstanovlenije funkcii mozga posle vojennoi travmy* [Restoration of brain functions after war trauma]. Moscow, Russia: Izdatel'stvo Akademii Medicinskih Nauk SSSR.

Luria, A. R. (1969). *Vyshije korkovyje funktsii tsheloveka i ikh narushenija pri lokal'nykh porazenijakh mozga* [Higher cortical functions in man and their disturbances in local brain lesions]. Moscow, Russia: Izdatel'stvo Moskovskogo Universiteta.

Luria, A. R. (1973). *Osnovy neiropsikhologii* [Foundations of neuropsychology]. Moscow, Russia: Izdatel'stvo MGU.

Luria, A. R. (1979). *Jazyk i soznanije* [Language and consciousness]. Moscow, Russia: Izdatel'stvo Moskovskogo Universiteta.

Ostrosky-Solis, F., Garcia, M. A., & Perez, M. (2004). Can learning to read and write change the brain organization? An electrophysiological study. *International Journal of Psychology*, *39*(1), 27–35.

Petersson, K. M., Reis, A., & Ingvar, M. (2001). Cognitive processing in literate and illiterate subjects: A review of some recent behavioral and functional neuroimaging data. *Scandinavian Journal of Psychology*, *42*, 251–267.

Petersson, K. M., Silva, C., Castro-Caldas, A., Ingvar, M., & Reis, A. (2007). Literacy: A cultural influence on functional left–right differences in the inferior parietal cortex. *European Journal of Neuroscience*, *26*, 791–799.

Polyakov, G. I. (1969). Sovremennyje dannyje o strukturnoi organizacii mozgovoi kory [Modern data about structural organization of the brain cortex]. In A. R. Luria (Ed.), *Vyshije korkovyje funktsii tsheloveka i ikh narushenija pri lokal'nykh porazenijakh mozga* (pp. 37–73). Moscow, Russia: Izdatel'stvo Moskovskogo Universiteta.

Toomela, A. (2000). Stages of mental development: Where to look? *Trames: Journal of the Humanities and Social Sciences*, *4*(1), 21–52.

Toomela, A. (2003a). Culture as a semiosphere: On the role of culture in the culture–individual relationship. In I. E. Josephs (Ed.), *Dialogicality in development* (pp. 129–163). Westport, CT: Praeger.

Toomela, A. (2003b). Development of symbol meaning and the emergence of the semiotically mediated mind. In A. Toomela (Ed.), *Cultural guidance in the development of the human mind* (pp. 163–209). Westport, CT: Ablex Publishing.

Toomela, A. (2007). Unifying psychology: Absolutely necessary, not only useful. In A. V. B. Bastos & N. M. D. Rocha (Eds.), *Psicologia: Novas direcoes no dialogo com outros campos de saber* (pp. 449–464). Sao Paulo, Brazil: Casa do Psicologo.

Toomela, A. (2008). Variables in psychology: A critique of quantitative psychology. *Integrative Psychological and Behavioral Science*, *42*(3), 245–265. doi: 10.1007/s12124-008-9059-6

Toomela, A. (2009). How methodology became a toolbox – and how it escapes from that box. In J. Valsiner, P. Molenaar, M. Lyra, & N. Chaudhary (Eds.), *Dynamic Process Methodology in the Social and Developmental Sciences* (pp. 45–66). New York, NY: Springer.

Toomela, A. (2010a). Biological roots of foresight and mental time travel. *Integrative Psychological and Behavioral Science*, *44*(2), 97–125. doi: 10.1007/s12124-010-9120-0

Toomela, A. (2010b). Methodology of idiographic science: Limits of single-case studies and the role of typology. In S. Salvatore, J. Valsiner, J. T. Simon, & A. Gennaro (Eds.), *Yearbook of Idiographic Science, Volume 2/2009* (pp. 13–33). Rome, Italy: Firera & Liuzzo.

Toomela, A. (2010c). Quantitative methods in psychology: Inevitable and useless. *Frontiers in Psychology, 1*(29), 1–14. doi: 10.3389/fpsyg.2010.00029

Toomela, A. (2010d). Systemic person-oriented approach to child development: Introduction to the study. In A. Toomela (Ed.), *Systemic Person-Oriented Study of Child Development in Early Primary School* (pp. 1–24). Frankfurt am Main, Germany: Peter Lang.

Toomela, A. (2010e). What is the psyche? The answer depends on the particular episte-mology adopted by the scholar. In S. Salvatore, J. Valsiner, J. T. Simon, & A. Gennaro (Eds.), *Yearbook of Idiographic Science, Volume 2/2009.* (pp. 81–104). Rome, Italy: Firera & Liuzzo.

Toomela, A. (2011). Travel into a fairy land: A critique of modern qualitative and mixed methods psychologies. *Integrative Psychological and Behavioral Science, 45*(1), 21–47. doi: 10.1007/s12124-010-9152-5

Toomela, A. (2012). Guesses on the future of cultural psychology: Past, present, and past. In J. Valsiner (Ed.), *The Oxford handbook of culture and psychology* (pp. 998–1033). New York, NY: Oxford University Press.

Toomela, A. (2014a). Mainstream psychology. In T. Teo (Ed.), *Encyclopedia of Critical Psychology* (pp. 1117–1125). New York, NY: Springer.

Toomela, A. (2014b). Modern qualitative approach to psychology: Art or science? In S. Salvatore, A. Gennaro, & J. Valsiner (Eds.), *Multicentric identities in a globalizing world* (pp. 75–82). Charlotte, NC: Information Age Publishing.

Toomela, A. (2014c). A structural systemic theory of causality and catalysis. In K. R. Cabell & J. Valsiner (Eds.), *The catalyzing mind: Beyond models of causality* (pp. 271–292). New York, NY: Springer.

Toomela, A. (2014d). There can be no cultural–historical psychology without neuropsy-chology: And vice versa. In A. Yasnitsky, R. van der Veer, & M. Ferrari (Eds.), *The Cambridge handbook of cultural–historical psychology* (pp. 315–349). Cambridge, UK: Cambridge University Press.

Toomela, A. (in press). *Kultuur, kõne ja Minu Ise* [Culture, speech, and My Self]. Tallinn, Estonia: Eesti Keele Sihtasutus.

Toomela, A., & Valsiner, J. (Eds.). (2010). *Methodological thinking in psychology: 60 years gone astray?* Charlotte, NC: Information Age Publishing.

Tsvetkova, L. S. (1985). *Neiropsikhologicheskaja reabilitatsija bol'nykh. Rech i intellektual'naja dejatel'nost* [Neuropsychological rehabilitation of a sick per-son: Speech and intellectual activity]. Moscow, Russia: Izdatel'stvo Moskovskogo Universiteta.

Vygotsky, L. S. (1982). Psikhologija i uchenije o lokalizacii psikhicheskih funktcii [Psychology and doctrine of localization of psychic functions]. In A. R. Luria & M. G. Jaroshevskii (Eds.), *L. S. Vygotsky. Sobranije sochinenii. Tom 1. Voprosy teorii i istorii psikhologii* (pp. 168–174). Moscow, Russia: Pedagogika.

Chapter 7

Socio-developmental aspects of apprenticeship

The case of musical tuition

Pablo Rojas

In this chapter we will address the central aspects of a process crucial to the apprenticeship of a musical instrument, which we will refer to as the *tuition principle*. Our aim here is to sketch its interactional qualities and distinguish it from formal instruction-based learning models, as well as to characterize it as a specific form of companionship and reciprocity between instructor and apprentice. The latter will ideally become a process of mutual alignment, which we will argue plays a central role in the "transmission" and development of instrumental skill.

The perceptual dispositions that arise in the encounter between the instrument's materiality and the musician's corporality resonate in a mesh of public, normative and stylistic values, converging in the harmonious efficacy characteristic of any skill. Such harmonious efficacy is often based upon an instructor-and-apprentice relationship. Here a mimetic dimension (the most elementary of its forms being "do as I do") is evidently present, but the relationship calls primarily upon a mode of companionship, which often finds its support in a relationship of *mutual alignment*. We will draw on the notion of *tuition* in order to qualify this relationship and the process that accompanies the development of the aforementioned harmonious efficacy. This distinguishes the tuition principle from traditional ways of conceiving teaching,[1] since it does not consist (or at least rarely) in the transmission of ready-made knowledge. It is rather about providing a framework for the development and sedimentation of gestures that, while being idiosyncratic to the apprentice, do participate in a tradition and strive for a holistic efficacy.

The mutual alignment we have just evoked is habitually characterized by a mimetic interplay between instructor and apprentice. Such alignment is mutual at a relational level (connivance, attachment, ways of attending to each others' doings, trust, etc.),[2] as well as at practical and dispositional levels: it is not that the apprentice alone responds to the demands of the instructor. The latter also adapts her or his gestures to the face-to-face (or rather side-by-side) situation by simplifying it, exaggerating some of its traits, and reproducing the apprentice's gesture (in order to show its "lacking" character or to highlight its "evenness"). Evidently, tuition does not limit itself to a mimetic interplay, for it is only the apprentice's commitment to the execution of a gesture that will allow the discovery of an expressive motif that was previously unreachable. Let us underscore that, although imitation has an important role in the tuition process, it certainly does not mean that we should seek an identical reproduction in it.

Otherwise, musical interpretation always implies a degree of variation, whether between different versions of a piece played by the same musician or by transformations happening from one generation to the next. Repetition and variation do constitute an indivisible couple in the defining of a skill and its development. At a musical level, the apprentice's discovery of several variants of a musical gesture promotes the enhancement of the instrument's potentialities, which goes alongside adapting a newly discovered gesture to the qualities of her or his morphology and motility. This will gradually allow the attainment of the expressive force that is so desired. Ultimately, just as repetition contributes to the constitution of musical form, the successive iteration of musical gestures from one generation of players to the next gives place to the revision of technical movements, as well as to the emergence of new expressive pathways that then become available to the musical community.

The didactic aspect of *tuition* covers a wide range of interventions, from expert listening (the role of an "auxiliary ear") and the qualification of the apprentice's performance, to both behavioural (e.g. orchestral-like gestures) and verbal indications (where its distinction with singing is blurred, privileging physiognomic orientation). At every level, we observe the physiognomic character of these interactions. For instance, the instructor will point out, "There, it's almost translucent", "Don't plunge into it all of a sudden", "Make the note bounce." Usually, these interventions come coupled with a programme structured around a repertoire that is sensed to be fundamental for a fluent progression of the learning path.

We will start by situating the phenomenon of tuition within the broader context of animal life and development, before returning to music as an exemplary case, to certain aspects of instructor/apprentice mutual alignment. The need for such kind of relational, practical and dispositional accompaniment in apprenticeship processes underscores intergenerational continuities and discontinuities between different generations. We will finally turn to the notion of *reprisal*, in order to look into the ways in which tuition practices configure threads where aesthetic, ethic and practical dimensions become tightly entrenched. Hence, we will suggest that the appropriation of musical skill reveals a fundamental continuity between present-time and further-reaching sociocultural developmental scales.

Tuition as a vital developmental process

Let us now briefly shift our focus into a broader context, which is that of animal life, where tuition configures the *developmental* and *relational* process that allows an animal to appropriate (actually, re-appropriate) the conducts, skills and technical dispositions or the "ways to do things" that are characteristic to the members of its species and vital in the context of their environment and their way of living. In this sense, the tuition principle does not convey a "technique of transmission and instruction" characteristic to humans, but refers to a much more general phenomenon that concerns all animal species that undergo an early period in their life span where reliance upon elders is crucial. We tend to confine this dependence to nursing—which is evidently true—forgetting that animal life consists of *conducts*. This period of reliance offers an instance to learn the *effective* ways (as Marcel Mauss, 2009, would have said) to feed, explore their environment, hunt, defend themselves, relate to others, and so forth. These are all vital conducts learnt in time while coexisting with other generations and requiring a fairly active situation (which goes well beyond mere mimicry). Such understanding of the tuition process evokes Oswald Spengler's (1934) formulation of *technics as the tactics of living*, according to which all animals develop (certainly, to various extents and degrees) a set of practices of hunting, scavenging, home building, and so forth. The idea that this kind of technique bears a biological weight without being reducible to it can be approached by means of Marcel Mauss' concept of *techniques of the body* (2009).

Mauss defined techniques of the body as "the traditional ways in which, from society to society, men know how to use their bodies" (2009, p. 365), accounting for the variety of bodily practices, such as walking, running, swimming and sleeping, to name a few. At least two aspects of his description are relevant to our discussion. First, the observation of such practices evidences the presence of a social idiosyncrasy in the gestures involved. Intergenerational re-appropriation does not arise from sheer individual imitation, but entails the sharing of collective values that are tangible in practice. Furthermore, Mauss underscored that the *efficacy* of such techniques does not depend on the use of extensional instruments (like an axe, or a bicycle), since there are equally effective techniques that do not suppose any tool intervention—at least in the traditional sense of the term.

Second, the traditional character of techniques makes them a dense entanglement, where bodily, aesthetic, ethic and mythical (for instance, magical) dimensions are intimately intertwined (cf. Mauss, 2009, p. 371). The transmission, and the tuition process that upholds these techniques, forces us to return to such traditional patterns, since their efficacy relies on the cohesion between these dimensions. For Mauss, traditional efficacy necessarily supposes a ritual dimension that neither physiology (contemporary neural correlates) nor the psychology of motor patterning in humans captures accurately.

Regretfully, it has been rare to see either anthropology or psychology moving from their usual indifference toward technical activity, particularly toward the tuition processes involved in it. After Mauss' intervention, works devoted to technical activity and its traditional dimensions have been scarce—among such works, we can count those of de Beaune (2013), Ingold (2013), Leroi-Gourhan (1965), Schlanger (2012), Sigaut (1985; 2003/2010), Simondon (1958/2012; 2014) and Berliner (2013). Returning to the appropriation of skill in the context of musical practice would allow us to grasp the unity between dexterous practice and its aesthetic and ethic dimensions.

For the time being, we will return to Tim Ingold's (2000) analyses as sketched in his volume's introduction, and particularly to his definition of the five main traits of skill, as they will serve us as a guideline in what follows: (1) every practice involves both *intentionality* and *functionality*, which are inherent to it and are therein merged, neither pre-existing in an agent's mind nor existing as pre-given properties of the instrument; (2) skill does not reside in a single individual, but strongly relies on the individual's participation in the experience and workings of a collective, and consequently on the ensemble of relationships that are nurtured within it; (3) skill does not rely on the exercise of mechanical force, but always supposes dimensions of exploration, caring and evaluation; (4) skills are "transmitted" from generation to generation by means of *in situ* practice, not by means of ready-made rules (in the case of music, we would first point out the role of ritualization); (5) skillful practice does not rely on the execution of a pre-established design, all the more since it contributes to regenerating tools (either "material" or not, as with the case of body techniques).

Tuning-in relationships

A key aspect of musicians' efficacy involves being able to listen accurately to their own playing, since they need to repeat and promptly respond to what they are hearing, reading or imagining on their own instrument. From the moment they start listening to themselves, they must evaluate the quality of their own playing in real time while keeping up with the musical flow, which presents a great difficulty for the newcomer (Rojas, 2015). This would gradually give place to an "evaluative attitude" toward their playing, which supposes that the performance is always directed to "another ear", irrespective of whether that listener is actually present, imagined or oneself.[3] The accompaniment exerted by a tutor is justified by the need of a trained ear that *listens with and for* the upcoming musician, which serves as a "resonating chamber", helping the practitioner find the acuteness so difficult to find on one's own. We will take the apprentice–tutor relationship as a paradigmatic scenario where musical skills are shared and developed.

As we will argue, tuition also supposes the re-appropriation of stylistic aspects that can be invisible to the foreign eye in side-by-side situations, but that will manifest themselves in musical gestures. Our focus will attempt to cover the contexts that capture the dynamic engagement between practitioners in their everyday tasks.

How, then, does the *mutual alignment* between practitioner and tutor come into play? Let us consider that the affective value of perceived forms (and of our relationship with others) is ingrained in their developmental processes (Krueger, 1928). This affective dimension invokes a kind of reciprocity: the tutor takes her or his own gestures and adapts them to the context, simplifying, exaggerating them, or imitating the practitioner's gesture in order to capture its "faulty" character or to underscore its "accuracy". This mimetic interplay seeks to involve the apprentice in the recreation of a musical gesture, which can lead into grasping what was previously unattainable (viz. perceived or performed, irrespectively). Part of the tutor's task is to make the expressive qualities of musical gestures manifest and palpable to practitioners, so they can effectively grasp what *motivates* a musical form. One could say that the latter bears a suggestive power, which alongside adequate instruction would promote the discovery of new qualitative layers of depth, strongly impacting bodily motion and feeling. In this sense, musical motion is not only kinetic, but also kinaesthetic (Francès, 1984; Vion-Dury & Besson, 2011). Langer (1953) has noted that such extension of felt motion does not correspond to a mere subjective projection, by which one would endow an original, "neutral" version of form with a separate affective value. Lived *participation* in musical configuration instantiates the relationship between perception and skill: it provides a direct, immediate comprehension of the field of musical forms—irrespective of how frail it might be at an initial point. From the moment attentive listening is present, I am no longer faced with homogeneous forms over a neutral background.

It should be underscored that, although imitative interplay might be an important aspect of tuition, mutual alignment does not seek identical reproduction.[4] When looking at musical gestures closely, it becomes clear that morphological differences between tutor and apprentice, as well as their respective gestures and posture, make such identical reproduction impossible. This mimetic alignment orients the development of an *attuned equivalent* at a functional and/or expressive level. Evidently, this equivalence does not remain constant throughout different phases of the tuition process, making this *mutual tuning-in* idiosyncratic to every tutor–apprentice relationship and their practice, despite traditional constraints.

In order to provide a better account for this mutual alignment, let us go back to Alfred Schütz's analysis of interpersonal engagement in joint activities. Taking the conditions of possibility for any social interaction as his point of departure, he took the example of musical activity to illustrate interpersonal engagement. In his 1951 article "Making music together", Schütz characterized the social interaction related to the musical process as a *mutual tuning-in relationship* (Schütz, 1951). On the one hand, the meaning shared among participants of the musical instance *hic et nunc* (here and now) does not require a derived conceptual formulation to be upheld. On the other hand, what happens within these side-by-side interactions does not fall under the conventional emitter–receptor scheme. In the mutual tuning-in relationship: "the 'I' and the 'Thou' are experienced by both participants as a 'We' in vivid experience" (Schütz, 1951, p. 79). When musicians share both a lived temporality and spatiality (e.g. performance situations, or musical instrument courses), Schütz says, they find themselves in a flow of reciprocal anticipations through their gestures: "The other's facial expressions, his gestures in handling his instrument, in short all the activities of performing, gear into the outer world and can be grasped by the partner in immediacy" (1951, p. 95). Musicians experience music making as an open-ended, unfolding continuum. Thus, from Schütz's perspective, their engagement with music is lived as forward-oriented motion. This *ongoing*, developmental character supposes that mutual involvement is constantly under re-evaluation (either tacit or explicit), so it can present moments of greater fluency, sudden rupture, opposition, tension, etc. Within the interactional situation described by Schütz, the other's action and my own are guided by an apodictic understanding of what is (musically) going on. It should be noted that, if Schütz returned to the example of playing together, it is precisely because music presents a setting where tuning-in relationships allow for things to go smoothly. Indeed, musicians share a kind of *common sense* that enables these alignments to take place as if they were spontaneous.

Mutual tuning-in relationships are characterized by the "sharing of the other's flux of experiences in inner time, this living through a vivid present in common" (Schütz, 1951, p. 92). Yet this is not limited by the here-and-now of the situation; as Schütz himself notes, there are stylistic norms at play that do not appear explicitly in these encounters, but act as a background *guiding their action*. Nevertheless, what we can borrow for our discussion is a description of the ongoing process by which tutor and apprentice become interlocked, and so tuned-into one another. This is a first step to understand the process by which they are able to re-evaluate their listening and performance on the spot, and to reorganize and move their practice forward.

Expressive indications

What is the role of these mutual alignments in promoting the introduction and further development of a "musical common sense"? Richard Sennett (2008) has pointed out the power of what he has termed "*expressive indications*" in the apprenticeship process. Although Sennett's examples are mostly culinary, he also calls upon his own experience as a cellist to convey his point. The latter can be boiled down to the need for a "show, don't tell" paradigm in tuning-in relationships. In practical terms, the tutor's most compelling manner of conveying his or her doings is not that of description; it consists rather of imagining *ad hoc* ways to render her or his *tacit knowledge* (cf. Polanyi, 1958) apparent. Verbal description is usually sterile (Sennett terms it "dead denotation") to the extent it lacks *in situ* relevance.

Alternatively, expressive instructions bring out a repertoire of gestures and language: "[it] is indeed full of analogies, but these analogies are loose rather than exact, and for a reason" (Sennett, 2008, p. 185). The lack of precision of the tutor's instructions (or, in positive terms, its generic quality) actually helps the practitioner establish an affective engagement with them. Such engagement is granted by the evocative power that analogies and other familiar tropes draw from the richness of different experiential registers. For instance, an instructor might say, "Try to make the note bounce at the end", in order to capture the subtle imbrication between sound and bodily gestures in a *ritardando*. The apprentice will gradually integrate these gestures into a musical situation. This has the advantage both of allowing the practitioner to see such situation anew and of infusing confidence and ease into her or his gestures.

However, in order to achieve this, instructors need to *sympathetically* (Scheller, 1971) put themselves in situations that have long escaped them, namely where they could not help but make mistakes, feeling awkward toward their instrument, or unable to focus their attention on a particular aspect of what is being played. These are precisely the kinds of situations where instructors will be able (or unable) to reveal such background of tacit knowledge to the practitioner. Sennett goes on to provide different ways in which "expressive imaginative language can serve the practical end of guidance" (2008, p. 193) in order to put practitioners in a situation where they will be increasingly able to find a thread that serves as a guide for their action. In this sense, expressive directions transcend dead denotation and *connect technical craft to imagination* (Sennett, 2008). Thus, the pieces of music's motions become intertwined with those of the other and my own, and are, to a certain extent, indistinct.

We would like to underscore another trait of expressive instructions found in Schütz's tuning-in relationships. Although another's action might present itself as an indication of what she or he might or might not do, *this action does not necessarily carry explicit communicational intent*. Non-denotative in nature, expressive instruction conveys the qualitative richness condensed in the act of showing. Let us recall that Rudolf Arnheim (1949) also stressed the importance of discovering an *expressive theme or motif* that will serve the practitioner as a principle to guide both listening and the gestures that attend its development. Arnheim depicts this by describing a drawing lesson, where students attempt to capture the model's physiognomy:

> The student will watch proportions and directions, but not as geometrical properties in themselves. Rather will these formal properties be perceived as being functionally dependent upon the primarily observed expression, and the correctness and incorrectness of each stroke will be judged on the basis of whether or not it captures the dynamic "mood" of the subject . . . whereas the artificial concentration on formal qualities will leave the student at a loss as to which pattern to select among innumerable and equally acceptable ones, an *expressive theme* will serve as a natural guide to forms that fit the purpose.
> (1949, p. 107, emphasis added)

Moving explicitly into the realm of musical expression, Arnheim insisted on this point by showing that, when listeners are asked about the formal qualities in a piece, they spontaneously draw on its expressive qualities (1949, p. 106), characterizing an instrument's timbre as "crystalline" or "sweet", a melodic movement as "jumpy" or "insistent", or a rhythmic pattern as "dense" or "spacious". Far from a kind of anthropomorphism, this supposes a general principle of direct relationship between stylistic or behavioural dimensions of forms, and their affective value. Additionally, this brings us back to the aforementioned mythic dimension of tuition, wherein there is nothing strange with looking for a "menacing sound". Quite to the contrary, it can make all the difference to the efficacy of a single gesture. As musical motion unfolds and permeates the perceptual field, the distinctive dynamics of affective life become attuned to the musical dynamics and to the tensions it generates. This goes back to Wolfgang Köhler, who summarized this interrelation as follows: "Quite generally, the inner processes, whether emotional or intellectual, show types of development which may be given names, usually applied to musical events, such as: *crescendo* and *diminuendo*, *accelerando* and *ritardando*" (Köhler, 1929, p. 248, emphases in the original).

The same dynamism transpires at the relational level in the tutor–apprentice alignment. In her autobiographical novel, *Lost in Translation*, Eva Hoffman (1989) describes the relationship with her teacher as a nine-year-old piano student as distinctly carrying expressive qualities with ethical overtones. Yet rather than presenting themselves as imposing explicit normative standards, her teacher's expressive indications helped articulate "the motions and the conduct of her inner life":

> Although she never raises her voice, and is unfailingly kind, Pani Witeszczak exercises great authority over me. She is the first in a sequence of music teachers to whom I owe the closest thing I get to a moral education. In this intimate, one-to-one apprenticeship—an apprenticeship mediated through the objective correlative of music—they teach me something about the motions and the conduct of my inner life. When Pani Witeszczak attempts to convey to me what tone to use in a Bach invention, or the precise inflection of a theme in a mazurka, she is trying, indirectly, to teach me the language of emotions. "Music is a kind of eloquence," she tells me. "Ask yourself what it says here. See? This is like someone pleading. And here someone is getting angry, more and more angry, and trying to persuade somebody else, who is not listening."
> (Hoffman, 1989, pp. 69–70)

Thus, expressive indications evoke a register of apodictic perception. Their efficacy resides precisely in their capacity to convey the dimensions of musical, affective and motor movement (e.g. singing becomes a way of talk, of indication, or of emphasis). Ultimately, it is about a way of becoming perceptually acute and sensitive to relevant aspects of musical configurations that are far from evident for the newcomer.

Tuning-into tradition

Thus far, we have placed special emphasis on the pervasive role of expression in tuition. However, acknowledging the role of expressive elements is not sufficient to describe the iterative dynamics at stake in musical tuition interactions. Aron Gurwitsch (1979, p. 95ff in "Part III: Consociate being together") explains how our engagement in the immediacy of expressive gestures does not necessarily exhaust a characterization of our relationship with the latter. In this sense, a seemingly identical gesture can be read quite differently according to the total situation in which it is immersed: it can be seen, for instance, as spontaneous or artificial, genuine or dishonest. Thus, added to the expressive engagement with a gesture or a course of action, all comprehension (including misunderstandings) is sustained by a normed background that remains implicit. Within it, a form of "contract" is assumed between the participants involved in the situation, which affects both the form and meaning of their effective gestures (musical or otherwise). Thus we enter the domain of collectively instituted forms or that of *stylistics*, which function in continuity with expressivity. In musical terms, this translates into the function of standards, which regulate the "appropriateness" and pertinence of a particular gesture in a given musical situation.

Thinking along these very lines, Merleau-Ponty (2010, pp. 539–570) noted the importance of tempering the role of expressivity, since it ultimately does not exhaust our relationship with music or with others. At a relational level, we do not need to be constantly imbued in the immediacy of physiognomic traits. It is only in rare occasions that we stay fixed in the particulars of a form (even if art empha- sizes them), but we see it as partaking in the complete situation, where a style is at stake, in turn capable of promoting various modalities—Wagner can evoke his contribution to opera as a genre as well as the use of his music as war propaganda. Thus the expressive dimension is side by side a *normativity*, emanating from col- lective, practical and symbolic life, as well as from our engagement to others: "To understand style . . . is fundamentally to take up a certain practical intention" (Merleau-Ponty, 2010, p. 442–443). Effectively, "we are not only a sensory body, but also a body that carries techniques, styles, behaviours that all correspond to a superior layer [*couche*] of objects: the modalities of our corporeal styles give cultural objects a certain physiognomy" (p. 438).

The development of expressive (musical) gestures includes a myriad of pub- licly available forms and values shaped by tradition, which defines the instituted character of musical forms. Elements that go from a particular system of tem- perament, a preference for a particular set of scales or modes, a choice of chord progressions that contributes to define a musical form (e.g. the recurrent II–V–I chord progression in bebop), to varieties of meter (e.g. the 2/4 meter so often found in numerous forms of Brazilian music), arrays of orchestration, and other stylistic idiosyncrasies, play a major role in granting the *recurrence* of expressive gestures, and developing what is usually called a musical vocabulary. Stylistic elements thus make up a constellation of normative resources shared by a com- munity, having a direct effect on musical *gestures* (perceived and performed, irrespectively). In terms of their expressive power, stylistic elements reveal the interpretative emphases that bestow a genre with its specific character. Expression is thus social by definition and cannot exist outside a cultural form. At the same time, it allows us to conceive the formation of both experience and culture as a part of the same holistic process.

The developmental aspect of tuition: a brief illustration

However, in concrete terms, which are the actual practices that enable the prac- titioner both to be immersed in the expressive immediacy of gestures and to recognize recurrent forms in different musical situations? Practice is often organized based on different "moments", as the ones denoted by the distinction between *studying* and *playing*, often used by both practitioners and instructors. These two moments correspond to different attitudes toward musical practice. *Studying* is generally an instance of self-observation, one where difficulties and cracks are to be detected, isolated and smoothed out, structures decomposed, and so forth. Briefly put, a re-evaluation of the relationship between bodily gestures and musical gestures is performed. Different alternatives are considered in order to achieve the desired musical motion, leading to the selection of most suitable one(s). However, *playing* calls for a *letting-go* disposition, so to speak, character- ized by a focalization on achieving music's expressive continuity *here and now*. Since it is *play*, it supposes an immersion in the ongoing present (as Schütz com- mented), where mistakes can even be overlooked or instantly dealt with (Klemp, McDermott, Raley, Thibeault, Powell, & Levitin, 2008) in favour of capturing both the local and the overall arc of the piece.

In a similar vein, Michael Polanyi (1958) characterized the alternation between instances of dexterous activity in a *principle of dual control* of action. Musicians can try out (study) different fingerings until they find the one that adjusts fluently to both their hands and the sought musicality. Yet after a number of repetitions, fingering will recede into the background, in favour of the phrase's expressive movement and quality. At this point, the musician will arrive at a *tacit integra- tion* between tonal movement and fingering, or equilibrium between focal and subsidiary awareness, in Polanyi's terms (1958). The importance of the func- tional relationship between focal and subsidiary poles of a course of action can be illustrated by its breakdown: if our hypothetical player focuses on following the fingers movement instead of the actual musical motion, the functional relation- ship would be broken, and her playing would become a mere fiddling exercise deprived of musicality. Nevertheless, it would be enough for this player to return her attention to the tonal motion and so get re-immersed in musical performance. The tacit integration would be quickly regained, making the subsidiaries—in this case, the fingering pattern—recede again into the background. Along the tuition process, this alternation between cyclic integrations serves as a regulator of prac- tice. The cycle introduces the possibility for an integration not to be definitely set, and brings in room for further developments and modulations. It is by virtue of this recursive *developmental cycle* that an instrumentalist can manoeuvre with the piece's different layers or dimensions and make new findings. In this scenario, the tutor serves as a moderator between these instances, suggesting that the practi- tioner stay in one or move to the other at different moments, according to what he or she might want the practitioner to attend (listen–feel) to. The objective of this example is to capture just one way in which the *organization of musical activity* involves developmental processes that need to be incorporated in accounting for the skilful couplings with music that practitioners achieve.

Development by reprisal

One could say, at first glance, that in musical terms a reprise is a repetition: "In composition, [it is] a return to the first section after an intervening and contrasting section. In the works of Rameau, Couperin, etc. the term means a short refrain at the end of a movement and intended to be repeated" (Kennedy & Kennedy, 2007, p. 618). Yet repetition, still in its most simplistic versions, Bergson observed, is perceived as contributing value (Bergson, 1998). It might be sheer insistence, or even lead into dullness, but it is never exact replication, as music based on rhythmical patterns or compositions by Steve Reich and Terry Riley have stressed. In musical contexts, reprises carry with them all the strength of previous developments, so that a theme might be heard anew. Reprise introduces variation and modulation, even though nothing has *seemingly* changed in the "outside" form.

Variation and repetition are indeed inseparable in skill genesis and development. When we turn to the tuition situation, reprises (whether of an expressive motif, specific repertoire, or the organization of work itself) serve to guide mutual alignment within a broader developmental scale. Reprises establish recurrent themes to work on (phrasing, dynamics, improvisation, reading, etc.), and allow practitioners to develop a personal rapport to their craft, beyond the immediacy of the here and now.

Let us introduce a counterpoint between musical reprisal and reprisal in tuition. On the one hand, all players, no matter how experienced, need to face the always-imminent risk of a piece's disintegration. This is, by repeating a piece or a section of music over and over, mechanization starts taking over—and inevitably, form starts loosing its cohesion. In order to prevent this from happening, musicians learn to listen to their own playing with a "fresh ear" every time. This means that the more one knows a piece and feels comfortable playing it, the more one might be prone to losing its overall balance if not paying the required care and attention. On the other hand, looking at the same example from the tuition process perspective, reprises help in establishing recurrences between different musical situations and genres, in order to approach them appropriately. This does not mean that practitioners need to deprive themselves of the ensemble of gestures that they have worked so hard for, as if they entered a different modality of playing (e.g. a different genre or composer) each time. Much to the contrary, a principle of reprise helps in establishing continuities between different musical gestures, since, as we have seen, the latter are often transposable.

Thus, variation and repetition constitute an inseparable couple in the definition and development of skill. The rearrangement of *technical gestures* in musical tuition can be organized along an axis that goes from tacit ways of doing (bodily positions, coordinative glances, mannerisms), to explicit stances of skill development (face-to-face instruction), to a register of well-instituted practices (incorporating stable normative and stylistic aspects) (Lassègue, Rosenthal & Visetti, 2009, pp. 92–95). The latter conceptualization, on the one hand, considers different *reprise* registers supporting a practice's stabilization process. On the other, it conveys a fundamental cohesion between the individual and the social in the appropriation of skill. Although mastering a musical instrument requires a specialization of one's own body, it is only by means of contact with values emanating from collective life that the re-appropriation of the instrumentalist's craftsmanship takes place. Thereby, skills are continuously undergoing a process of semiotization (Lassègue, Rosenthal & Visetti, 2009): even considering different degrees of expertise, from the moment musicians evaluate their own capabilities and adjust their performance to the threads of a tradition, they are already involved in these endlessly iterative dynamics regardless of the level we choose to look at: genre, historical period, a particular musical form, etc.

The successive *iteration* of musical gestures through *several generations* of players engenders a reconfiguration of *perceptual–technical knots* (to use one of Tim Ingold's, 2007, metaphors), which involve aesthetic, ethical, practical and traditional open-ended threads. Such reconfiguration ultimately leads to the emergence of new expressive pathways that become available to the musical community; as said before, repetition *and* variation constitute an indivisible couple in defining skill and its development. In turn, this stereotypical relationship shows the continuity that practical skills gain from one generation to the next. However, such continuity supposes a dimension of variation and auto-evaluation as a condition for the stabilization and permanence of skill (e.g. in unintended *and* intended ways, practitioners transform their actions concerning a trend or a tradition). This iterative process directs our attention toward the social dimension of skill: it is only in the context of these intergenerational encounters that the player's craft may be (re)developed. A characterization of these encounters that assumes the roles of an "ignorant" apprentice and a "proficient" tutor would certainly fail to account for their skillful action. Only the permanent *mutual alignment* between apprentice and tutor can evidence both the ignition and perpetuation of this developmental process.

Concluding remarks

Musical craft involves a heterogeneous weave that nevertheless conveys a captivating efficacy. In the case of music, this efficacy is accompanied by an expressive mastery that can render a performance unforgettable. A knot is tied between the instrument's materiality and the musician's corporality (to stick to Ingold's metaphor). Its tightness is provided by public, normative and stylistic motifs and values that accord themselves to perceptual dispositions in order to provide the harmonic efficacy characteristic of skilful action. Such an effective, intricate fabric, stemming from collective life, can only develop through an apprenticeship that certainly involves a mimetic aspect, but relies heavily on what we have termed a *principle of tuition*. The development of the cohesive mesh that a skill embodies is often triggered by means of a *mutual alignment* between practitioner and tutor in an imitative interplay. Similarly to the way repetition contributes to the musical piece, the intergenerational *reprise* of musical gestures sets forth the reconfiguration of *perceptual–technical knots* and to the emergence of novel expressive gestures that become available to the musical community. More importantly, it is not that expressive themes are "transmitted" as schemata; rather, they are reprised in the practical endeavours that make up musical craft. The notion of *tuition* covers a myriad of modes of participation that go from attentive listening and characterization to the practitioner's performance to *in situ* behavioural and verbal indications, which require aesthetic and physiognomic specificity. Such indications involve the totality of visual, auditory, aesthetic and stylistic dimensions, which goes well beyond what is traditionally called "didactics".

Certainly, our aim here has not been to provide a definitive account of tuition. Indeed, it falls short even when we have just limited ourselves to the domain of the musical skill. However, we have succinctly covered some issues that suggest an accurate description of the *tuition process* strongly relies on its bonds to a developmental approach and its corollaries.

Notes

1 This would suppose a rupture between pre-established designs (maintained throughout time) and its behavioural implementation.
2 Certainly we do not seek to provide an idyllic account for musical tuition: as is the case with any intense and lasting relationship, the one between instructor and apprentice is also bound to tensions and conflicts that may or may not eventually end up in a relationship crisis. This, however, is not our subject at hand.
3 The difficulty of listening accurately to oneself become tangible, for example, in the awkwardness or unease felt when listening to a recording of one's own voice.
4 While discussing children's imitation, Merleau-Ponty (2010, p. 30) observed that it is not about copying behaviour (an identical imitation), but rather to accomplish a meaningful action. A child who grabs a crayon to draw has no interest in the way she or he holds it, but rather in the drawn lines themselves.

References

Arnheim, R. (1949). The priority of expression. *Journal of Aesthetics and Art Criticism, 8*(2), 106–109.

Bergson, H. (1998). *La pensée et la mouvant* [The creative mind]. Paris, France: Quadrige/ Presses Universitaires de France.

Berliner, D. (2013). New directions in the study of cultural transmission. In L. Arizpe & C. Amescua (Eds.), *Anthropological perspectives on intangible cultural heritage* (pp. 71–77). Berlin, Germany: Springer.

de Beaune, S. A. (Dir.) (2013). L'esthétique du geste technique [Aesthetics of technical gesture]. *Gradhiva, 17*(1), 26–49.

Francès, R. (1984). *La perception de la musique* [The perception of music]. Paris, France: Vrin.

Gurwitsch, A. (1979). *Human encounters in the social world*. Pittsburgh, PA: Duquesne University Press.

Hoffman, E. (1989). *Lost in translation*. London, UK: Vintage.

Ingold, T. (2000). *The perception of the environment: Essays in livelihood, dwelling and skill*. London, UK: Routledge.

Ingold, T. (2001). From the transmission of representations to the education of attention. In H. Whitehouse (Ed.), *The debated mind: Evolutionary psychology versus ethnography* (pp. 113–153). Oxford, UK: Berg.

Ingold, T. (2007). *Lines: A brief history*. London, UK: Routledge.

Ingold, T. (2013). *Making: Anthropology, archaeology, art and architecture*. London, UK: Routledge.

Kennedy, M. & Kennedy, J. (2007). *Oxford concise dictionary of music* (5th ed.). Oxford, UK: Oxford University Press.

Klemp, N., McDermott, R., Raley, J., Thibeault, M., Powell, K., & Levitin, D. (2008). Plans, takes and mis-takes. *Critical Social Studies, 10*(1), 4–21.

Köhler, W. (1929). *Gestalt psychology.* New York, NY: Liveright.

Krueger, F. (1928). The essence of feeling: Outline of a systematic theory. In M. L. Reymert (Ed.), *The Wittenberg Symposium: Feelings and emotions,* Worcester, MA: Clark University Press.

Langer, S. (1953). *Feeling and form: A theory of art.* New York, NY: Charles Scribner's Sons.

Lassègue, J., Rosenthal, V. & Visetti, Y.-M. (2009). Économie symbolique et phylogenèse du langage [Symbolic economy and the phylogenesis of language]. *L'Homme, 192,* 67–100.

Leroi-Gourhan, A. (1965). *Le geste et la parole II: La mémoire et les rythmes.* [Gesture and speech II: Memory and rhythms]. Paris: Albin Michel.

Mauss, M. (2009). *Sociologie et anthropologie* [Sociology and Anthropology]. Paris, France: PUF.

Merleau-Ponty, M. (2010). *Child psychology and pedagogy: The Sorbonne Lectures 1949–1952.* Evanston, IL: Northwestern University Press.

Polanyi, M. (1958). *Personal knowledge: Toward a post-critical philosophy.* Chicago, IL: Chicago University Press.

Rojas, P. (2015). To become one with the instrument: The unfolding of a practical topography. *Culture & Psychology, 21*(2), 207–230.

Rosenthal, V. (2014). Ways of mindreading. Paper presented in the 6th Conference on Language, Culture and Mind (LCM VI), Lublin, Poland.

Scheller, M. (1971). *Nature et formes de la sympathie* [The nature of sympathy]. Paris, France: Payot.

Schlanger, N. (2012). Une technologie engagée. Marcel Mauss et l'étude des techniques dans les sciences sociales [Committed techology: Marcel Mauss and the study of techniques in the social sciences]. In N. Schlanger (Ed.) *Marcel Mauss: Techniques, technologie et civilisation* (pp. 17–134). Paris: PUF.

Schütz, A. (1951). Making music together: A study in social relationship. *Social Research, 18*(1), 76–97.

Sennett, R. (2008). *The Craftsman.* London, UK: Penguin.

Shanon, B. (2008). *The representational and the presentational: An essay on cognition and the study of mind.* Charlottesville, VA: Imprint Academic.

Sigaut, F. (1985). More (and enough) on technology! *History and Technology, 2,* 115–132.

Sigaut, F. (2003/2010). La formule de Mauss [Mauss' formula]. *Techniques & Culture, 40,* Retrieved October 21, 2014 from http://tc.revues.org/1538

Simondon, G. (1958/2012). *Du mode d'existence des objets techniques* [On the mode of existence of technical objects]. Paris: Aubier.

Simondon, G. (2014). *Sur la technique (1953–1983)* [On technique (1953–1983). Paris: PUF.

Spengler, O. (1934). *El hombre y la técnica: Contribución a una filosofía de la vida* [Man and technics: Towards a philosophy of life]. Santiago, Chile: Editorial Cultura.

Vion-Dury, J. & Besson, M. (2011). L'électro-encéphalographie et la musique: Apports, limites et perspectives épistémologiques [Electro-encephalography and music: Contributions, limitations, and epistemological perspectives]. In L. Guirard (Ed.), *Cinquante ans de psychologie de la musique: L'Ecole de Robert Francès* (pp. 74–107). Montauban, France: Alexitère.

Part III

Representing what is yet to happen

Ideas for new pathways into developmental science

On the "Ganzheit" and stratification of the mind

The emergence of Heinz Werner's developmental theory

Martin Wieser

Though overshadowed by his contemporaries Jean Piaget and Lev Vygotsky, Heinz Werner (1890–1964) was without doubt one of the most creative thinkers in 20th-century developmental science. His works covered such seemingly distant areas as logic substitution (Werner, 1912b), psychophysiology (Werner, 1914), the origin of metaphor and lyric (Werner, 1919, 1924c), the physiognomy of language (Werner, 1932), symbol formation (Werner & Kaplan, 1963) and, most prominently, developmental psychology (Werner, 1926). In this commentary, I do not want to provide an intellectual biography of Heinz Werner (cf. Müller, 2005; van der Veer, 2005). Instead, I want to show how his early theorizing emerged out of contemporary psychological discourses and debates; this was a time when defenders of Gestalt Psychology and holistic psychology argued against psychophysics and associationist psychology, followers of Dilthey's conception of psychology as an interpretative "Geisteswissenschaft" (Dilthey, 1894; Spranger, 1921) opposed experimental psychologists who wanted to bring psychology closer to the natural sciences (e.g., Ebbinghaus, 1896; Müller, 1904), and Karl Bühler and Wilhelm Wundt publicly argued whether or not "higher" psychological functions, such as verbal reasoning, could be investigated experimentally (Wundt, 1907, Bühler 1908). All these debates between different psychological theories and methodologies culminated in the widespread talk of a crisis in psychology during the 1920s (Bühler, 1927; Vygotsky, 1927/1997). During the two decades of his academic career, Werner was confronted with these major epistemological and methodological debates within German psychology before World War II. Werner's answer to these debates was his proposition of his radically *developmental* approach within psychology, which suggests grasping all psychological phenomena as dynamic, functional parts of an organismic whole ("Ganzheit") that is unfolding over time, rather than a set of distinct timeless elements that should be studied in isolation from each other.

In the following pages, I will outline the most influential schools of thinking within philosophy and psychology that prepared the conceptual grounds for Werner's idea of how this crisis should be overcome through a developmental turn in academic psychology. Besides the well-known influences of Mach, Stöhr, Wundt and Krueger, I will also mention a current of psychological thinking that has remained largely unnoticed in historical literature so far: stratification theory, a theoretical current that became increasingly popular in many different disciplines in the first half of the 20th century and which provided key concepts that we can also find in Werner's developmental writings.

Genesis and Ganzheit: on the emergence of Werner's developmental thinking

The historical influences that inspired Werner's developmental thinking are well known. First of all, there are Ernst Mach and Adolf Stöhr, who both taught an empirically oriented philosophy at the University of Vienna. Both of them were convinced that philosophy had to include results of experimental psychology to construct an empirical foundation for epistemology by studying how abstract concepts emerged out of complex sensations. Werner's early publications followed this evolutionary perspective by genetically reconstructing the emergence of concepts out of immediate practice (i.e. as mental "tools"), perceptual sensations and inner feelings (Mach, 1905; Stöhr 1910; cf. Müller, 2005). While Werner's teachers, Mach and Stöhr, endorsed the inclusion of psychological experiments in philosophical research to gain deeper insights into how scientific knowledge is acquired, his superior at the Physiological Institute in Vienna from 1915 to 1916, Sigmund Exner, served as a role model for blurring the lines between psychological and physiological territories (Exner, 1894). Werner's next teachers in Munich, Karl Bühler and Oswald Külpe, also expanded the application area of psychological experimentation by investigating "higher" psychological functions. The most remarkable fact about Werner's publications during this period is that all of his teachers seemed to have inspired him to transition between physiological, psychological, cultural–historical and ethnological–comparative methods: besides his publications on the genesis of concepts (Werner, 1912a, 1915), he experimentally investigated the blind spot in human perception (Werner, 1913b) as well as the phenomena of "optical fusion" (Werner, 1913a) and "optical rhythm" (Werner, 1918), and he also published on the origin of metaphor (Werner, 1919) and lyric (though written at the same time, this book was published five years later: see Werner, 1924c).

Werner could only write about such divergent topics because he had an overall theoretical goal in mind, namely to explore and exemplify the laws of development that cover all of these areas. In his book on metaphor, he states: "there is a general developmental law that deeper levels of consciousness and culture are preforming certain mental forms [Gestaltungen] which are taken up again in higher stages of development when needed and used for higher purposes" (Werner, 1919, p. 3). On the level of "premagical" thinking, for instance, a hunter would imitate the appearance and behavior of animals purely for hunting purposes, whereas in cultures of "magical thinking" this mental "form" is transformed into a magical ritual to induce the hunter's luck. The mental and behavioral "form" survives, but its motive has shifted and is transformed to fit into different contexts. This transformation, however, generates new aspects and properties of the "form": in every stage of development, Werner states, something new emerges out of the old. If we compare his book on the origins of metaphor with his earlier publication on the genesis of concepts (Werner, 1912a), we can recognize a very similar idea: concepts arise out of simple sensations that are repeatedly presented through different sensory channels. The sensation (e.g., "round") is isolated from circumstantial properties of perceived objects (e.g., color or size) and develops into a new, higher form, a complex of sensations that identifies the typical properties of a concept (a shape with no edges), a process that was described as "apperception" by Wundt (1893, pp. 266–285), as the activity of a subject raising a group of sensation into the focal point of consciousness. The highest form is achieved when a complex of sensations has developed into an abstract, scientific concept that can be applied deductively on various objects and situations.

While the idea of a genetic perspective on consciousness and concepts, as they were developed by Mach, Stöhr and Wundt, was most prominent in Werner's early publications, the Leipzig school of holistic psychology provided the most important intellectual inspiration for Werner's grand scheme of psychology as a science of development. The most prominent representative of the Leipzig school of holistic psychology was Felix Krueger, the successor to Wilhelm Wundt's chair in Leipzig in 1917, who was frequently cited by Werner as a source of his developmental thinking. While Wertheimer, Köhler and Koffka proposed a rather static view of Gestalt and searched for Gestalt laws both in the physical and the subjective realm (Ash, 1995), holistic psychologists such as Krueger, Hans Volkelt or Friedrich Sander emphasized the fluent, biological nature of "Ganzheit", which was understood as the creation of a spontaneous, intentional subject. For holistic psychologists, the emergence of a Gestalt in perception (such as a melody or a geometrical figure) was just one example of the manifold appearance of "Ganzheiten", which also included emotional, biological, phylogenetic and social processes (Krueger, 1926, pp. 92–107). The concept of development played a key role in Krueger's mission to create a new foundation for scientific psychology:

> Holism is the highest principle of development. Just like all the other branches of the sciences of life, psychology is depending on systematic genetic comparison, analysis and conceptualization. . . . Only as a theory of development, psychology can arise to a system. . . . The laws of the structure of the psyche refer to the necessity of its genesis.
>
> (Krueger, 1926, p. 120)

In Werner's *Introduction to Developmental Psychology*, we can find a very similar statement on the concept of Ganzheit as the universal foundation of psychological thinking: "every type of wholeness, be it the wholeness of a nation [*Volk*], an ethnic group or the wholeness of objective goods, such as language, religion, or customs, has to be understood as an organically grown and operating totality" (Werner, 1926, p. 7). Both Werner and Krueger understood development as a goal-directed, teleological process that is determined by structural laws of the whole, be it a single organism, a group or even a whole nation. Although parts of a whole may be transformed or interchanged, the integrity of the Ganzheit as an evolving, dynamic living system is still maintained. Development is not seen as a mere addition of functions, properties or abilities, but as a continuous restructuring of the whole towards a higher level of internal organization.

Werner's studies on microgenesis (1924a, 1924b, 1927; Werner & Lagercrantz, 1924; Werner & Creuzer, 1927; Zietz & Werner, 1928) put this concept of development into practice within an experimental context, developing a methodology to analyze the emergence of clear and unambiguous mental structures out of undifferentiated, vague and intuitive sensations. He studied the emergence of clear patterns in human perception (e.g., hearing a melody) and behavior (e.g., drawing a geometrical figure) by varying the complexity of stimulus configurations and observing the behavior and analyzing the introspective reports of his subjects. As Werner expected, mental and behavioral structures become clearer, more focused and unambiguous over time on all sensory levels when subjects are forced to elaborate and reproduce them. Following Krueger and the Leipzig school, Werner emphasized the gradual unfolding of Ganzheiten over time:

> It is the fundamental path of experience that every individual has to follow: an object becomes more meaningful, more objective, the more it is formed *unambiguously* through all psychophysical layers of the individual. The unambiguousness takes place in experience by an assimilation and adjustment of all layers of the psychophysical subject.
>
> (Werner, 1927, p. 181)

From a historiographical point of view, I want to argue that this holistic and goal-directed concept of development, as it was put forth by Krueger and his colleagues, was the most important influence for Werner's approach to developmental psychology. It is true that Goethe is cited in the first German edition of Werner's introduction to developmental psychology, where Werner explicitly refers to him as the discoverer of a universal developmental law of a continuous differentiation and subordination of parts under a unified whole (Werner, 1926, p. 32). Therefore, one may rightfully argue with Müller and Graves (this volume) that Goethe has paved the way for a holistic–developmental approach in the life sciences that was reincarnated in German holistic psychology—but the same argument would apply to Herder, Schlegel, Schiller, Fichte, Schelling and Hegel too, who also contributed to the construction of a teleological–idealistic system of "natural philosophy" and the principle of orthogenesis (van der Veer, 2005, pp. 76–77; see also Harrington, 1996). Taking into account the fact that Goethe is mentioned only incidentally and very infrequently in Werner's writings, in contrast to the works of Krueger and other holistic psychologists, I would classify the relation between Goethe and Werner rather as a byproduct of Werner's allegiance to contemporary holistic psychology and the revival of holistic thinking in Germany after World War I than as a special connection beyond this context between Werner and Goethe.

Layers of the mind: the structure of Werner's theorizing

Besides genetic and holistic thinking, I just want to give a hint on another influence on Werner's theorizing that, to my knowledge, has not been mentioned in historical literature so far: stratification theory, also referred to as "stratology" or "layer theory". The basic assumption of this intellectual current is the idea that the structure of the world, the human brain, the personality and the mind are all structured as a system of "layers". The most prominent philosopher of stratification theory was Nicolai Hartmann, who developed a metaphysical theory of a system of layers that covers all areas of being (Hartmann, 1921, 1940, 1943). The fundamental layer of being is inorganic matter (first layer), out of which living organisms have evolved (second layer). Some organisms show signs of sensitivity (the layer of the soul), while organisms of the highest layer also incorporate mind and reason. The point of Hartmann's system is to analyze how these layers, which are built up gradually over time, relate to each other: younger layers are always dependent on older ones (no organism could exist without matter, the existence of mind requires a sensory system); yet although the younger layers "rest" upon the older ones, they also control and steer them—organisms absorb and repel inorganic substances, the mind is supposed to control the body's movements, but not vice versa. While every layer follows its own laws and has its own structure, there are some categories (e.g., time or space) that some layers share and enable their integration into a unified whole.

While Hartmann was the most outspoken representative of layer theory within philosophy, there are numerous other advocates of stratological thinking that spread widely among a number of disciplines in the first half of the 20th century. Max Scheler proposed a stratological theory of the person and of feelings (Scheler, 1928). Neurologists such as Constantin Monakow (1910) and Ludwig Edinger (1912), both cited by Werner (1926, p. 36), differentiated between "lower" and "higher" layers of the nervous system (e.g., the brainstem, the diencephalon and the neocortex) and speculated about their relationship with "deeper" and "older" parts of the personality. In the same vein, psychiatrists such as Friedrich Kraus (1926) and Karl Kleist (1934) developed psychopathological taxonomies based on different layers of the nervous system and the brain. The connection between Freud's metapsychological systems (Freud, 1900/1953, 1923/1961, 1933/1964) and stratological thinking is quite obvious; the same goes for Jung's theory of a conscious, individually unconscious and collective unconscious layer of the psyche (Jung, 1921). An example from a different field is Theodor Geiger's sociological work *The Social Stratification of the German Nation* (1932). In German psychology, especially within the psychology of personality, stratology was extremely popular in the first half of the 20th century: Heinrich Heider's *Structure of the Human Soul* (1929), Hermann Hoffmann's *Theory of Layers* (1935), Philipp Lersch's *Structure of the Character* (1938) and Erich Rothacker's *Layers of Personality* (1938) are just a few examples out of the long list of stratological theories in German psychology (for a full list, see Ruttkowski, 1974; for an

English introduction into layer theory see Gilbert, 1951). Although some of these stratological thinkers were also holistic psychologists, most of them were not, so these two currents are not to be conflated with each other. Rather, stratological thinking should be seen as a distinct attempt to visualize the mind on the basis of a spatial metaphor (cf. Wieser & Slunecko, 2013; Wieser, 2013).

A closer look into Werner's writings reveals his close affiliation with stratological thinking and its key concepts. In his major work on developmental psychology, he states that "one and the same individual . . . depending on the situational conditions, can experience and think in different layers of his inner life" (Werner, 1926, p. 2), a perspective that completely overlaps with the stratological view that older, more primitive layers form the basis of human experience and personality. In Werner's writings, we often find statements asserting that older layers are still present in the sane educated adult, but they are usually overshadowed by younger, "higher" layers of the psyche. In every activity of the psyche, every single layer is involved, and the partial involvement of every layer is a key interest for Werner's experimental studies: "Just as the process of thinking is running through layers in the normal human being, also human perception can be regarded as layered, and this stratification can be explored through psychological experimentation" (Werner, 1926, p. 31).

In his works on the structural laws of perception, Werner states that human perception, although located on a "lower" level of the psyche, operates in a similar fashion to the "higher layers of the soul" (1924a, p. 251): while perception aims to determine a clear and concise perceptual Gestalt, reason aims towards the definition of clear and precise abstract concepts. Holistic psychology provided Werner with a concept of development as a goal-oriented, continuous process towards differentiation and centralization of parts as a whole. Stratification theory, however, gave him an idea of *what* it is that is going through this process: a hierarchical order of layers that, as they are piled up in chronological order, "have to be understood as stages of development" (Werner, 1926, p. 3). Werner finds this chronological order of layers not just on the level of microgenesis and ontogenesis, but also in phylogeny and cultural history:

> Rising from step to step we will see from the most primitive and instinctive forms up to the most complicated folk psychological systems how every developmental sphere of the mind bequeaths its inheritance to higher cultural areas.
> (Werner, 1919, p. 8)

From this perspective, the psyche of "the abnormal, the child, the animal and the madman" (Werner, 1926, p. 31) has one thing in common: the fact they are functioning in (or have fallen back to) a more "primitive", less differentiated layer of the psyche. If we take a look at the structure of Werner's *Introduction to Developmental Psychology*, we can we find sections within every one of its chapters that is devoted to the "primitive" (or "archaic") layers of perception, reasoning and "magical thinking", which he finds in the child, the "primitive" and the "madman". The last chapter of the book sums up his findings and integrates them into his theory of the "structure of the primitive personality" (Werner, 1926, pp. 297–337), which, in his view, represents an architecture of mental layers that all human beings once shared, and which, in the case of the "madman" and the "primitive", still prevails. Layer theory does not contradict holistic psychology or the principle of orthogenesis, but it adds another set of concepts into Werner's theorizing that helped him to systematize the experimental, neurological, psychiatric and anthropological studies into one grand theoretical scheme.

Concluding remarks

I want to emphasize that Werner's theoretical work was prepared to a considerable extent by his teachers and colleagues within German-speaking psychology, biology, philosophy and physiology. That is not to downplay his achievements within the field of developmental psychology by any means, but to note the intellectual heritage that he skillfully integrated into his grand scheme of a universal psychology of development. Werner's career occurred within the heydays of stratification theory and holistic thinking in psychology, and his writings show clear traces of these intellectual currents. As every intellectual currents has its ancestors and pioneers, Goethe definitely is one for holistic thinking in 20th-century Germany, though it must be added that a whole generation of "natural philosophers" at the end of 18th century also contributed to this line of thinking (Harrington, 1996).

Since Werner has become of major interest in the last few years within cultural–psychological communities (e.g., Valsiner, 2004) it may be adequate to conclude this commentary with a reminder of the political implications and contexts of the holistic movement, since this line of thinking played a key role in the rise of German psychology during the Nazi era. The hierarchical conceptualization of "higher" and "lower" organization of personalities and ethnicities was completely in line with National Socialist race ideology (Harrington, 1996; Benetka, 1997; Ash, 2002). Although Werner became a victim of political suppression himself when he was expelled from the University of Hamburg in 1933, his description of "primitives" and the "abnormal" remind us how scientific knowledge can support what Thomas Teo called "epistemological violence" (Teo, 2008), i.e. a scientific legitimization of suppression by constructing the "other" as an inferior being. I do not want to imply that Werner may have approved of the actions done in the name of science during the Nazi regime in any way. But it is our task to see how much of his holistic theorizing is entangled with epistemological violence—and how much of it still stands when these parts would be removed.

References

Ash, M. (1995). *Gestalt psychology in German culture, 1890–1967: Holism and the quest for objectivity*. Cambridge, UK: Cambridge University Press.

Ash, M. (2002). Psychologie [Psychology]. In F. Hausmann (ed.), *Die Rolle der Geisteswissenschaften im Dritten Reich 1933–1945* (pp. 229–264). München, Germany: Ouldenburg.

Benetka, G. (1997). "Im Gefolge der Katastrophe . . .": Psychologie im Nationalsozialismus ["Following the catastrophe . . .": Psychology during National Socialism]. In P. Mecheril & T. Teo (Eds.), *Psychologie und Rassismus* (pp. 43–72). Hamburg, Germany: Rohwolt.

Bühler, K. (1908). Antwort auf die von W. Wundt erhobenen Einwände gegen die Methode der Selbstbeobachtung an experimentell erzeugten Erlebnissen [Answer to W. Wundt's objections to the method of self-observation of experimentally generated experiences]. *Archiv für die gesamte Psychologie, 12*, 93–122.

Bühler, K. (1927). *Die Krise der Psychologie* [The crisis of psychology]. Jena, Germany: Fischer.

Dilthey, W. (1894). Ideen über eine beschreibende und zergliedernde Psychologie [Ideas about a descriptive and dissecting psychology]. *Sitzungsberichte der Königlich Preußischen Akademie der Wissenschaften zu Berlin, 26*, 1309–1407.

Ebbinghaus, H. (1896). Über erklärende und beschreibende Psychologie [On explanatory and descriptive psychology]. *Zeitschrift für Psychologie und Physiologie der Sinnesorgane, 9*, 161–205.

Edinger, L. (1912). *Einführung in die Lehre vom Bau und den Verrichtungen des Nervensystems* [Introduction to the doctrine of the structure and the functions of the nervous system]. Leipzig, Germany: Vogel.

Exner, S. (1894). *Entwurf zu einer physiologischen Erklärung der psychischen Erscheinungen* [Draft of a physiological explanation of psychical phenomena]. Leipzig, Germany: Deuticke.

Freud, S. (1953). The interpretation of dreams. In J. Strachey (Ed.), *The standard edition of the complete psychological works of Sigmund Freud* (Vols. IV–V). London, UK: Hogarth. (Original work published in German 1900)

Freud, S. (1961). The ego and the Id. In J. Strachey (Ed.), *The standard edition of the complete psychological works of Sigmund Freud* (Vol. XIX) (pp. 1–66). London, UK: Hogarth. (Original work published in German 1923)

Freud, S. (1964). New introductory lectures on psychoanalysis. In J. Strachey (Ed.), *The standard edition of the complete psychological works of Sigmund Freud* (Vol. XXII) (pp. 1–182). London, UK: Hogarth. (Original work published in German 1933)

Geiger, T. (1932). *Die soziale Schichtung des deutschen Volkes* [The social stratification of the German nation]. Stuttgart, Germany: Enke.

Gilbert, A. R. (1951). Recent German theories of stratification of personality. *The Journal of Psychology, 31*(1), 3–19.

Harrington, A. (1996). *Reenchanted science: Holism in German culture from Wilhelm II to Hitler*. Princeton, NJ: Princeton University Press.

Hartmann, N. (1921). *Grundzüge einer Metaphysik der Erkenntnis* [Foundations of metaphysics of knowledge]. Berlin, Germany: de Gruyter.

Hartmann, N. (1940). *Der Aufbau der realen Welt: Grundriss der allgemeinen Kategorienlehre* [The structure of the real world: Outline of a general doctrine of categories]. Berlin, Germany: de Gruyter.

Hartmann, N. (1943). *Die Anfänge des Schichtgedankens in der alten Philosophie* [The beginnings of the idea of strata in old philosophy]. Berlin, Germany: Akademie der Wissenschaften.

Heider, H. (1929). Die Struktur der menschlichen Seele [The structure of the human soul]. *Archiv für die gesamte Psychologie, 71*, 409–480.

Hoffmann, H. (1935). *Die Schichttheorie: Eine Anschauung von Natur und Leben* [Theory of layers: A view of nature and life]. Stuttgart, Germany: Enke.

Jung, C. G. (1921). *Psychologische Typen* [Psychological types]. Zürich, Switzerland: Rascher.

Kleist, K. (1934). *Gehirnpathologie* [Pathology of the brain]. Leipzig, Germany: Barth.

Kraus, F. (1926). *Allgemeine und spezielle Pathologie der Person* [General and special pathology of the person]. Leipzig, Germany: Thieme.

Krueger, F. (1926). Zur Einführung: Über psychische Ganzheit [Introduction: On psychical wholeness]. *Neue psychologische Studien, 1*, 1–122.

Lersch, P. (1938). *Der Aufbau des Charakters* [The structure of the character]. Leipzig, Germany: Barth.

Mach, E. (1905). *Erkenntnis und Irrtum: Skizzen zur Psychologie der Forschung* [Knowledge and error: Sketches of a psychology of research]. Leipzig, Germany: Barth.

Monakow, C. (1910). *Über Lokalisation der Hirnfunktion* [On localization of brain functions]. Wiesbaden, Germany: Bergmann.

Müller, G. E. (1904). *Die Gesichtspunkte und die Tatsachen der psychophysischen Methodik* [Perspectives and facts of physophysic methods]. Wiesbaden, Germany: Bergmann.

Müller, U. (2005) The context of the formation of Heinz Werner's ideas. In J. Valsiner (Ed.), *Heinz Werner and developmental science* (pp. 25–53). New York, NY: Springer.

Rothacker, E. (1938). *Die Schichten der Persönlichkeit* [The layers of personality]. Leipzig, Germany: Barth.

Ruttkowski, W. (1974). *Typologien und Schichtenlehren* [Typologies and doctrines of stratification]. Amsterdam, Netherlands: Rodopi.

Scheler, M. (1928). *Die Stellung des Menschen im Kosmos* [The place of man in the cosmos]. Darmstadt, Germany: Reichl.

Spranger, E. (1921). *Lebensformen: Geisteswissenschaftliche Psychologie und die Ethik der Persönlichkeit* [Forms of life: Humanistic psychology and the ethics of personality]. Halle (Saale), Germany: Niemeyer.

Stöhr, A. (1910). *Lehrbuch der Logik in psychologisierender Darstellung* [Textbook of logic from a psychological perspective]. Leipzig, Germany: Verlag Franz Deuticke.

Teo, T. (2008). From speculation to epistemological violence in psychology: A critical–hermeneutical reconstruction. *Theory & Psychology, 18*(1), 47–67.

Valsiner, J. (Ed.) (2004). *Heinz Werner and developmental science*. New York, NY: Kluwer.

van der Veer, R. (2005). The making of a developmental psychologist. In J. Valsiner (Ed.), *Heinz Werner and developmental science* (pp. 75–105). New York, NY: Springer.

Vygotsky, L. (1997). The historical meaning of the crisis in psychology: A methodological investigation. In R. R. Rieber & W. Wollock (Eds.), *The collected works of L. S. Vygotsky* (pp. 233–343). New York, NY: Springer. (Original work written in 1927)

Werner, H. (1912a). Begriffstafel auf genetischer Grundlage [A concept table on genetic foundation]. *Archiv für systematische Philosophie, 18*, 45–62.

Werner, H. (1912b). Ein Beitrag zur Lehre logischer Substitutionen [A contribution to the doctrine of logical substitution]. *Archiv für systematische Philosophie und Soziologie, 18*, 431–444.

Werner, H. (1913a). Ein Phänomen optischer Verschmelzung [A phenomenon of optical fusion]. *Zeitschrift für Psychologie, 66*, 263–270.

Werner, H. (1913b). Untersuchungen über den "blinden Fleck" [Investigations of the blind spot]. *Pflüger's Archiv für die gesamte Physiologie, 153*, 475–490.

Werner, H. (1914). Eine psychophysiologische Theorie der Übung [A psychophysiological theory of training]. *Vierteljahrsschrift für wissenschaftliche Philosophie und Soziologie, 38*, 417–441.

Werner, H. (1915). Begriffspsychologische Untersuchungen [Investigations of the psychology of concepts]. *Archiv für systematische Philosophie, 21*, 162–172.

Werner, H. (1918). Über optische Rhythmik [On optical rhythm]. *Archiv für die gesamte Psychologie, 38*, 115–163.

Werner, H. (1919). *Die Ursprünge der Metapher* [The origins of metaphor]. Leipzig, Germany: Engelmann.

Werner, H. (1924a). Studien über Strukturgesetze. I. Über Strukturgesetze und deren Auswirkung in den sogenannten geometrisch-optischen Täuschungen [Studies on structural laws. I. On structural laws and their effect in so-called geometrical–optical illusions]. *Zeitschrift für Psychologie, 94*, 248–264.

Werner, H. (1924b). Studien über Strukturgesetze. II. Über das Problem der motorischen Gestaltung [Studies on structural laws. II. On the problem of motoric organization]. *Zeitschrift für Psychologie, 94*, 265–272.

Werner, H. (1924c). *Die Ursprünge der Lyrik: Eine entwicklungspsychologische Untersuchung* [The origin of lyric: A developmental–psychological investigation]. München, Germany: Reinhardt.

Werner, H. (1926). *Einführung in die Entwicklungspsychologie* [Introduction to developmental psychology]. Leipzig, Germany: Barth.

Werner, H. (1927). Studien über Strukturgesetze. V. Über die Ausprägung von Tongestalten [Studies on structural laws. V. On the formation of sound Gestalts]. *Zeitschrift für Psychologie, 101*, 159–181.

Werner, H. (1932). *Grundfragen der Sprachphysiognomik* [Basic questions of the physiognomy of language]. Leipzig, Germany: Barth.

Werner, H. & Creuzer, H. (1927). Über einen Fall von "Schichtspaltung" beim Bewegungssehen [A case of "layer division" during the perception of motion]. *Zeitschrift für Psychologie, 102*, 333–337.

Werner, H. & Kaplan, B. (1963). *Symbol formation*. New York, NY: Wiley.

Werner, H. & Lagercrantz, E. (1924). Experimentell–psychologische Studien über die Struktur des Wortes [Experimental–psychological studies of the structure of words]. *Zeitschrift für Psychologie, 95*, 316–363.

Wieser, M. (2013). From the eel to the ego: Psychoanalysis and the remnants of Freud's early scientific practice. *Journal of the History of the Behavioral Sciences, 49*(3), 259–280.

Wieser, M. & Slunecko, T. (2013). Images of the invisible: An account of iconic media in the history of psychology. *Theory & Psychology, 23*(4), 435–457.

Wundt, W. (1893). *Grundzüge der physiologischen Psychologie* [Outlines of physiological psychology] (Vol. 2). Leipzig, Germany: Engelmann.

Wundt, W. (1907). Über Ausfrageexperimente und über die Methoden zur Psychologie des Denkens [On interrogation experiments and the methods of psychology of thinking]. *Psychologische Studien, 3*, 301–390.

Zietz, K. & Werner, H. (1928). Studien über Strukturgesetze. VIII. Über die dynamische Struktur der Bewegung [Studies on structural laws. VIII. On the dynamic structure of movement]. *Zeitschrift für Psychologie, 105*, 226–249.

Reconsidering equipotentiality

Agency and the directions of development

Vanessa Lux

"[B]iology . . . is in great need of a general theory of living systems. As our recent advances in genomic sciences show, the empirical work has outpaced theoretical advances and so it has become a blind search for simple solutions—where there can only be complex ones" (Valsiner, this volume, Chapter 2, p. 000). I strongly support this diagnosis. Especially for my area of expertise, working at the intersections of epigenetics, neuroscience, and psychology, the need for a general theoretical framework, as well as individual models, which allow integration of the daily growing amount of molecular and neuroimaging data, has become quite urgent. At the core of this current need for theory and modeling is the conceptualization of development (see Lux, Chapter 3, this volume). As Valsiner points out, any theory of development needs to address its special nature, being something that "happens always 'in-between'" (Valsiner, this volume, Chapter 2, p. 000), which we should conceptualize as "being of the becoming". Indeed, developmental processes always refer to a potential future. They do not fit into the convertible structure of formal logic, but, as Valsiner writes with reference to James Mark Baldwin, they "operate with non-convertible propositions" (Valsiner, this volume, Chapter 2, p. 000).

For Valsiner, the former diagnosis and the special nature of development are only two starting points from which he revisits the works of Hans Driesch. He discusses Driesch's three key concepts of embryological development—regulation, equifinality, and equipotentiality—and their use for developmental issues in contemporary psychology and genomics. On this, Valsiner concludes: "While the notion of *regulation* has found its honorable place in contemporary epigenetics . . . and the concept of *equifinality* has been maintained within the general systems theory (as a defining characteristic of open systems), the third notion with which Driesch operated—*equipotentiality*—has become lost" (Valsiner, this volume, Chapter 2, emphasis in the original, p. 000). According to Valsiner, the notion of (constrained) equipotentiality allows conceptualization of the prospective nature of development, as reflected by the difference between competence and performance. He argues that, together with the notion of hierarchical organization, equipotentiality could serve as a bridging concept within the interdisciplinary field of developmental sciences from genomics to psychology. But the "vitalist branding" of Driesch's theoretical heritage, especially of his *entelechy* concept, is an ongoing burden to such an endeavor.

I very much support the effort made by Valsiner to grasp Driesch's non-mechanistic approach to development and use it for current issues in developmental sciences. Most importantly, Driesch's approach seems to fit with the experimental data, especially for the field of epigenetics. Here, as Valsiner suggests, Driesch's concept of equipotentiality could stimulate a more precise theoretical modeling. I am convinced that this is also the case for a number of areas in developmental neuroscience.

In the following, I outline the potential of Driesch's concept of equipotentiality for two examples from the fields of epigenetics and developmental neuroscience. In addition, I argue that the vitalist tendency of Driesch's concept of equipotentiality is not just a matter of branding, but points to a basic epistemological problem of developmental sciences in general: the question of agency.

Epigenetic reprogramming and the "non-convertible proposition"

When considering examples of equipotentiality in epigenetics, the production of induced pluripotent stem (iPS) cells immediately comes to mind. iPS cells are transformed adult soma cells that are capable of developing anew in every other cell type in the body, hence pluripotent. Originally, pluripotency was thought to be an exclusive characteristic of non-differentiated embryonic stem (ES) cells. However, in 2006, Takahashi and Yamanaka showed that the introduction of only four transcription factors into mouse embryonic or adult fibroblasts, under ES cell culture conditions, facilitates subsequent differentiation of these cells into a diverse range of cell types when injected back into body tissue (Takahashi & Yamanaka, 2006). Thus, through the experimental modulation of epigenetic mechanisms such as DNA methylation and histone modifications non-ES cells acquired a partial pluripotent character. It seems that, in the case of iPS cells, the injected transcription factors restructure the epigenetic mechanisms channeling cell-specific gene expression patterns, although the exact mechanisms are still unknown.

This phenomenon, discussed under the term "(epigenetic) reprogramming", has been interpreted as a "complete reversal" (*komplette Umkehr*, Niemann, 2014, p. 47) of the cell differentiation process. At first glance, epigenetic reprogramming of adult soma cells into iPS cells seems to violate the Dewey's non-convertible proposition logic. However, this would imply that DNA methylation patterns, histone modifications, RNA interference etc. are exactly the same in iPS and ES cells, which is probably not the case. It is more likely that the four transcription factors target key epigenetic mechanisms with structural functions in cell differentiation— something I would rather call "developmental epigenetic mechanisms" (see Lux, 2013). Within this concept of epigenetic reprogramming and the related notion of reverse development, differences between iPS and ES cells are framed as failure of the reprogramming procedure. However, when we interpret the state of iPS cells as expression of a constraint or relative equipotentiality of adult soma cells, both communalities and differences with ES cells could be considered as contributing to the cell state of iPS cells and studied accordingly.

Thus, in the case of iPS cells the notion of equipotentiality suggests that we should consider those cells as an additional cell state. This means that we should model the developmental potential of adult soma cells as manifold, with several outcomes. For example, a skin cell, blood cell, or neuron could develop a certain shape, maybe migrate to a certain position in its target tissue, or build certain connections with surrounding cells to fulfill a specified function. These micro-differentiations could all be considered as expressions of equipotentiality. When we take one of these micro-differentiated cells and inject the four transcription factors, and the cell develops a certain degree of pluripotency, this iPS cell status could also be considered as further cell differentiation—under specific (experimental) conditions. Therefore, interpreting the iPS cell state as expression of equipotentiality and further cell differentiation rather than "reprogramming" of cells would enable us to study differences and communalities between iPS and ES cells not as failure but as alternative developmental outcomes. This would not only increase the number of known potential developmental outcomes and pathways for adult soma cells; it would also allow us to further study the therapeutic potential of iPS cells without getting lost in trying to mimic ES cells and reverse development.

Neuroplasticity as expression of constraint equipotentiality

In the case of neural plasticity, however, the notion of equipotentiality seems to emphasize the constraints of development. The term "neuroplasticity" is commonly used to describe the lifelong ability of the brain, its areas, groups of neurons, and even single neurons, to change their structure and function in response to experience (see Fuchs & Flügge, 2014). Thus: "Brain plasticity can be conceptualized as nature's invention to overcome limitations of the genome and adapt to a rapidly changing environment. As such, plasticity is an intrinsic property of the brain across the lifespan" (Pascual-Leone, Freitas, Oberman, Horvath, Halko, Eldaief et al., 2011, p. 302). The most striking example is the incredible ability of patients with brain lesions who are able to re-acquire lost functions. At the level of single neurons, plasticity is exhibited by changes in morphology and synaptic activity, including inter-neural connections and number of synapses (Fuchs & Flügge, 2014). For instance, stress reduces the length of apical dendrites of pyramidal neurons (Watanabe, Gould, & McEwen, 1992); in turn, dendrite reduction shrinks the surface of the neurons and therefore the number of synapses (see Fuchs & Flügge, 2014). In contrast, brain regions and networks seem to exhibit different degrees of plasticity; for instance, neurons in the medial prefrontal cortex also retract their dendrites in response to stress, but the effects of such retraction depend on the brain hemisphere where this change takes place (Perez-Cruz, Müller-Keuker, Heilbronner, Fuchs, & Flügge, 2007). Therefore, it seems that the equipotentiality of single neurons and groups of neurons with regard to their morphological structure, biochemistry, and neural functions depends on their embeddedness in neural pathways and surrounding tissue as well as their prior developmental history.

Therefore, the notion of (constraint) equipotentiality would allow emphasis of the mechanisms of locality and placement within which neuroplasticity is exhibited. Instead of attributing a general plasticity to the brain or to single neurons, the idea of local specification would direct the attention to those developmental mechanisms that enable or constrain plasticity. Furthermore, it points to a model of development accounting for multi-level coactions—between single neurons, neural networks or brain areas, and the developmental sources of plasticity from molecular mechanisms to psychic functions.

The question of agency

These two examples show the productivity of Driesch's thinking and especially of the concept of equipotentiality for current theoretical issues in epigenetics and neuroscience. However, compared with Valsiner, I am more skeptical about whether the resonance of vitalist ideas in Driesch's concept of *entelechy* is only a question of branding, or labeling. Driesch conceptualized entelechy as neither a material substrate nor a type of energy, but an acting *something* that is capable of suspending possible manifestations and enabling development of form through regulation: "Entelechy, we know, is an intensive manifoldness, i.e. it is an agent acting manifoldly without being in itself manifold in space or extensity. Entelechy therefore is only an agent that arranges, but not an agent that possesses quantity" (Driesch, 1908, p. 250). Thus, entelechy is a form of non-materialistic action potential, inherent and specific to living organisms.

In my opinion, Driesch's turn to such non-materialistic agency is a symptom of an unsolved—and eventually unsolvable—epistemological problem concerning all of the developmental sciences: how can we conceptualize causal relationships in a non-deterministic fashion, but still identify constrained potentialities and causal factors without assuming "agency" and "will"[1] to the chemical and physical compounds of organic matter? This problem, constitutive to the emergent forms of the organic, has probably occupied every generation of biologists trying to uncover the mechanisms of development. One of these figures was Conrad H. Waddington (see Lux, Chapter 3, this volume). He not only coined the term epigenetics and argued for a systematic study of the mechanisms regulating gene expression in organ development and evolution (Waddington, 1942, 1947); he also proposed the model of the epigenetic landscape that has become a thought model for epigenetics in general and stem cell research in particular (see Baedke & Brandt, 2014). Following Driesch and others, Waddington also identified a certain degree of organization (or form) as a key characteristic of living organisms:

A living organism is not just a bag of chemicals each produced by the influence of some particular gene. It has a character which we acknowledge by calling it a living organism. This phase admits that it exhibits the property of organization; but what exactly is organization? It is a rather tricky concept to define, and it is probably sufficient to say here that it implies that if an organized entity is broken up into parts, the full properties of these parts can only be understood by reference to their relations with the other parts of the whole system.

(Waddington, 1963, p. 53)

According to Waddington, such organization is the result of development. A single cell, tissue, organism, or species develops along a developmental pathway (chreode), which is defined by complex self-stabilizing mechanisms of gene–gene and gene–environment interactions (see Waddington, 1957, p. 26). His lifelong aim was to identify the exact mechanisms for individual chreodes and to isolate their defining characteristics in general.

Within this attempt, Waddington particularly struggled with the problem of directedness of development and the emergence of new properties. Following Alfred North Whitehead's relational materialism (see Waddington, 1963, p. 19; Waddington, 1975), he argues that the individual parts (such as atoms, electrons, or genes) show different properties (potentials) that emerge only in relation to the structure or form in which they are arranged:

When it turns out that certain arrangements of the atoms of carbon, nitrogen, hydrogen, oxygen, etc., exhibit properties which we recognize by the name of enzymes; when other still more complicated arrangements turn out to be able to duplicate themselves identically like the genes in the cell nucleus, or to be able to conduct electrical impulses like nerve cells, or to exhibit the correlate electrical phenomena found in the staggeringly complex systems of nervous cells in the brain; it is completely out of the picture to suggest that we have to add something of a non-mechanistic kind to an already fully comprehended material atom. What we have done is simply to discover something about atoms that we did not know before; namely, that when they are arranged in certain special ways the total complex can exhibit another behavior that we might not have expected at first sight. . . . The secret of their performance in this way is architecture, or, to use the Aristotelian term, form.

(Waddington, 1963, p. 21)

According to Waddington, instead of an inherent potential—Driesch's *entelechy*—, the developmental manifold emerges out of the relationships between the individual parts and their organization. Despite this relationalism, Waddington still searched for a mechanistic solution of the problem of agency. His lifelong efforts included the use of early computer simulation and several attempts of mathematization—all without success. Finally, his notion of "emergent properties" of individual parts in their relationships still attributes a certain degree of agency to these parts as a result of their relational embeddedness.

As the examples of Driesch and Waddington show, the question of agency is at the core of developmental theory. It results from the epistemological problem of how we explain directedness of development and the emergence of form and higher degrees of organization without assuming intentionality to the physical and chemical compounds of living matter. Driesch's merit here undoubtedly is his direct and highly reflexive addressing of this issue, while Waddington's work shows the epistemological limits of a pure mechanistic approach to development. Taking their theoretical reflections and empirical attempts a bit further, I would argue that on a molecular level developmental mechanisms can only be studied ex post, as developmental outcome. However, on the level of psychological functions, where we have agency of the individual subject and where this plays a key role with regard to the potential developmental outcome, e.g. in learning, developmental theory has the potential to take the perspective of the acting subject into account. As Valsiner discusses, the notion of equipotentiality enables us to model both: the developmental potential at the molecular or cell level and the developmental potential at the level of psychological functions and agency of the subject. This does not solve the epistemological problem of agency in the developmental sciences. But it allows us to think consistently throughout all levels of development about different ways to model the potential future in developmental processes for each of these levels. This would be one step further to those complex solutions we all are looking for.

Note

1 Driesch notes: "In this way, regarding it only as a kind of description, I see no fundamental difficulty in speaking of entelechy's *primary* 'knowing and willing'; at least no other description of what happens seems to be derivable from any species of analogy" (Driesch, 1908, p. 145).

References

Baedke, J. & Brandt, C. (2014). Die andere Epigenetik: Modellbildungen in der Stammzellbiologie und die Diversität epigenetischer Ansätze [Another epigenetics: Modelling in stem cell biology and diversity of epigenetic approaches]. In V. Lux & J. Richter (Eds.), *Kulturen der Epigenetik: Vererbt, codiert, übertragen* (pp. 23–41). Berlin, Germany: De Gruyter.

Driesch, H. (1908). *The science and philosophy of the organism*. London, UK: Adam and Charles Black.

Fuchs, E. & Flügge, G. (2014). Adult neuroplasticity: More than 40 years of research. *Neural Plasticity*, doi: 10.1155/2014/541870.

Lux, V. (2013). With Gottlieb beyond Gottlieb: The role of epigenetics in psychobiological development. *International Journal of Developmental Science*, 7, 69–78.

Niemann, H. (2014). Somatisches Klonen und Epigenetik bei Nutztieren [Cloning and the epigenetics of livestock]. In V. Lux & J. Richter (Eds.), *Kulturen der Epigenetik: Vererbt, codiert, übertragen* (pp. 43–55). Berlin, Germany: De Gruyter.

Pascual-Leone, A., Freitas, C., Oberman, L., Horvath, J., Halko, M., Eldaief, M., et al. (2011). Characterizing brain cortical plasticity and network dynamics across the age-span in health and disease with TMS-EEG and TMS-fMRI. *Brain Topography*, *24*(3–4), 302–315, doi: 10.1007/s10548-011-0196-8.

Perez-Cruz, C., Müller-Keuker, J. I. H., Heilbronner, U., Fuchs, E., & Flügge, G. (2007). Morphology of pyramidal neurons in the rat prefrontal cortex: Lateralized dendritic remodeling by chronic stress. *Neural Plasticity*, *14*, doi: 10.1155/2007/46276.

Takahashi, K. & Yamanaka, S. (2006). Induction of pluripotent stem cells from mouse embryonic and adult fibroblast cultures by defined factors. *Cell*, *126*(4), 663–676, doi: 10.1016/j.cell.2006.07.024.

Waddington, C. H. (1942). The epigenotype. *Endeavour*, *1*, 18–20.

Waddington, C. H. (1947). *Organisers & genes*. Cambridge, UK: Cambridge University Press.

Waddington, C. H. (1957). *The strategy of the genes: A discussion of some aspects of theoretical biology*. London, UK: George Allen & Unwin.

Waddington, C. H. (1963). *The nature of life*. London, UK: Allen & Unwin.

Waddington, C. H. (1975). The practical consequences of metaphysical beliefs on a biologist's work: An autobiographical note. In C. H. Waddington (Ed.), *The Evolution of an Evolutionist* (pp. 3–9). Ithaca, NY: Cornell University Press.

Watanabe, Y., Gould, E., & McEwen, B. S. (1992). Stress induces atrophy of apical dendrites of hippocampal CA3 pyramidal neurons. *Brain Research*, *588*(2), 341–345.

Observations on Karl and Charlotte Bühler's perspective of development

Gerhard Benetka

In her reconstruction of the concept of development in life sciences, Vanessa Lux (Chapter 3, this volume) identifies a notorious gap between the conceptualization and study of the individual level of development—ontogenesis—and the population level of development—phylogenesis. As the concept of development in psychology has its roots in the field of biology, the author traces a matching theoretical discrepancy back in the history of developmental psychology. Here, too, Lux differentiates an initial embryological notion of development—individual-based—from a later epidemiological—population-based—concept. Following this distinction, however, Lux's position about the psychological theories of development discussed remains vague. Ultimately, her reflections on epigenetics and neurobiology suggests that an integration of both perspectives into a unitary, comprehensive concept of development would be a desirable scientific progress—yet it is not specified why this would be beneficial beyond data integration.

I am not in a position to adequately comment on the latter argument, nor on the merit of Waddington's and Oyama's Developmental Systems Theory approach, as I do not have the background knowledge that the author has on these subjects. Regarding the implications of Lux's argument for developmental psychology, however, I think that her optimistic view on this integration seems a little inappropriate. My pessimism is based in the fact that such integrative concepts have already existed, yet they have not been able to relativize the basic biological bias of psychological development theory—namely, assuming development as growth.

In this commentary, I would like to focus specifically on the reference made by Lux to the work of Karl Bühler, as a representative of the "early developmental psychology" movement in Germany. In particular, in her text (p. 000) Lux refers to Bühler's seminal book *Die geistige Entwicklung des Kindes* [The mental development of the child]—first published in 1918—as an exemplar of the embryological concept of development in psychology. Although this appears obvious for Lux, I am not certain that Bühler's work represents a case of the abovementioned gap between ontogenetic and phylogenetic levels of interpretation. This is mostly because the entire early child psychology—in German psychology the term "developmental psychology" is introduced only much later—had Ernst Haeckel's "biogenetic law" as a common reference. Thereby, most authors—Bühler included—subscribed to the speculative assumption that ontogeny would always represent an abbreviated recapitulation of phylogenetic development, which would be the opposite of an embryological approach. If anything, the transmission of the embryonic logic to the child's development, and from there further to the whole of human history, is rather rooted in the close ties between early child psychology and anthropology. How pristine this way of thinking was can be seen, for instance, in Freud's works; not in vain does his *Totem and Taboo* bear the subtitle *Resemblances between the Mental Lives of Savages and Neurotics* (Freud, 1919). Interestingly, for Freud, the neurotic is someone who in almost all areas of his or her life acts as a child rather than as a grown-up adult.

Going back to Bühler's book, at its core it is possible to find the idea of a *three-stage theory of mental development*:

> The human being is not isolated in the world, but related to animals. When all meaningful actions, i.e. objectively goal oriented [*zweckmaessige Betaetigungsweisen*], of animals and humans are observed, a very simple and transparent structure comprising three major stages moving from bottom to top can be seen: instinct, training, and intellect.
>
> (Bühler, 1924, p. 2)

Instinct here refers to a rigidly fixed repertoire of behavior, while *training* points to the ability to learn via association. In turn, *intellect* refers to the ability to plan inventions via *ideas*, and, on the highest human level, via *insight* into complex situations and conditions (Bühler, 1924, p. 88). Intriguingly, the idea that the child *must* pass through this three-stage development does not come from Bühler but from Haeckel. In fact, in his book Bühler mostly supports these phylogenetic postulates on the basis of empirical, ontogenetic material. In this vein, the elaboration on the sequence of stages related to "objective goal oriented actions" is actually oriented to deepen on the phylogenetic concept of adaptation:

> The Darwinian adaptation proceeds through the elimination of less favourably equipped individuals, with their lives at stake. Adaptation by training takes place within the individual . . . the area affected here is that of physical activity and the price paid is no longer lives, but bodily movements that are produced in abundance and are wasted. Only further development of thinking is needed to formulate an alternative form of adaptation on the basis of the knowledge of human relations. If body movements are still too costly in psychical terms, or are not enough to achieve their goals, the area affected should be shifted to the field of ideas and thoughts: if they are wasted, this is probably cheaper and certainly in many respects a more efficient process.
>
> (Bühler, 1924, p. 434)

In the above extract it is possible to observe the contradiction, following Lux's ideas, present in the work of Bühler: while he tries to advance tenets coming from a phylogenetic model of development—those of Haeckel's three-stage model—, in empirical terms his approach is embryological, as it is grounded in ontogenetic observations. This is interesting not only because of the questions it opens— whether the phylogenetic observations made by Bühler only have a metaphorical significance for his empirical work—, but also because of the relation with the *data generation* gap described by Lux, which points to the difficulties of integrating the data collected at individual and population level, without falling into logical or theoretical inconsistencies.

It is worth noting here that Karl Bühler's wife, Charlotte Bühler, precisely tried to evaluate an embryological concept of development through epidemiological, statistical data, even though she rudimentarily sought to conduct the evaluation at a population level—something that Lux reproaches her for. While Charlotte Bühler familiarized herself in the United States with behavioristic methods of observation, she later based her own concept of child development on a comparative psychology approach. For her theoretical framework, the concept of *deferred instincts* was central. This notion points to those instincts whose manifestation is delayed due to the lack of biological maturity, yet they surface in correspondence with the attainment of a certain physiological level—all of which is quite compliant with those models Lux refers to as embryological. "In addition to the innate and acquired," Charlotte Bühler writes, there is "that which reaches full potential only through personal development, only through maturing" (1927, p. 8).

Accordingly, the empirical evaluation of this concept of development was carried out through continuous 24-hour observations of infants and young children at different ages at the Viennese municipal transfer house for orphans (*Städtische Kinderübernahmestelle*)—an institution that served to house children who were transferred, in most cases by the police, to the public child and youth welfare system. However—enacting the gap described by Lux—the aim of these investigations was to construct behavior schemes for every age range, in which mainly those behaviors that newly came into appearance during particular developmental stages, but were not yet visible in the preceding age group, were recorded. Hence the relevance of the abovementioned deferred instincts. These statistical, population-based analyses served as a stepping stone for developing a program to examine child's development, namely the Viennese Toddler Tests (*Wiener Kleinkindertests*) (Bühler & Hetzer, 1932), which built upon Binet and Simon's intelligence tests.

What is remarkable about Charlotte Bühler's concept is that her statistical evaluation does not entail the biologistic constriction, as it is built upon an open-ended set of behavioral observations. In my work on the Vienna Psychological Institute (Benetka, 1995), I have shown that it is exactly under these research conditions where a panoptic institution mutated into a living environment, where the maturation of predisposed aptitudes can be observed—without being contaminated by social contingencies. In this sense, the work of Charlotte Bühler may well serve as an example of integrating individual- and population-based approaches to development and data generation.

Regrettably, this interesting perspective has proven to be more flexible for political uses than for developmental research. As later became apparent, in Viennese urban educational institutions, children from broken homes performed worse on the development tests than children from intact middle-class families. This result, it was finally explained, was due to the social structure of the family being the "natural" environment for a child—an explanation that fitted perfectly with the Catholic and fascist ideologies ruling at the time (Bühler, Baar, Danzinger-Schenk, Falk, Gedeon & Hortner, 1937).

References

Benetka, G. (1995). *Psychologie in Wien: Sozial- und Theoriegeschichte des Wiener Psychologischen Instituts 1922–1938.* [Psychology in Vienna: Social history and history of theories of the Viennese Psychological Institute 1922–1938]. Vienna, Austria: WUV University Publishing.

Bühler, Ch. (1927). Die ersten sozialen Verhaltungsweisen des Kindes. [The first social behavior patterns of the child]. In Ch. Bühler, H. Hetzer & B. Tudor-Hart (Eds.), *Soziologische und psychologische Studien über das erste Lebensjahr* [Sociological and psychological studies of the first year of life] (pp. 1–102). Jena, Germany: G. Fischer.

Bühler, Ch. & Hetzer, H. (1932). *Kleinkindertests: Entwicklungstests für das erste bis sechste Lebensjahr* [Toddler tests: Development tests for the first until the sixth year of life]. Leipzig, Germany: Hirzel.

Bühler, Ch., Baar, E., Danzinger-Schenk, L., Falk, G., Gedeon, S. & Hortner G. (eds.) (1937). *Kind und Familie* [Child and family]. Jena, Germany: G. Fischer.

Bühler, K. (1924). *Die geistige Entwicklung des Kindes* [The cognitive development of the child] (4th ed.). Jena, Germany: G. Fischer. (Original work published 1918)

Freud, S. (1919). *Totem and taboo: Resemblances between the mental lives of savages and neurotics.* New York, NY: Moffat, Yard and Company.

The dangerous look of development and developmental science

Jeanette A. Lawrence and Agnes E. Dodds

Elite: Dangerous (2015) is a newly released computer game in which players make their individual ways through an open-ended, competition-filled galaxy. Players' choices and moves are critical for the unfolding of the game. They affect them directly, but they also affect what thousands of other players can do, thus shaping the possible patterns of relationships in the entire galaxy. Playing the game is *dangerous*, because the possibilities are open ended, and because players' choices and actions can have unexpected, embedded, long-term and unforeseen consequences. The workings of this virtual world, however, do not seem very different from the processes of development involved in our actual world, either in the experiences of developing persons, or in the progress of the *developmental science* that Jaan Valsiner (Chapter 4, this volume) ascribes to Bob Cairns and his colleagues through the Carolina Consortium on Human Development. In the quest to understand human development experientially or scientifically, Valsiner claims, "Development can look dangerous" (p. 000). How can this be? What makes development look dangerous as a life experience? What makes scientific research that seeks to make sense of those experiences look dangerous as a research program and as a social agenda for developmental scientists to pursue?

Valsiner's analysis of the creation of developmental science works forward from a set of observations about the nature of development that together give clues about why development suggests danger. In this vein, Valsiner proposes that *development*: is the process of becoming (p. 000); involves the emergence of new phenomena, particularly the emergence of developmental surprises and novelty (pp. 000–000); is an ever-moving structure of past–present–future in irreversible time (p. 000); and, by bringing about substantial transformation, also involves loss (p. 000). These defining characteristics of development point to why the view of development as transformational change may have provoked feelings of danger in developmental psychologists who encountered Cairns' passion for developmental science. As a set, they center on development as the kind of change that brings new experiences that are distinctive from those that have gone before, and, with that newness, some loss of what was previously experienced.

Having established that it was Bob Cairns' passion to understand this transformational sense of developmental change, and having established how the emerging developmental science was developmental at its heart, Valsiner shows how the scientific shift to seeing development in this way moved the thinking of Cairns and his colleagues away from traditional, pseudo-developmental accounts. These had been more concerned with stability and steady states than with the processes of change. Developmental psychology could not make the move toward understanding development as transformational change, embedded as it was in a psychology wrapped in models and methods looking for sameness and predictability. The new science was designed to bring about its own change: to replace developmental psychology by drawing on concepts from other disciplines and by opening up new avenues of research. It was not an incidental movement and it was not an historical accident. The shift was a purposive transformational change in research agendas and research progress.

Valsiner describes the creation of the new research agenda and its early progressions over time, first as they arose in the transformation of Cairns' ideas about child development, and then how they developed as he pioneered new ways of studying human development through the synthesis of perspectives and methodologies belonging to developmental biology, sociology, anthropology and psychology. He traces the changes in Cairns' core concepts and language through three key history-oriented publications from 1979, 1983 and 1998 (see Table 4.2 in Valsiner, Chapter 4, this volume). Cairns was moving toward understanding development as transformation, upheaval, and the emergence of novelty, and so he was advancing toward an account of relations between developing children and their environments that went beyond his own roots in social learning theory. The transforming nature of human development demanded a change in how developmentalists theorized and studied developmental phenomena.

Core developmental phenomena could not be understood appropriately in terms of states or of relentlessly unfolding predetermined trajectories. They could not be tracked using retrospective models and methods of analysis. The open-endedness and the possibility of novelty needed dynamic and prospective models and methods that the traditional approaches of developmental psychology could not provide. These new kinds of developmental approaches were proposed in the dialogue and debates of the Carolina Consortium that introduced accounts of development that were engaging the attention of colleagues from other developmental disciplines. Cairns was transforming his ideas—and those of the field—into a new meta-theoretical framework with developmental (as opposed to non-developmental) methods of studying children's life experiences and trajectories.

The introduction of new concepts and multidisciplinary approaches came as a shock and potential *danger* to consortium colleagues and visitors steeped in the stability models and methods of twentieth-century psychology. Gottlieb's (1991) model of bi-directional, co-acting levels of human functioning, for example, was a shock for our Australian empiricist colleagues when we introduced it in post-Carolina conversations. It took decades for some developmental psychologists to cope with the co-acting fundamental levels and their multi-directional effects that were proposed in such a systemic model. Similarly disturbing were anthropological insights into the pervasiveness, immediacy and plasticity of cultural thought in the development of personal identity (e.g., Holland & Skinner, 1997). The time-related and age-related significance of historical events in individual people's lives, such as war and the Great Depression, also forced psychologists to re-assess their understanding of environmental influences on development (e.g., Elder & Conger, 2000). The field would be changed irrevocably if these kinds of analyses were incorporated into the new developmental science, especially if it also embraced the thought—untenable for some traditional developmentalists—that development could be experienced beyond adolescence and throughout the whole life-course (e.g., Elder, 1996). That developmental science looked dangerous: such outrageous proposals must be ignored or colonized and taken over. Developmental psychologists involved in the shift must be encouraged back into the fold.

The sense of novelty and newness, nevertheless, was explicit and persisted in both the academic discourse and the organization of the Carolina Consortium. It was owned in the 1996 volume as a statement attributed to the consortium, and as such, no doubt, was carefully composed:[1]

> Developmental science refers to a fresh synthesis that has been generated to guide research in the social, psychological, and bio-behavioral disciplines. It describes a general orientation for linking concepts and findings of hitherto disparate areas of developmental inquiry, and it emphasizes the dynamic interplay of processes across time frames, levels of analysis, and contexts.
>
> (The Carolina Consortium on Human Development, 1996, p. 1)

The new developmental science was called a "fresh synthesis" for a particular purpose. It emphasized the shift away from the constraints of developmental psychology toward a broader and more integrative meta-level framework for developmental research. It also was a shift out of the constraints of one discipline into multi-disciplinarity. As a movement, it offered scholars theoretical ideas about development, and a social organization in which those ideas and concepts could be generated, debated, refined and tested in research studies.

This shift into the new developmental science can be appropriately interpreted as a *theory change* in the account of scientific progress proposed by the philosopher Alan Chalmers (1979). His concept is a looser and more appropriate descriptor of the progress of a research program than a Kuhnian revolution because his account did not propose a theoretical change from within an existing science. This fresh synthesis of disparate ideas simply could not have emerged within developmental psychology, which could hardly be seen as a science on any basis. Rather, developmental psychology was a branch of psychology that never represented itself as having the theoretical unity or the social organization of a science in Kuhn's terms. Twentieth-century psychology was much more a disparate set of divisions with little by way of any unifying meta-theoretical or methodological approach, apart from perhaps the pursuit of sameness or difference, but not change.

Chalmers (1979, p. 227) proposed his *objectivist account of theoretical change* as a way of avoiding the constraints of either Kuhnian or Lakatosian accounts of the progress of scientific research. As he described it, theoretical change seems to be a concept that is readily applicable to the shift into and through the new developmental science. It concerned, in his terms, "research strategies and the guidance and evaluation of the choices and decisions of scientists" (Chalmers, 1979, p. 228). In this scheme, Chalmers proposed a criterion for judging research progress and productivity that can be directly applied to the shift into developmental science, because the new synthesis presented researchers precisely with the kind of "objective opportunity" (p. 227) that Chalmers argued would progress a science. His criterion involved the "degree of fertility" accompanying the theoretical change that he identified as "the extent to which it [a research program] offers opportunities for future development, the number of new avenues it opens up" (Chalmers, 1979, p. 229). Explaining how that opening of avenues could be used to assess the progressive—or degenerative—nature of a shift, he gave Galileo's mechanics example, which opened up the study of motion by bringing mathematics, physics and astronomy together in his theory. Cairns and colleagues similarly opened up the study of development by bringing together and synthesizing accounts of developmental change from multiple disciplines with overlapping and unique interests in developmental phenomena.

For Chalmers, a suitably fertile change opened up the field. Let avenues open up and proliferate, let ideas emerge and multiply, and their numbers will attest to the value of the change from the old theory. The old would be left behind and be marked as degenerative by its stagnant closing-down of ideas and blocked avenues of research. He demonstrated the contrast between progressive and degenerative theories by comparing the fertility of Einstein's general formulation of relativity theory with that of Lorentz. Einstein's theory was more general, had greater application, and produced greater fertility. Under this criterion, there can be little doubt that the new developmental science outstripped developmental psychology—especially U.S.-dominated, twentieth-century developmental psychology. Once the theoretical change had been initiated, its high levels of fertility could be observed in many new avenues for research it opened up. Meta-theoretical and multi-disciplinary dialogue suggested numerous research programs, filling the future developmental science with possibilities. How the synthesis would proceed and what research programs would emerge in future dialogues were matters beyond prediction as the dialogue promoted creativity and novelty.

Chalmers acknowledged that the burgeoning avenues of any theory change would be affected by the number of scientists taking up the new possibilities. Developmental science did not have the connected and vast community of scholars that was able to progress nineteenth-century physics along multiple lines. Developmental science did attract, however, numbers of younger and older scholars who had the will and the skill to take up the available offers to work in a range of different avenues. The fertility of developmental science, accordingly, was worked out in directions that could not only co-exist but also cross-fertilize each other within the free-flowing and rich dialogue. For example, Magnusson's early collaborations with Cairns on person-centered approaches to studying individuals led off in one avenue that productively developed "the person-oriented approach" (e.g., Bergman, Magnusson & El-Khouri, 2003). Related are the pursuits of Valsiner and colleagues along the avenue of studying the individual that has issued in analyses of idiographic psychology that moved further away from contemporary, mainstream English language psychology (e.g., Salvatore & Valsiner, 2010). The systemic view of the intertwining of the person and the environment generated several lines of ecological and systemic models (e.g., Bronfenbrenner & Evans, 2000; Lerner, 2012). Multi-disciplinary avenues took up the interactions of personal and environmental factors in neuroscience (e.g., Fahrbach, 2013) and criminology (e.g., Le Blanc, 2012). These avenues could not all have been envisaged at the beginning, nor would such a vision have been productive. Predictability would not have been admitted by the diverse avenues that were generated in the early and continuing fertility of developmental science. How, then, could this account of research fertility and progress be seen as dangerous?

Danger came with the unpredictability for researchers who were used to the self-assurance of twentieth-century psychology. It lurked around questions about ownership of the field, challenges of accepted wisdom, and tensions between competing approaches. Perhaps more significantly, however, danger was suggested by new formulations of basic developmental processes, and by questions about the appropriate methods for uncovering and tracking developmental as opposed to non-developmental phenomena. The Carolina Consortium's dialogues meant that psychology could no longer determine, without challenge, developmental research agendas and their desirable social outcomes. Valsiner illustrates the importance of holistic (as opposed to separated, exclusivist) analyses of the developmental transformations of the individual with Cairns' (1979) early case study of the social behaviors of 5-year-old Peter. Any trans-context continuity in his patterns of social behavior, for example, could only be developmentally analyzed in juxtaposition with the context-specificity of others of his behaviors. To try promoting either one of these aspects of development exclusively as the goal of interventions in the lives of Peter and other disadvantaged children would involve determining a social end-point that was not properly informed by developmental theory. It would ignore the repertoire of possibilities that exist in any individual child in any population. Focusing research and training on parenting activities without attending to the agentic role of the child similarly would be non-developmental at heart, because the developmental experiences of children and adults in dynamic, interactive situations are not predictable.

By 1998, Cairns had already marked out the general tendency of developmental psychology to be self-assured in its approaches and predictions, and in his words, "to give short shrift to competing findings, concepts and interpretations" (p. 26). Chalmers' fertility criterion underlines the appropriateness of Cairns' concern about this tendency, and also underlines the emphases added by Valsiner on how that territorial tendency impedes research progress (p. 21). From their perspectives, it is clear that simple assertions of the scientific and developmental status of psychology represent retreat from the dialogue and from fertility; for instance, assertions like, "psychology is, after all, a developmental science" (Greenberg, Callina & Mueller, 2013, p. 99).

Claims of researcher certainty and authority in the face of the perspectives of researched persons also incur stagnation while they seek to avoid the danger of surrendering control. A nice counter-example of turning from this self-assurance of psychology can be seen in Schwarz's (2009) discovery that his research method for understanding the quality of life of cancer patients was not fulfilling his agenda. There was a disassociation between Schwarz's measurement apparatus questionnaires (tools) and the psychological experience of his cancer patients (sentient agents) who were asserting their own well-being despite their illness. The test of correspondence brought Schwarz to the view that, in his case, the toys in the researcher's playpen were broken. Along the same lines, Toomela (2011) makes a powerful argument that standard quantitative methods can never uncover the nature of psychological phenomena. The studied phenomenon itself disappears because quantitative methodology is used for studying *relationships* between events and things; therefore it is not—and cannot—be used for understanding what a thing or phenomenon *is* (Toomela, 2011, p. 24).

Transformations are especially closed to standard statistical methods, because of the multiple levels and directions of change that intertwine and co-act at the transforming event (Gottlieb, 1991). Individual researchers and research teams, nevertheless, have the license and ability to reject a shift into enlightenment. They also have license to follow their own priorities and preoccupations in their choices of research avenues and approaches. According to Chalmers, the subjective choice of researchers can keep some researchers working on research programs despite their being clearly (to others) degenerative.

When political, economic and social forces have interest in the status quo, transformational change becomes especially dangerous for researchers with careers at stake and standard reviewers to impress. The possibility of many research avenues and the opportunity to choose among them do not guarantee success in practice. The possibility of dead-end avenues and research failure persists. Bukowski, Li, Dirks and Bouffard (2012), for instance, sought to address the issue of competing research programs in developmental science. Their solution was to broaden the concept and thus make it easier to judge between competing agendas. The expansion involved adding the criterion of *successful* development and using it as a measure of comparison, which was identified as, "the capacity to effectively respond to the challenges inherent in particular parts of the life span and to be prepared to respond to the challenges of subsequent periods" (p. 58). However, this expansion seems to miss the point of change as open ended, novel and transformational. The end-point of developmental change in this account would be pre-defined in terms of the person's negotiation of reliably succeeding states (stages).

Transformational change in the form that we, with Valsiner, see as inherent to developmental science naturally provokes reactions. Reactions other than reasonable challenge may be retreat or redefinition, specialization and closing-down, or persistence with degenerate preoccupations. It should not be surprising, then, that the new developmental science provoked a range of reactions from developmental psychologists and others with an interest in children if not in developmental processes. To work toward understanding something as inherently dynamic and transforming as human development is to engage in activities that look and potentially are dangerous. Does it avoid or heighten the potential danger for the 2015 Wiley edition of the handbook to be titled *The Handbook of Child Psychology and Developmental Science*? (Lerner, 2015). The powerful basis has been laid by Cairns and his colleagues. The challenge to follow the shift is open and available, and it still looks dangerous.

Note

1 We leave aside the question of whether Cairns and the Carolina Consortium *created* developmental science with their new synthesis, accepting that this meta-theoretical and multi-disciplinary framework emerged in the dialogues, debates and inquiries that were raised over time.

References

Bergman, L. R., Magnusson, D. & El-Khouri, B. M. (2003). *Studying individual development in an interindividual context: A person-oriented approach. Paths through life, Vol. 4.* Mahwah, NJ: Lawrence Erlbaum Associates.

Bronfenbrenner, U. & Evans, G. W. (2000). Developmental science in the 21st century: Emerging questions, theoretical models, research designs and empirical findings. *Social Development, 9*(1), 115–125.

Bukowski, W., Li, K., Dirks, M. & Bouffard, T. (2012). Developmental science and the study of successful development. *International Journal of Developmental Science, 6,* 57–60.

Cairns, R. B. (1979). *Social development: The origins and plasticity of interchanges.* San Francisco, CA: W.H. Freeman.

Cairns, R. B. (1983). The emergence of developmental psychology. In W. Kessen (Ed.), *Handbook of child psychology. 4th Ed. Vol. 1. History, theory, and methods* (pp. 41–102). New York, NY: Wiley.

Cairns, R. B. (1998). The making of developmental psychology. In W. Damon & R. M. Lerner (eds.), *Handbook of child psychology. 5th Ed. Vol. 1. Theoretical models of human development* (pp. 25–105). New York, NY: Wiley.

Chalmers, A. (1979). Toward an objective account of theory change. *British Journal for the Philosophy of Science, 30*(3), 227–233.

Elder, G. H., Jr. (1996). Human lives in changing societies: Life course and developmental insights. In R. B. Cairns, G. H. Elder, Jr. & E. J. Costello (Eds.), *Developmental science* (pp. 31–62). New York, NY: Cambridge University Press.

Elder, G. H., Jr. & Conger, R. D. (2000). *Children of the land: Adversity and success in rural America.* Chicago, IL: University of Chicago.

Elite: Dangerous (2015). Retrieved April 4, 2015 from http://www.elitedangerous.com

Fahrbach, S. E. (2013). *Developmental neuroscience: A concise introduction.* Princeton, NJ: Princeton University Press.

Gottlieb, G. (1991). Experiential canalization of behavioral development: Theory. *Developmental Psychology, 27,* 4–13.

Greenberg, G., Callina, K. S. & Mueller, M. K. (2013). Emergence, self-organization, and developmental science. In R. M. Lerner & J. Benson (Eds.), *Advances in child development and behavior* (pp. 95–126). Oxford, UK: Elsevier.

Holland, D. C. & Skinner, D. G. (1997). The co-development of identity, agency and lived worlds. In J. Tudge, M. J. Shanahan & J. Valsiner (Eds.), *Comparisons in human development: Understanding time and context* (pp. 193–221). Cambridge, UK: Cambridge University Press.

Le Blanc, M. (2012). Twenty-five years of developmental criminology: What we know, what we need to know. In R. Loeber & B. C. Welsh (Eds.), *The future of criminology* (pp. 124–133). New York, NY: Oxford University Press.

Lerner, R. M. (2012). Developmental science: Past, present, and future. *International Journal of Developmental Science, 6,* 29–36.

Lerner, R. M. (2015) (Ed.). *Handbook of child psychology and developmental science, 7th Edition.* New York, NY: Wiley.

Salvatore, S. & Valsiner, J. (2010). Idiographic science on its way: Towards making sense of psychology. In S. Salvatore, J. Valsiner, S. Strout-Yagodzynski & J. Clegg (eds.), *Yearbook of idiographic science, Vol. 1.* (pp. 9–22). Rome, Italy: Firera & Liuzzo.

Schwarz, M. (2009). Is psychology based on a methodological error? *Integrative Psychology and Behavioral Science, 43,* 185–213.

The Carolina Consortium on Human Development (1996). Developmental science: A collaborative statement. In R. B. Cairns, G. H., Elder Jr. & E. J. Costello (Eds.), *Developmental science* (pp. 1–6). New York, NY: Cambridge University Press.

Toomela, A. (2011). Travel into a fairy land: A critique of modern qualitative and mixed methods psychologies. *Integrative Psychology and Behavioral Science, 45,* 21–47.

Knowledge in mind
Piaget's epistemology

Leslie Smith

Eduardo Martí (Chapter 5, this volume) has presented a perceptive account of Piaget's intellectual journey comprising a biographical sketch with pointers to his constructs, reasons for their decline, and an inventory of principles for further attention in developmental science. These principles merit attention, even though they are merely listed without adequate guidance about their interpretation. Thus, my commentary includes an outline of Piaget's research programme and a critique of the factors cited by Martí as related to its decline. Following this, I present an analysis of the six principles proposed as a valuable legacy of Piagetian thinking, namely: epistemology of development; interdisciplinarity; explanatory non-reductionism; action, organization, development; epigenesis; and methodological diversity.

Piaget's programme: outline

Kant addressed an epistemological problem: what legitimates anyone's demarcation of objective knowledge from other kinds of human experiences? Piaget was captivated by this problem, but not by Kant's answer, namely a fixed set of rational categories to be used in *a priori* judgments. In particular, he objected to the omission of an empirical check on the availability of these categories to all knowers (Piaget, 1922). His objection was extended by his peers' collateral arguments, regarding the factual origin (genesis) of all knowledge (Baldwin, 1906), and the failure to reflect the development of knowledge in the history of science (Brunschwicg, 1922).

Piaget presented an alternative answer in the form of an epistemology focused on the relations between "one's self [*le moi*] and objective reality" (1929a, p. 1*[1] [see Note 1 for my use of an asterisk]). This crucial assumption concerned the organization of the self as a part of, but non-reducible to, bio-social reality. At stake were the relations between dual historical sequences, the formation of knowledge in persons, and the development of knowledge in adult science. Clearly, the content of these sequences differed, but what about their form and structure? Inhelder astutely declared that Piaget's epistemology is "to my knowledge, the only theory which links the most basic biological mechanisms to the most superior achievements of human thought" (1971, p. 149).

Critique of the factors cited in the decline

Martí acknowledges the historical importance of the Geneva School during the early 20th century, and attributes its fall from grace to three main factors: Piaget's *modus operandi*, methodological biases, and a change in paradigm.

Regarding the *modus operandi*, Marti includes an *ad hominem* comment on Piaget's preferred way of commuting, which appears as an irrelevant anecdote. He also mentions an alleged mismatch between Piaget's commitment to intellectual discussion and tendency to assimilate alternative positions to his own. True, Piaget repeatedly engaged in critical commentaries on rival positions. Yet these attested the nuances in and fertility of his position rather than deficient accommodation to, for example, the work of Bruner or Monod (Piaget, 1971, pp. 20, 163, 294n). Interestingly, wise counsels continue to be issued about refraining from the premature dismissal of Piagetian insights (Chandler, 2009; Flavell, 1996).

Martí shrewdly remarks that methods in psychology currently dominate principles. Unfortunately, he is right. This domination, however, is itself flawed: an experimental method is not a methodology, which contributes only one part of a research programme. The other part comprises a specific metaphysics as its "hard core" preferably with a progressive, not degenerating, problem-shift. An implication is that *crucial* experiments are limited to refuting principles within a programme, but not the programme itself (Lakatos, 1970). Piaget's programme is a case in point, whose evaluations run in opposite directions: negatively about language construction (Piattelli-Palmarini, 1994), but positively about epistemic mechanisms (Boom, 2009; Messerly, 1996; Niaz, 1998).

Kuhn's (1970) influential argument defined the history of science as changes in a paradigm, i.e. what different scientists share during normal science. Any paradigm is liable to gradual revision but can only be recast to become a new paradigm in a scientific revolution; including value judgments about which problems to address, and how to explain them. From the outset, Piaget's epistemology was confronted by alternative paradigms, such as socio-cultural anthropology (Lévy-Bruhl, 1922) and bioscience (Le Dantec, 1912). He acknowledged biology and society as necessary conditions of human development – necessary but not sufficient. He argued that bio-social coordination in specific cases was itself lawful, thereby requiring explanation in its own right. His argument amounted to a novel answer to Kant's problem.

In brief, the factors presented by Martí regrettably provide insufficient ground for the omnibus rejection of the research programme in Piaget's epistemology.

Analysis: guiding principles for developmental science

In the following, I re-visit the six principles outlined in Martí's conclusion to clarify their interpretation within Piaget's epistemology, and to identify pointers for their further elaboration.

Epistemology of development

An epistemology is a theory of knowledge with three different kinds available: conceptual analysis, critical analysis, and scientific epistemology.[2] These kinds are similar in requiring a disciplinary contribution from philosophy, but dissimilar in the rest of their disciplinary requirements. Piaget (1924) named his theory of knowledge *epistémologie génétique*, usually translated as genetic epistemology, in line with Baldwin's *genetic theory of knowledge* (1906). To offset any confusion with the genetics of DNA, it is more transparently named *developmental epistemology* (Smith, 1996, 2009a), complementing the critical analysis of knowledge in adult science (Brunschwicg, 1922; Duhem, 1906; Meyerson, 1908). Here Piaget addressed the formation of knowledge through its history, for instance, during childhood. His basic question was, "how does knowledge grow, what is the mechanism of its growth?" (1929b, p. 152), and his answer comprised an explanation of "the development of knowledge by appealing to a central process of equilibration" (Piaget, 1985, p. 3). Thus his research programme was primarily epistemological about knowledge development, not psychological about children's development. Contrariwise, in evaluating his work, the relevance of psychological perspectives to epistemology has to be demonstrated, not merely asserted, still less assigned privileged status.

Two substantive implications stem from Piaget's epistemology. First, any conceptual analysis in epistemology is incomplete unless an empirical check is included on the origin and development of knowledge at levels of life other than adult levels. Typically, no version of conceptual analysis has included this kind of check. In this vein: "Platonic, rationalist or apriorist epistemologies suppose themselves to have found some fundamental instrument of knowledge that is extraneous, superior or prior to experience . . . . Such doctrines, though careful to characterise the properties which they attribute to this instrument . . . have omitted to verify that it was actually at the subject's disposal. Here whether we like it or not, is a question of fact" (Piaget in Smith, 1993, p. 7). All epistemic instruments make demands on knowers, and it is simply question begging to assume their availability throughout every population. A converse tendency is evident in psychologies where factual conclusions about knowledge are presented independently of conceptual/critical analysis (e.g., Carey, 2009; Spelke, Breinlinger, Macomber, & Jacobson, 1992; Wellman, 2002).

Second, any critical analysis is a step forward in requiring the re-analysis of scientific knowledge, yet a comparable omission recurs. Although Kuhn (1964) made approving references to the correspondence between his work on the history of science and Piaget's on the epistemic history of children, these were not systematically followed through. In general, three problems would have to be addressed (Piaget & Garcia, 1989): (1) Is there any continuity in epistemic histories from infants to savants? (2) Are there correspondences between the epistemic instruments in these sequences? (3) Is the form of these instruments invariant or a variable construction through their use? Piaget argued for continuity, correspondences, and construction, respectively. Falsifiability provides a test-case: defined through contraposition (an inference rule notoriously hard to control), falsifiability is difficult to master even by adolescents, with further constraints in causal and counter-factual reasoning (Barrouillet & Gauffroy, 2013; Johnson-Laird, 2006).

Interdisciplinarity

Piaget's epistemology required interdisciplinarity, a commitment evident in *Recherche* as a circle of sciences (1918), or better as a spiral admitting expansion in new directions (1924). Thus, interdisciplinarity was retained throughout (1985). It comprised integrated explanations by analogy with mathematical physics (1929b); psychology and logic, however, were required disciplines in an indicative list that was left intentionally open (1979).

An integrated explanation was required to explain the structure of action and thought from children to scientists. Its focus was holistic rather than atomistic, directed on "totalities in the serial levels of a child's logical development" (Piaget, 1921, p. 154). Piaget's epistemology required two elements: first, psychological evidence about children's reasons for their beliefs or judgments, i.e. reasons as criteria of the respects in which the structure of their action and thought is lawful or lawless; second, psychological laws to be checked against normative rules in a logical model. At issue was their goodness of fit, i.e. their degree of correspondence (1968). To that end, different systems of logic were used, since: "It is for the observer to find out and to analyse which structures do, and which do not, exist [*que les structures existent*] in the mind" (1973, p. 46*). Dual process theories of reasoning tend to downplay mental structure in favour of a conception of mind as a bunch of heuristics (Evans, 2008; Gigerenzer & Gaissmaier, 2011). Rational models of logic were not thereby officially denied; otherwise any route to rationality would be a dead-end.

Psychology made a required contribution to Piaget's epistemology by providing empirical evidence about mental functioning. Its unit of analysis comprised norms (rules), values, and meanings (1950a), all implying a public component in their factual applications, and thereby other disciplines. Piaget remarked that each kind of thinking (insane, infantile, primitive, mystical, etc.) was psychologically investigable, regardless of being true or false. For all these cases, the fundamental, epistemological question was: how does the notion of truth arrive at all? Piaget's one-word answer was: logic, standardly defined as the formal science of truth (1949; cf. Peirce, 1898; Wundt, 1883). Frege (1897), the founder of modern logic, had the same view, insisting on the difference between logic and psychological logic. When asked about a society whose psychological laws of thought were in flat contradiction with logical laws, yet accepted in theory and in practice, he answered: "we have here a hitherto unknown type of madness" (Frege, 1964, p. 14; commentary in Smith, 2006, 2009b). Piaget accepted this verdict with the reminder that his epistemology steered clear of dual fallacies, i.e. psychologism and logicism (1966). Furthermore, he accepted its consequence: that the application of (formal) logic in (factual) psychology was hypothetico-deductive (1923).

Explanatory non-reductionism

The part–whole distinction underlies different conceptions of the mind, the atomism of sensations (Mach, 1959), and the holism of gestalts (Köhler, 1959). An explanation of a gestalt solely by reference to its parts is illicit reductionism. Piaget's conception of mind was thus a version of holism: any scheme or structure was a central organ of the mind as "a gestalt with a history" (1953, p. 384*). The qualification attested plasticity and amelioration in the organization of the self: "what we call 'structure' amounts to this: it is a form or organisation of experience, and a form subject to endless revisions under the influence of success or failures due to reality" (Piaget, 1931, p. 149). Structures change endlessly in their use, and these changes are developmental if they consist "in regular or even sequential series of qualitative transformations guaranteeing progressive structuring" (1974, p. 6). In turn, differences in power between (weaker/stronger) structures are amenable to qualitative analysis in terms of their principles.

Psychological reductionism was defined by Piaget (1968) as the reduction of the mind's structural complexity to causal principles, whose three main variants were social, physicalist, or biological. His objections were twofold. From the perspective of the self, reality is complex due to the causality of its physical, biological, and social relationships, as Comte (1830) already acknowledged. Piaget went further, insisting on the normative complexity in their comprehension by a developing self. Second, causal principles provide factually indeterminate grounds of normatively necessary implications and obligations. Contemporary versions of the three variants are evident (e.g., Daniels, 2008; Thagard, 2005; Changeux, 2010). An open question is how each explains a commonality in the life of any person or in the history of science, the formation and development of structures bound by necessary relations.

Action, organization, development

A theory of truth should explain what a truth is true of, a hard problem about empirical truth, and harder still for logical truth (e.g., $A \Rightarrow A$). Piaget was not presenting a conceptual analysis of truth, but instead a scientific analysis of the formation of truth during childhood. His proposal was that its origin lay in action in advance of language (1918, p. 50; 1954, p. 360; cf. Goethe in Müller & Graves, this volume). Seemingly a non-starter about truth, this proposal is substantive. Piaget acknowledged that pre-linguistic infants cannot state truths (1953). Yet the logic of their actions contains properties with formal truths about, e.g., means–end relations and object conservation in terms of actions "yielding to norms of truth" (1954, p. 359). A key insight was realized by St. Anselm that doing something is always doing something to be the case; doing something means to bring about a fact, i.e. a truth-maker (Henry, 1964) – this insight has not been lost on Brandom (2000). Agents recognize the meaning of their own intentional actions, but this does not automatically extend to the rationality of the logic in their action coordination. Thus what is done is an indicator of what an agent regards as true, converting to a criterion of truth if and only if what is done is rational. Rationality in turn is intelligible through layers of meaning. Meaningful recognition requires reason, defined by Piaget as "one of the meanings of an object or event . . . a meaning that entails others through signifying implications" (2006, p. 7). Meanings link a reason to other reasons related by implications in exponential explosions, and reason-giving develops in the lives of any person, child, or scientist (Henriques, Dionnet, & Ducret, 2004). Actions are intelligible only through reasons, those of their agent, or those of other agents (von Wright, 1983).

Epigenesis

The notion of epigenesis was introduced by Aristotle (1943) as a living process generating the organization of novel structures. In his seminal analysis, emergence was teleologically directed to an end. Further, an end was not actually pre-existent, and yet potentially present in, for example, growth from nutritive seed to perceptual animal. In particular, he noticed that interpreting intellectual generation was especially difficult as the emergence of reason in embodied beings. Later on, a contrast was drawn between epigenesis and evolution as an unfolding mechanism based on preformation (Wolff, 1759). Currently, epigenesis is interpreted either inclusively, merging to become genetic/probabilistic processes (Karmiloff-Smith, 2007), or exclusively as the inter-dependent coordination of bio-social processes (Molenaar & Raijmakers, 2000).

Piaget's interpretation was exclusive: epistemic processes in each person, and in the history of science, were epigenetic as manifestations of the organization of the self (1950a). Their outcomes included novel kinds of structures of thought, without preformation (1950b). This process was not itself innate and, even though it depended on genetic enabling conditions, it was contrary to the central dogma in genetics since its information flow was bi-directional (1971, 1980). Manifestations included the "horizon" of an action scheme, notably through recursive feedback in negative judgment (1985). From the cradle to the grave, the self's intentionality of action was culturally contextualized interacting with other selves. "Human knowledge is essentially collective, and social life constitutes an essential factor in the formation and growth of knowledge, both pre-scientific and scientific" (1950a, p. 187)

A paradigm case was the development of necessary knowledge (see Smith, 2009a, p. 69). Any necessary truth is knowable *a priori*. The analysis of apriority continues to be a major outstanding problem in epistemology (Casullo, 2011), although in psychology it has attracted almost zero attention (cf. Moshman, 2015). To the best of my knowledge, the sole exception is Piaget's work (1921, 1971). His starting-point was Kant, who interpreted the generation of *a priori* categories not as evolution, but as epigenesis (1933, 2000). Piaget agreed, provided the two senses of temporal and logical priority in Kant's analysis were separated (1971; cf. Smith, 2010). That is, children's understanding of the necessity of an *a priori* judgment was neither innate nor ready-made in early life (e.g., Leibniz,

Chomsky), but was instead emergent from their applications of more advanced structures, A good example was the advance from non-conservation to conservation based on an "*a priori* analytic deduction" (Piaget, 1952b, p. 18). The classical factors of biology and society were required as necessary conditions, but denied to be sufficient for advances due to "joint organic and behavioral self-regulations [*autorégulations*] that determine this epigenesis" (1980, p. 31*).

Methodological diversity

A psychology consisting in experimental tasks is vulnerable to two deficiencies: a method is neither a theory, nor a methodology, i.e. theory of scientific knowledge. Piaget's psychology was a contribution to methodology devoid of these deficiencies. He repeatedly referred to his "experiments" (1922, 1952a) that have attracted polarized comments both as paragons of reliability (Gelman, 1979), and as not being "proper" experiments (Elkind, 1971).

Piaget's experiments had a tenable rationale. His "clinical [*clinique*] method" (1929a, p.2) was used during the 1920s for the diagnosis of belief and attendant logic of thought. From the 1930s onwards, it was recast as a "critical [*critique*] method" (1947, p. 7) for the diagnosis of judgment and attendant logic of action (1950b[3]). About any belief, re-visit his question about truth in that it can always be asked, "Why believe that?" The answer "No reason, I just do" is admissible, but epistemically suspect: if the belief is correct, how does this believer understand its truth? And if it is incorrect, how is its falsity demarcated from truth? A comparable question can always be raised about judgment, but the same answer is self-refuting. A singleton judgment is a contradiction in terms since to judge is to assert something to be true/false. A reason for a judgment makes explicit its relations with other judgments through the logical relations of implication, contradiction, and the like (1949, 2006). Piaget was arguing that the origin of judgment-making was in infants' actions (cf. 1953, p. 410), later recast serially in children's acts of judgment. To that end, logic was required as the formal science of truth along with psychology for evidence about extent of correspondences: re-visit the three issues identified by Piaget and Garcia. Merely asking veracity questions is indeterminate (e.g., Gathercole, Pickering, Ambridge, & Wearing, 2004): a person's reasons comprise the grounds for recognizing a truth, its meaning as a truth, and its necessary implications for the infinitude of other truths/falsehoods. Thus, ascertaining reasons requires constraints on experimentation relevant to a scientific epistemology.

Ambiguity of test/task invariance

Repeating the same procedure for presenting a problem to everyone in a sample does not guarantee its semantic identity throughout anyone's train of thought. Piaget argued that the self has dual properties, spontaneity and novelty (1918, 1929a). Their emergent manifestations include both irrationalities and new forms of reasoning (1947), even if both originated through reasons. Instances of this duality are not predictable in advance in human history, neither in science, nor in any person. Consequently, an experimental design has to include non-standardized elements that are activated "live" in dialogical exchanges.

Twin pre-conditions of full standardization, ne varietur [let nothing vary]

Piaget and Inhelder argued that full standardization had two pre-conditions, that "we know in advance what we want to get from any child and believe we are capable of interpreting the obtained responses" (1961, p. xii). They added that neither was met in experimentation in epistemology. The first pre-condition concerned the spontaneity and novelty of the self, both inherently unpredictable. The second concerned the development of novel structures in the mental acts invoked in their expression. No structure has been predictable in the history of science, e.g. Riemann's geometry from Euclid's; and "childhood is the maximum creative time in the life of a human being" (Piaget, 1972, p. 228).

Logic of action

Piaget's "critical method" required questions to be asked concurrently with, or consequent to, specific actions. First, he argued that the logic of action coordination during infancy was temporally prior to a logic of language (1950b). He also argued that a logic of action was epistemically prior as a necessary, but not sufficient, condition of a logic of thought. By way of illustration (1947), he referred to his studies of classification and transitivity that did not (1928), and that did (1952b), respect his argument. Acts of judgment, manifest in action or in thought, are intentional without the logic of their coordination having to be consciously explicit to their agent; in other words, fuller conscious realization is a later development.[4]

Conclusion

Currently, Piaget's epistemology is widely disregarded. This is a self-fulfilling prophecy in view of the practices of journal editors and developmentalists content with, first and foremost, *ignoratio elenchi* in converting Piaget to a straw-man; uncritical trust in caricatures of his position; reducing empirical to empiricist psychology; conflating psychology and epistemology; replacing hard problems by more tractable successors; unwitting reliance on ubiquitous mistranslation; and abstaining from reading Piaget on affective instead of intelligent grounds.

My analysis is intended to show how six principles in Piaget's epistemology could make distinctive contributions to advances in developmental science. It turns out that connections with complementary work elsewhere abound. The potential is there; its actualization is another matter.[5]

Notes

1 An asterisk * indicates a personally amended translation.
2 *Conceptual analysis* involves an analysis of the concept of knowledge through criteria linked to allied notions − e.g. justified true belief (Plato, 2014), *a priori* categories (Kant, 1933). The focus is on criteria for possession of knowledge as opposed to belief, intuition, perception, etc. The analysis is intended to cover all knowledge independently of any scientific discipline. Contemporary surveys (Audi, 2010) attest major disagreement, though an exception is that knowledge implies the truth of what is known − no truth, no knowledge (Moser, 1999). *Critical analysis* refers to the analysis of knowledge through its development in the history of science. Not all cases of knowledge in the history of science can be true since contradictory theories abound, and scientific revolutions usually comprise contrary paradigms. A methodological criterion is falsifiability: knowledge true of reality has to be refutable, irrespective of its truth's verifiability. Its later generalization covered all knowledge from the amoeba to Einstein (Popper, 1979). Its adequacy has proved to be ambiguous and controversial (Feyerabend, 2010; Kuhn, 1970; Lakatos, 1970; Maxwell, 2005). *Scientific epistemology* includes positivism (Comte, 1830), phenomenology (Husserl, 1965), and dialectics (Cornforth, 1963). They share a feature characterized by Piaget as the conversion of an epistemology of science into "an epistemology which thereby seemed to me really scientific" (1952a). Recall that, in the citation to his Distinguished Scientific Contribution award, Piaget was acknowledged for creating an "epistemology as a science" (APA, 1970).
3 He augmented his rationale in two short papers (1947; Piaget & Inhelder, 1961); neither in English translation, but reviewed in Smith (1993, 2002).
4 The interpretation of the logic of rules in Piaget's epistemology has affinities with their interpretation in Wittgenstein's (1958) rule-following paradox (Smith, 2009b). No rule, even in mathematics, is ready-made with a complete specification, but is instead capable of variable re-constitution in its applications. This issue has received scant attention in psychology, as too have constraints on experimentation with epistemological relevance.
5 Companion work on Piaget's evidence is in Smith (2014), and on his ideas in Smith (in preparation).
6 The first edition of this book was published in French with the same title in 1941, and translated in English in 1974 as: Piaget, J. & Inhelder, B. (1974). *The child's construction of quantities*. London, UK: Routledge & Kegan Paul.

References

APA (1970). Distinguished Scientific Contribution awards 1969: Jean Piaget. *American Psychologist, 25*, 65–79.

Aristotle (1943). *Generation of animals*. Cambridge, MA: Harvard University Press.

Audi, R. (2010). *A contemporary introduction to the theory of knowledge* (3rd ed.). London, UK: Routledge.

Baldwin, J. M. (1906). *Thought and things*, Vol. 1. London, UK: Swan Sonnenschein.

Barrouillet, P. & Gauffroy, C. (2013). *The development of thinking and reasoning*. London, UK: Psychology Press.

Boom, J. (2009). Piaget on equilibration. In U. Müller, J. Carpendale, & L. Smith (Eds.), *Cambridge companion to Piaget* (pp. 132–149). Cambridge, UK: Cambridge University Press.

Brandom, R. B. (2000). *Articulating reasons: An introduction to inferentialism*. Cambridge, MA: Harvard University Press.

Brunschwicg, L. (1922). *L'expérience humaine de la causalité physique* [The human experience of physical causality]. Paris, France: Alcan.

Carey, S. (2009). *The origin of concepts*. New York, NY: Oxford University Press.

Casullo, A. (2011). *A priori* knowledge. Retrieved May 22, 2015 from: http://www.oxford-bibliographies.com

Chandler, M. (2009). Commentary: Piaget on Piaget. *British Journal of Psychology*, *100*, 225–228.

Changeux, J.-P. (2010). *Du vrai, du beau, du bien* [On truth, beauty, goodness]. Paris, France: Odile Jacob.

Comte, A. (1830). *Cours de philosophie positive* [Course on positive philosophy]. Paris, France: Hermann.

Cornforth, M. (1963). *Dialectical materialism: Volume 3 Theory of knowledge*. London, UK: Lawrence & Wishart.

Daniels, H. (2008). *Vygotsky and research*. London, UK: Routledge.

Duhem, P. (1906). *La théorie physique, son objet et sa structure* [Physical theory, its object and structure]. Paris, France: Chevalier et Rivièr.

Elkind, D. (1971). Two approaches to intelligence: Piagetian and Psychometric. In D. R. Green, M. P. Ford, & G. B. Flamer (Eds.), *Measurement and Piaget* (pp. 12–28). New York, NY: McGraw-Hill.

Evans, J. S. (2008). Dual-processing accounts of reasoning, judgment, and social cognition. *Annual Review of Psychology*, *59*, 255–278.

Feyerabend, P. K. (2010). *Against method* (3rd ed.). London, UK: Verso.

Flavell, J. H. (1996). Piaget's legacy. *Psychological Science*, *7*, 200–202.

Frege, G. (1897). Logic. In G. Frege (1979), *Posthumous writings* (pp. 126–151). Oxford, UK: Blackwell.

Frege, G. (1964). *The basic laws of arithmetic*. Berkeley, CA: University of California Press.

Gathercole, S. E., Pickering, S. J., Ambridge, B., & Wearing, H. (2004). The structure of working memory from 5 to 15 years of age. *Developmental Psychology*, *40*, 177–190.

Gelman, R. (1979). Why we will continue to read Piaget. Paper presented at the meeting of the Society for Research in Child Development, San Francisco, CA.

Gigerenzer, G. & Gaissmaier, W. (2011). Heuristic decision making. *Annual Review of Psychology*, *62*, 451–482.

Henriques, G., Dionnet, S., & Ducret, J.-J. (2004). *La formation des raisons: Étude sur l'épistémogenèse* [The formation of reasons: study of epistemogenesis]. Sprimont, Belgium: Mardaga.

Henry, D. P. (1964). *The De Grammatico* [*On grammar*] *of St Anselm*. Notre Dame, IN: University of Notre Dame Press.

Husserl, E. (1965). *Phenomenology and the crisis of philosophy*. New York, NY: Harper Torchbooks.

Inhelder, B. (1971). Developmental theory and diagnostic procedures. In D. G. Green, M. P. Ford, & G. B. Falmer (Eds.), *Measurement and Piaget* (pp. 148–167). New York, NY: McGraw Hill.

Johnson-Laird, P. N. (2006). *How we reason*. Oxford, UK: Oxford University Press.

Kant, I. (1933). *Critique of pure reason* (2nd ed.). London, UK: Macmillan.

Kant, I. (2000). *Critique of the power of judgment*. Cambridge, UK: Cambridge University Press.

Karmiloff-Smith, A. (2007). Atypical epigenesis. *Developmental Science*, *10*, 84–88.

Köhler, W. (1959). Gestalt psychology today. *American Psychologist, 14*, 727–734.

Kuhn, T. S. (1964). A function for thought experiments. In T. S. Kuhn (1977) *The essential tension* (pp. 240–265). Chicago, IL: University of Chicago Press.

Kuhn, T. S. (1970). *The structure of scientific revolutions* (2nd enlarged ed.). Chicago, IL: University of Chicago Press.

Lakatos, I. (1970). Falsification and the methodology of scientific research programmes. In I. Lakatos & A. Musgrave (1972). *Criticism and the growth of knowledge*, corrected edition (pp. 91–196). Cambridge, UK: Cambridge University Press.

Le Dantec, F. (1912). *La science de la vie* [Science of life]. Paris, France: Flammarion.

Lévy-Bruhl, L. (1922). *La mentalité primitive* [Primitive mentality]. Paris, France: Alcan.

Mach, E. (1959). *The analysis of sensations*. New York, NY: Dover.

Maxwell, N. (2005). Popper, Kuhn, Lakatos, and aim-oriented empiricism. *Philosophia, 32*, 181–239.

Messerly, J. (1996). *Piaget's conception of evolution*. Lanham, MD: Rowman & Littlefield.

Meyerson, E. (1908). *Réalité et identité* [Reality and identity]. Paris, France: Alcan.

Molenaar, P. C. M. & Raijmakers, M. (2000). A causal interpretation of Piaget's theory of cognitive development: Reflections on the relationship between epigenesis and nonlinear dynamics. *New Ideas in Psychology, 18*, 41–55.

Moser, P. K. (1999). Epistemology. In R. Audi (Ed.). *The Cambridge dictionary of philosophy*, 2nd edition (pp. 80–88). Cambridge, UK: Cambridge University Press.

Moshman, D. (2015). *Epistemic cognition and development: The psychology of justification and truth*. New York, NY: Psychology Press.

Niaz, M. (1998). The epistemological significance of Piaget's developmental stages: A Lakatosian interpretation. *New Ideas in Psychology, 16*, 47–59.

Peirce, C. S. (1898). Logic: dispute between Nominalists and Realists. Retrieved May 8, 2015 from: http://www.helsinki.fi/science/commens/terms/logicnarrow.html

Piaget, J. (1918). *Recherche* [Search]. Lausanne, Switzerland: La Concorde.

Piaget, J. (1921). Une forme verbale de la comparaison chez l'enfant [A verbal form of comparison in children]. *Archives de Psychologie, 18*, 141–172.

Piaget, J. (1922). Essai sur la multiplication logique et les débuts de la notion de partie chez l'enfant [Report on logical multiplication and the origins of the notion of part in children]. *Journal de psychologie normale et pathologique, 19*, 222–261.

Piaget, J. (1923). La psychologie des valeurs religieuses [Psychology of religious values]. Association Chrétienne d'Etudiants de la Suisse Romande. *Sainte-Croix 1922* (pp. 38–82). Lausanne, Switzerland: La Concorde.

Piaget, J. (1924). Etude critique: *L'expérience humaine et la causalité physique* de L. Brunschwicg [Critical notice: Human experience and physical causality]. *Journal de psychologie normale et pathologique, 21*, 586–607.

Piaget, J. (1928). Les trois systèmes de la pensée de l'enfant [Children's three systems of thought]. *Bulletin de la Société française de philosophie, 28*, 97–141.

Piaget, J. (1929a). *The child's conception of the world*. London, UK: Routledge & Kegan Paul.

Piaget, J. (1929b). Les deux directions de la pensée scientifique [The dual directions of the scientific thought]. *Archives des sciences physiques et naturelles, 134*, 145–162.

Piaget, J. (1931). Le développement intellectuel chez les jeunes enfants [Intellectual development in young children]. *Mind, 40*, 137–160.

Piaget, J. (1947). Avant-propos de la troisième édition. *Le jugement et le raisonnement chez l'enfant* [Foreword to the 3rd edition. Judgment and reasoning in the child] (pp. 5–10). Paris, France: Delachaux et Niestlé.

Piaget, J. (1949). *Traité de logique* [Treatise on logic]. Paris, France: Colin.

Piaget, J. (1950a). *Introduction à l'épistémologie génétique. Tome I. La pensée mathématique* [Introduction to developmental epistemology. Tome I. Mathematical thought]. Paris, France: Presses Universitaires de France.

Piaget, J. (1950b). *Introduction à l'épistémologie génétique. Tome III. La pensée biologique, la pensée psychologique, et la pensée sociologique* [Introduction to developmental epistemology. Tome III. Biological thought, psychological thought, sociological thought]. Paris, France: Presses Universitaires de France.

Piaget, J. (1952a). Autobiography. In C. Murchison (Ed.), *History of psychology in autobiography*, Vol. 4 (pp. 237–256). New York, NY: Russell & Russell.

Piaget, J. (1952b). *The child's conception of number*. London, France: Routledge & Kegan Paul.

Piaget, J. (1953). *The origins of intelligence in the child*. London, UK: Routledge & Kegan Paul.

Piaget, J. (1954). *Construction of reality in the child*. New York, NY: Basic Books.

Piaget, J. (1966). Part II. In E. Beth & J. Piaget (Eds.), *Mathematical epistemology and psychology* (pp. 131–304). Dordrecht, Netherlands: Reidel.

Piaget, J. (1968). Explanation in psychology and psychophysiological parallelism. In J. Piaget & P. Fraisse (Eds.), *Experimental psychology, its scope and method*. Vol. 1, *History and method* (pp. 153–192). London, UK: Routledge & Kegan Paul.

Piaget, J. (1971). *Biology and knowledge*. Edinburgh, UK: Edinburgh University Press.

Piaget, J. (1972). Creativity. In J. M. Gallagher & D. K. Reid (1981). *The learning theory of Piaget and Inhelder* (pp. 221–229). Monterey, CA: Brooks/Cole.

Piaget, J. (1973). *Main trends in psychology*. London, UK: George Allen & Unwin.

Piaget, J. (1974). *The place of the sciences of man in the system of sciences*. New York, NY: Harper Torchbooks.

Piaget, J. (1979). Relations between psychology and other sciences. *Annual Review of Psychology*, *30*, 1–8.

Piaget, J. (1980). The psychogenesis of knowledge and its epistemological significance. In M. Piattelli-Palmarini (Ed.), *Language and learning: The debate between Jean Piaget and Noam Chomsky* (pp. 23–34). London, UK: Routledge & Kegan Paul.

Piaget, J. (1985). *Equilibration of cognitive structures*. Chicago, IL: University of Chicago Press.

Piaget, J. (2006). Reason. *New Ideas in Psychology*, *24*, 1–29.

Piaget, J. & Garcia, R. (1989). *Psychogenesis and the history of science*. New York, NY: Columbia University Press.

Piaget, J. & Inhelder, B. (1961). Introduction à la seconde edition [Introduction to the second edition]. In J. Piaget & B. Inhelder (1962). *Le développement des quantités physiques chez l'enfant* [The development of physical quantities in children], 2nd edition (pp. ix–xxvii). Neuchâtel: Delachaux et Niestlé.[6]

Piattelli-Palmarini, M. (1994). Ever since language and learning: Afterthoughts on the Piaget Chomsky debate. *Cognition*, *50*, 315–346.

Plato (2014). *Theaetetus* (J. McDowell, trans.). Oxford, UK: Oxford University Press.

Popper, K. (1979). *Objective knowledge: An evolutionary approach*. Oxford, UK: Oxford University Press.

Smith, L. (1993). *Necessary knowledge: Piagetian perspectives on constructivism.* Hove, UK: Lawrence Erlbaum Associates.

Smith, L. (1996). Conclusion: Piaget's epistemology. In L. Smith (Ed.), *Critical readings on Piaget* (pp. 478–521). London, UK: Routledge.

Smith, L. (2002). *Reasoning by mathematical induction in children's arithmetic.* Oxford: Pergamon Press.

Smith, L. (2006). Norms and normative facts in human development. In L. Smith & J. Vonèche (Eds.), *Norms in human development* (pp. 103–137). Cambridge, UK: Cambridge University Press.

Smith, L. (2009a). Piaget's developmental epistemology. In U. Müller, J. Carpendale, & L. Smith (Eds.), *Cambridge companion to Piaget* (pp. 64–93). Cambridge, UK: Cambridge University Press.

Smith, L. (2009b). Wittgenstein's rule-following paradox: How to resolve it with lessons for psychology. *New Ideas in Psychology, 27*, 228–242.

Smith, L. (2010). Knowledge *a priori*: From Plato and Kant to Piaget. In E. Nairz-Wirth (Ed.), *Aus der Bildungsgesichte lernen* (pp. 135–147). Vienna, Austria: Erhard Löcker.

Smith, L. (2014), Jean Piaget. Annotated bibliography, Childhood Studies. Retrieved May 8, 2015 from: http://www.oxfordbibliographies.com

Smith, L. (in preparation). Piaget's developmental epistemology. Cambridge, UK: Cambridge University Press.

Spelke, E., Breinlinger, K., Macomber, J., & Jacobson, K. (1992). Origins of knowledge. *Psychological Review, 99*(4), 605–632. DOI: 10.1037/0033-295X.99.4.605.

Thagard, M. (2005). *Mind: Introduction to cognitive science* (2nd ed.). Cambridge, MA: MIT Press.

Wellman, H. M. (2002). Understanding the psychological world: Developing a theory of mind. In U. Goswami (Ed.), *Blackwell handbook of childhood cognitive development* (pp. 167–187). Oxford, UK: Blackwell.

Wittgenstein, L. (1958). *Philosophical investigations* (2nd ed.). Oxford, UK: Blackwell.

Wolff, C. F. (1759). *Theoria generationis.* Halle an der Saale, Germany: Typis et sumtu Io. Christ. Hendel.

Wright, G. H. von (1983). *Practical reason.* Oxford, UK: Basil Blackwell.

Wundt, W. (1883). *Logik, eine Untersuchung der Prinzipien der Erkenntnis und der Methoden Wissenschaftlicher Forschung.* Vol. 2, Methodenlehre [Logic, an investigation of the principles of knowledge and methods of scientific discovery. Vol. 2. Methodology]. Stuttgart, Germany: Verlag von Ferdinand Enke.

Time is of the essence

From the estimation of single points to the description of functions

Felipe Munoz-Rubke

Of the several topics present in Toomela's chapter (this volume), in this commentary I will focus on only two of them. First, Toomela claims that it is impossible to understand the mind/brain without resorting to developmental accounts. Thinking along the same lines, in the first part of this chapter I propose that taking the variable time into consideration, and therefore estimating change, is the most fruitful way to study brain and mental processes together. In the second part, I move into recent advances in neuroimaging methods. By doing this, I show that we can also obtain valuable information about mental processes by evaluating changes in brain structure and function.

On time

The position of Toomela is crystal clear: we cannot learn anything about the mind/ brain if we do not look at its development. In his conceptualization, this involves describing a dynamic system of interacting components creating a whole, which has qualities that cannot be captured by studying the system's elements in isolation. At the same time, he rejects the notion that development could be studied as a description of cause–effect relationships, where it is irrelevant whether we look at long sequences or at separate events. Although I partially agree with his argument, my own perspective is more moderate since I do not consider non-developmental studies to be worthless, uninformative works. Even if those studies cannot provide us with a comprehensive account of mental phenomena, the accumulation of such scientific evidence ultimately gives us access to tentative and reasonable approximations.

Let us first introduce a graphical representation in order to expand on this idea. Imagine that our psychological phenomenon of interest follows a non-linear function $f(x) = x^2$, which has a U-shaped representation when considering positive and negative values for x. The x-axis is given by time, while the y-axis represents our phenomenon of interest. Provided that the x-axis cannot really assume negative values, since something like negative age does not exist, we deal with an increasing function starting at 0 and moving into higher values. A group of imaginary researchers interested in studying this phenomenon are not aware of this basic truth, and so they decide to conduct an initial cross-sectional experiment. Under the assumption that their methods are appropriate, their results represent something like a single point in our Cartesian coordinate system. It is unlikely that such a single point is exactly on the path described by the function due to an estimation error, but we will assume that it is close enough. However, regardless of how close the observation point may be to the function, a point cannot provide us with the same information that is conveyed by the function itself. In contrast to this isolated estimation, functions give us the highly desirable possibility of predicting what may come next—and what has come before—given the current position. A single cross-sectional study, however, does not provide enough data points to infer previous or future conditions; that is its main limitation.

Nevertheless, cross-sectional investigations are not totally uninformative, as Toomela (this volume) claims. Through their accumulation we amalgamate several estimates of our phenomenon of interest, presumably at different points in the developmental trajectory. By plotting those points together, we bring forth a more informed approximation to the underlying function. Logically, approximating a function by means of several discrete points can never be as good as accessing the function itself, unless the distance between points is infinitesimal. However, something like this is unmistakably impossible with cross-sectional studies. Indeed, it is unattainable with any type of study design. The closest we can get to this ideal is by means of longitudinal studies, given that by estimating changes of the same people we significantly reduce the error variance thanks to the participants' autocorrelation—a person is more similar to itself, at the next time point, than to anybody else.

Thus, based on the assumption that there are multiple ways to gather information about the mind/brain, what I want to suggest here is that studies and experiments do give us privileged access to essential information *whenever they consider the time it takes for a psychological process to manifest itself, and to change from one psychological state (moment) to the next.*[1] Hence, it is only through appropriate timescales that we can capture the unfolding of certain phenomena and the dynamic interplay of their constituents. Different phenomena demand different timescales. To study how adults shift their gaze as a reaction to unexpected events, it would be appropriate to design a study where unexpected events happen over a short period while eye gaze positions are estimated several times per second. In contrast, in order to understand how children learn to read, it would be more reasonable to design a longitudinal study over several months/years, during which we could observe how different psychological factors interact to allow a person to acquire such a skill.

If that is the situation, it would seem that all studies, irrespective of their design, take time into consideration. However, this is not exactly true. Studies may estimate a variable without providing instances for the psychological phenomenon to manifest itself. For instance, whenever we measure performance on mathematical problem solving, or ask a subject to complete a survey, time is not a variable of interest. Even if we do measure how much time it takes someone to solve those problems, or participants provide self-reports, we are not really studying the temporal dynamics involved in these processes. Such studies usually generate limited information for understanding the mind/brain because they involve a measurement of conditions or states that they assume to be fixed—and can be represented just by estimating a set of parameters. Thus, by calculating a person's score on a test we might get an estimation of the parameter related to that person's skills, but we do not get very much on how that person actually solved those problems.[2]

Another criticism involves the selection of the appropriate temporal scale of analysis. Resuming our hypothetical example, someone could argue that the reaction to unexpected events in a single experimental situation does not give us enough information to understand such processes. Then, multiple measures are suggested as a better alternative. Yet the problem with such an argument is that it could be extended ad infinitum. That is why the criterion needs to be defined both in terms of the scientific question of interest and the expectations we have about the application of our results (i.e. what are we going to do with them).

To close this section, I would like to summarize what I have said so far as two preliminary conclusions: (1) the best way to understand the brain/mind is through carefully considering the timescale in our experimental designs; (2) scientific knowledge can only approximate the nature of underlying processes by means of an everlasting gathering of information.

Can our knowledge of the brain inform our knowledge of mental processes?

Toomela considers that we need to understand the nervous system in order to fully understand the mind. However, as he suggests, that does not mean that any type of knowledge suffices for that purpose. For instance, mapping a psychological process to a unique brain region is just partially informative. Answering the "where" question alone provides useful information to the neurosurgeon, but it might not tell us much about the psychological process itself. However, by complementing that knowledge with the information of "which" areas or components interact to instantiate brain networks, together with the dimension of "when" those components are taking part in such process, a different picture emerges.[3]

The idea I put forward here is that when localizations, interactions, and temporal dynamics are all taken into account, we get an understanding of the brain that informs our knowledge of mental processes better. Once again, timing is crucial, since we need to investigate how those dynamics unfold throughout time periods relevant to our phenomena of interest. On a more practical level, I will suggest that those questions will be better answered if we transition from studies focusing on the localization of function and move into analyzing the brain as a dynamic complex network. In order to introduce the latter idea, I review a little bit of the history of neuroscience.

The brain as (is) a network

Two contending perspectives on brain organization have been present in the history of neuroscience over the last 200 years. One underscores the functional specialization of segregated brain areas, with each region in charge of an exclusive task. This point of view has been called localizationism. An opposite frame of reference highlights the functioning of the brain as an undivided system, where no division of labor takes place. For instance, Flourens (1824) proposed his aggregate field theory after observing that the brain reorganizes itself after injury—something we now call neuroplasticity. This theory suggested that, after sustaining damage, the initially diminished mental capacities could be partially or even totally recovered because the brain as a whole could take over the functions. This second point of view has been called holism.

Thanks to the work of Jackson (1884), Broca (1861), and Wernicke (1874)—among others—the pendulum swung towards the localizationist or functional segregation perspective, as it is called now. Since then, this approach has dominated the field and even today it is the default theoretical frame when it comes to understand brain functioning (Kanwisher, 2010). Despite this, certain concerns addressed by the holistic perspective have not been forgotten but rather incorporated into a new paradigm. This new theoretical account emphasizing brain connectivity is an alternative to the apparently irreconcilable localizationist and holistic positions. It combines the ideas of local specialization and global organization by modeling the brain in terms of networks (Rubinov & Sporns, 2010). Thus, the brain is conceptualized as a large-scale network comprising a set of functionally discrete areas, each having their own roles, that are nonetheless integrated (Friston, 2011; van den Heuvel & Hulshoff Pol, 2010; Wig, Schlaggar, & Petersen, 2011). Then, information is not only analyzed within specialized modules in the segmented regions, but is also transferred among them.

So far, three different characterizations of brain connectivity have been defined (Friston, 1994, 2011): structural, functional, and effective. *Structural* connectivity pertains to the physical, biological substrate of the network: according to the level of description, the nodes might be neurons, neuronal assemblies, or brain regions, and the edges might be individual axons or tracts connecting the nodes. *Functional* connectivity describes statistical dependencies—in terms of correlations, coherence, or transfer entropy—between brain nodes (Friston, 2011). We start with the assumption that each region presents a pattern of involvement given a specific context or situation. When activity from all nodes is considered together,[4] statistical patterns of co-participation in the temporal domain might be found. Those patterns are what we call functional connectivity. According to Friston (2011), functional connectivity does not rest on any model and it is essentially descriptive since there are only two possible alternatives: either a pair of nodes shows statistical dependency or not. In turn, effective connectivity models the flow of information within a network. Instead of just describing the dependencies between areas, as functional connectivity approaches do, the focus is on the chain of influences between regions. Due to the complexity of the topic, from now on we will focus on structural and functional connectivity only.[5]

Changes in structural and functional connectivity

Structural and functional connectivity are different ways to study localizations, interactions, and temporal dynamics. For instance, by studying transformations in structure, we tackle the localization issue. We do this by assessing how changes in gray and white matter relate to the acquisition of new skills or the involvement in new experiences. For instance, Draganski et al. (2004) used voxel-based morphometry[6] to assess brain changes in participants learning a juggling routine over a period of 3 months. The comparison to a group of non-jugglers indicated bilateral changes in V5, which is a visual motor area.

Focusing on structural connectivity can also help us to understand how interactions might occur as well. After all, we can expect structurally connected areas to be more functionally connected to each other, and for the structural architecture to partially restrict the pattern of those interactions. Research by Honey et al. (2009) supports this idea by showing that human resting-state functional connectivity and structural connectivity are more strongly related in regions with stronger structural connections.

Functional connectivity also attempts to answer the same problems. In this vein, recent studies have focused on functional brain networks under contexts of both cognitive task and resting-state (van der Heuvel & Hulshoff Pol, 2010), thus providing insights about interactions and long-term temporal dynamics. A good example is a study conducted by Bassett et al. (2015), in which they ran 4 fMRI scans in a period of 6 weeks while participants learned a complicated visually guided motor task. Throughout those training weeks, the participants went from a naïve to an expert level of achievement. Interestingly, the interactions between the motor and visual areas were considerably decreased as a function of task expertise. In other words, motor and visual functions became more autonomous from each other due to visual–motor practice on a specific task. These results suggest that the brain goes from an initial state of global integration to a later stage of higher specialization when dealing with complicated motor tasks.

Yet, why is brain connectivity useful for our understanding of mental processes? In any network, we define the components and the links among those components. If you look at those elements and their links at relevant timescales, as was suggested in the first section, then you have the chance to observe the dynamics of a process. If you observe dynamics, you can begin to evaluate contributions. In other words, given some knowledge concerning the standard function of brain regions—as revealed by studies of functional specialization—and the interactions among those areas, we can suggest that the psychological phenomenon of interest is made up from the reciprocal non-linear action of those multiple components. For instance, as in the study of Bassett et al. (2015), we could hypothesize that motor expertise is based on the partial autonomy of motor and visual elements, which nonetheless need to interact intensively during initial stages of learning. Another example comes from studies linking language and action, where Hauk, Johnsrude, and Pulvermuller (2004) showed that understanding action verbs elicits patterns of activity in frontal areas, including the premotor and primary motor cortices. These results suggest that language understanding may not be circumscribed to the canonical language brain regions, but supplemented by other components as well.

Once again, when looking at the appropriate timescale, we are provided with a more comprehensive account. That is exactly what James and Swain (2010) did. They taught novel verbs to children by making use of 3D novel objects and actions. All children took part in the following two conditions: one where they were allowed to perform an action on an object themselves (active); another where they observed how the experimenter performed an action on an object (passive). In both situations, a researcher provided them the novel verb describing the action. Following the training session, the children were tested on their understanding of the novel verbs to ensure their comprehension of the terms. A subsequent fMRI session was conducted. Children were presented with the newly learned words, new unlearned words, photographs of learned objects, and photographs of unlearned objects; they performed no actions inside the scanner. It was found that motor areas were activated for the newly learned verbs only when the verbs were learned through the active condition. With respect to pictures, both actively manipulated objects and passively observed objects generated significant activation in the left precentral gyrus (M1). However, the greater engagement was observed for the former rather than for the latter. The authors concluded that self-generated actions accounted for the recruitment of motor regions in the case of auditory stimuli, but that both active and passive object perception could generate—to a different degree—the involvement of motor regions as well. James and Swain's (2010) experiment makes it evident that the core of action verbs is not only visual, but also motor,[7] thus providing us with valuable information about the mental process behind verb learning. Following this, I wonder if it would be possible to derive such conclusion from behavioral studies alone.

Conclusions

In this commentary, I have emphasized the importance of considering the time it takes for a mental phenomenon of interest to manifest itself and the ability of neuroscience and its methods to enrich our understanding of its unfolding. Toomela suggests that we can only understand the mind through developmental accounts. Connected to that, I have proposed that conducting studies at relevant timescales could better allow us to study the non-linear dynamic interactions among a phenomenon's constituents. In the case of studying the human mind/brain phenomena, the physical reality of the brain is a crucial element, as Toomela points out. Here, I have suggested that estimating changes in brain connectivity significantly informs our understanding of mental processes, providing us with explanations for behaviors that are grounded within the physical constraints of the organism, and that could not be inferred from behavioral studies alone. In spite of the level of complexity we might face, that is the pathway that can take us to a higher level of understanding of the mind/brain.

Notes

1 Here I want to focus on the concept of time more than on concepts like development and maturation. In spite of its importance, which factors and how they influence change belong to a different discussion (Johnson & de Haan, 2010).
2 I am not claiming that evaluations that do not take time into consideration are not useful. They can serve multiple purposes, like deciding which topics should be taught in a classroom. Instead, what I am suggesting is that they do not provide much information on the psychological processes behind the performance.
3 The "how" problem is also crucial since it is connected to the mechanisms of change in the brain. Long-term potentiation (LTP) and long-term depression (LTD) are fundamental to addressing this issue, but they cannot be covered here.
4 To be more precise, all the information is analyzed at the same time when using multivariate methods (e.g. PCA, ICA). In turn, univariate analyses of connectivity are conducted voxel by voxel.
5 See Stephan and Friston (2010) and Friston (2011) to learn more about effective connectivity. See also Goldenberg and Galván (2015) to learn more about effective connectivity in the developing brain.
6 VBM is not a method of structural connectivity per se. However, because networks are made up of both nodes and edges, looking at changes at level of nodes also informs our models of structural networks.
7 However, this remains an open debate, as some critics have been directed towards the interpretation of sensorimotor activation as an important component of language understanding (see Mahon & Caramazza, 2008).

References

Bassett, D. S., Yang, M., Wymbs, N. F., & Grafton, S. T. (2015). Learning-induced autonomy of sensorimotor systems. *Nature Neuroscience*, *18*(5), 744–751.

Broca, P. (1861). Remarques sur le siege de la faculté du langage articulé, suivies d'une observation d'aphémie (perte de la parole) [Remarks on the seat of the faculty of articulated language, following an observation of aphemia (loss of speech)]. *Bulletin de la Societé Anatomique*, *36*, 330–357.

Draganski, B., Gaser, C., Busch, V., Schuierer, G., Bogdahn, U., & May, A. (2004). Neuroplasticity: Changes in grey matter induced by training. *Nature*, *427*, 311–312.

Flourens, P. (1824). *Recherches expérimentales sur les propriétés et les fonctions du système nerveux, dans les animaux vertébrés* [Experimental studies of the properties and functions of nervous system in the vertebrate animals]. Paris, France: Crevot.

Friston, K. J. (1994). Functional and effective connectivity in neuroimaging: A synthesis. *Human Brain Mapping*, *2*(56), 56–78.

Friston, K. J. (2011). Functional and effective connectivity: A review. *Brain Connect*, *1*(1), 13–36.

Goldenberg, D. & Galván, A. (2015). The use of functional and effective connectivity techniques to understand the developing brain. *Developmental Cognitive Neuroscience*, *12*, 155–164.

Hauk, O., Johnsrude, I., & Pulvermuller, F. (2004). Somatotopic representation of action words in human motor and premotor cortex. *Neuron, 41*, 301–307.

Honey, C. J., Sporns, O., Cammoun, L., Gigandet, X., Thiran, J. P., Meuli, R., & Hagmann, P. (2009). Predicting human resting-state functional connectivity from structural connectivity. *Proceedings of the Natural Academy of Sciences USA, 106*(6), 2035–2040.

Jackson, J. H. (1884). Evolution and dissolution of the nervous system (Croonian Lectures). In J. Taylor (Ed.), *Selected writings of John Hughlings Jackson* (pp. 739–744). New York, NY: Basic Books.

James, K. H. & Swain, S. (2010). Only self-generated actions create sensorio-motor systems in the developing brain. *Developmental Science, 14*(4), 673–678. doi: 10.1111/j.1467-7687.2010.01011.x

Johnson, M. & de Haan, M. (2010). *Developmental cognitive neuroscience* (3rd ed.). Oxford, UK: Wiley-Blackwell.

Kanwisher, N. (2010). Functional specificity in the human brain: A window into the functional architecture of the mind. *Proceedings of the Natural Academy of Sciences USA, 107*(25), 11163–11170.

Mahon, B. & Caramazza, A. (2008). A critical look at the embodied cognition hypothesis and a new proposal for grounding conceptual content. *Journal of Physiology—Paris, 102*, 59–70.

Rubinov, M. & Sporns, O. (2010). Complex network measures of brain connectivity: Uses and interpretations. *Neuroimage, 52*(3), 1059–1069.

Stephan, K. E. & Friston, K. J. (2010). Analyzing effective connectivity with fMRI. *Wiley Interdisciplinary Reviews: Cognitive Science, 1*(3), 446–459.

van den Heuvel, M. P. & Hulshoff Pol, H. E. (2010). Exploring the brain network: A review on resting-state fMRI functional connectivity. *European Neuropsychopharmacology, 20*(8), 519–534.

Wernicke, C. (1874). *Der aphasische Symptomencomplex* [The aphasic symptom complex]. Breslau, Poland: Kohn und Weigert.

Wig, G. S., Schlaggar, B. L., & Petersen, S. E. (2011). Concepts and principles in the analysis of brain networks. *Annuals of New York Academy of Science, 1224*, 126–146.

Reprise in musical tuition

Hints on the helical nature of development

David Carré

In this commentary I expand on a specific aspect of Rojas' chapter (this volume) that has major relevance for developmental thinking at large: the idea that repetition, in the form of reprise, leads to novelty rather than replication. This notion, drawn by him from musical tuition, goes way beyond the musical domain in—at least—three ways. In the first place, Rojas' observation challenges the common assumption that development only relates to novelty, i.e. *old* ways lead to *maintain* what is already there, while *new* means lead to *novel* outputs. Second, it moves us to reflect on whether it is really possible to do *exactly the same* two or more times if we are thinking from a developmental, i.e. time-based, ontology. Lastly, the case of musical reprise becomes a clear example of how tuition relationships condense in a single moment different developmental scales, particularly by weaving microgenetic gestures and traditional ways of doing together. In the following, I address these three ideas in consecutive order.

Repetition as source of novelty

In his chapter, Rojas—following Bergson—stresses an apparent contradiction for common sense: "[R]epetition, still in its most simplistic versions . . . is perceived as contributing value" (p. 000). Moreover: "It might be sheer insistence, or even lead into dullness, but it is never exact replication" (p. 000). This, for Rojas, is based in the fact that: "In musical contexts, reprises carry with them all the strength of previous developments, so that a theme might be heard anew" (p. 000). In sum, doing the same many times might not necessarily lead to the same results. But why does this idea seem so counterintuitive?

If we go back to daily life, it is not difficult to see why the former sounds strange. A commuting routine—going from home to the study/workplace, back and forth—shows how, for instance, driving the same road every workday does not lead to anything new. Likewise, cleaning the dishes and cutlery used for dinner every single evening probably does not bring much novelty to our lives either. However, it is also possible to think of ordinary routines that go in the opposite direction. Case in point: sports training, gym workout, or—especially— yoga are all activities that are performed through repetitions of a certain set of movements. Yet probably anybody who has practiced any of those would argue against how much change, and bodily skill development in particular, all these activities convey over time. Similarly, the case of cooking reminds us that following the same recipe over and over hardly leads us to prepare the exact same dish—especially when we are still struggling to do it. All in all, these ordinary examples show something interesting: *as long as we are learning or training something*—as in musical tuition—, *repetition is essential for development*, particularly for bodily skills.

The development of such skills, however, is probably obscured—or turned subsidiary in terms of Polanyi (1958)—by the notorious levels of dexterity we already have achieved for most of our daily activities. These, in turn, are certainly based in tireless yet unconscious repetitions over years. In fact, it is possible for us to observe the opposite case, i.e. the lack of dexterity, just by looking to those who are still learning. For instance, think of the case of infants, particularly of how many repetitions they need to perform in order to achieve something as simple as standing up by themselves, granted they have the muscular capacity for doing it. A similar case—in terms of structure—might be observed in adults: whenever we learn a new language, we do experience the strange feeling of not being able to even pronounce words properly. Similarly, we observe with dismay how foreigners learning our own mother tongue cannot make sentences that 5-year-old children can effortlessly produce. Ultimately, experience shows that persistence and practice are the only ways of achieving something as "simple" as speaking—a different language.[1]

A theoretical note on this is necessary. As thoroughly elaborated by Valsiner in Chapter 2, had developmental thinking been closer to Hans Driesch's *equipotentiality* concept, the idea of repetition as source of novelty would be anything but surprising to us. In this vein, it is our assumption that the same developmental path *necessarily* leads to the same output (i.e. *uni*potentiality) that renders blurry the contribution of repetition. On the contrary, following Driesch, *for living, developing organisms* repetition could not be equated to replication, as they—starting from the same point—can develop into multiple, open-ended directions.

Reprise in irreversible time

As seen, the importance for development of repetition and reprisal is rooted not only in its stabilizing role but also in the way it facilitates the emergence of novelty. Here, however, it is reasonable to question something that has been taken for granted so far: to what extent it is possible *in ontological terms* to repeat something? In other words, is it still possible to talk about *the same* activity as an exact duplicate, since, as noted by Rojas, every reprisal or repetition brings something new into the field of practice?

On the one hand, this question seems absurd: it sounds quite strange to ask, for example, whether playing the same musical score twice is actually a repetition or not.

Since the score guiding the performance has not transformed itself, and so it contains the same arrangement of musical notes, it appears to be evident that—potential mistakes apart—both performances should be identical. When looking closer at this situation, however, the conclusion is not trivial at all.

Despite being based in the same materiality, there is something missing in the former account: *time*. Performing the *same* musical score twice with no flaws might certainly lead to almost *physically identical* performances in terms of sound waves. Yet, for the performer—as a human being—*time passed* along these performances; and it passed irreversibly. In this sense, *from the performer perspective*, playing the score immediately after the previous performance makes it something different than, for instance, playing the score for the very first time, or performing it for the tenth time in the day.

Such difference is based in the first of the four axiomatic features of development proposed by Valsiner (2006a): "The irreversible nature of development based on the irreversibility of time" (p. 177). The latter idea, inspired by the works of Bergson (1907/1911), establishes that, for living systems, development cannot be reversed because it happens in a stream of time that is irreversible by nature. Looking back to the case of an apprentice reprising a certain musical piece, the idea of irreversible time does not mean that, after mastering a particular piece, the apprentice cannot lose touch with it—even forgetting how to perform it. In this sense, the development of the specific dexterity required for performing such piece could certainly be reversed. Such oblivion, however, does not imply that the apprentice can go back and revert his/her organismic development back to the state it had before being able to perform the piece. Even if the apprentice learns, then forgets, and finally re-learns how to perform the piece, the latter moment of development could not be equated to the first moment of learning. Both in phenomenological and developmental terms, such re-learning is *learning anew*. Therefore, previous experiences, and so previous stages of development, cannot be taken out of the present time. Just as in a helix, it is possible to go through similar positions many times; but when time is considered, those positions could be similar but never identical. Hence development, happening over irreversible time, is not reversible either.

In this vein, musical reprise brings forward an ontological tension between continuity—keep being the same—and discontinuity—turning into something else. There is continuity as the apprentice musician keeps striving to achieve or master the same musical form in acoustic terms; but there is also a discontinuity since every reprise aims to transform the way in which the piece is approached and performed. This tension, however, fades away when our perspective on this phenomenon turns into a time-based ontology. Here the main question is not about what forms, objects, or organisms *are*, but how—under what conditions—they *might develop* into something else, or *remain* the same. By doing this, continuity is not the opposite of discontinuity, just a different—and necessary—moment of development.

Intergenerational reprise

Finally, I would like to further comment on a specific term used by Rojas, namely intergenerational reprise. Thinking in terms of developmental scales, we have so far discussed reprise mostly in its microgenetic (Werner & Kaplan, 1963; see also Wagoner, 2009) and ontogenetic dimensions. In other words, we have focused on those actions involved in reprising that happen in a moment-to-moment time-scale,[2] and the potential influence they could have over apprentices' personal development. Furthermore, we have addressed reprise as a local activity where apprentice, instructor, and the musical piece are the only interactants, something similar to the interactants involved in Bühler's triadic Organon Model (1990): sender, receiver, and object/state of affairs.[3] Rojas' ideas, however, allow us to go beyond this triadic perspective and look closer into the traditional, cultural mesh holding this interaction. Thus he draws attention to this matter through the notion of intergenerational reprise.

The theoretical framework for Rojas' intergenerational reprise is twofold: on the one hand the well-known Mauss concept of techniques of the body, and on the other hand Tim Ingold's five traits of skills. As noted by Rojas, Marcel Mauss defined the techniques of the body as, "the *traditional* ways in which, from society to society, men know how to use their bodies" (1950/2009, p. 365, emphasis added). Meanwhile Ingold (2001), in Rojas' words, defines the second trait of skills as follows: "skill does not reside in a single individual, but strongly relies on the individual's participation in the experience and workings of a collective, and consequently on the ensemble of relationships that are nurtured within it" (p. 000).

As seen, both Ingold and Mauss emphasize the fact that skills are *inherited* from previous generations rather than created—developed—from scratch, thus rendering the socio-cultural scale of development also relevant for activities that we have assumed to be developed individually so far. Here it is worth noting that the term "inheritance" is probably as misleading as Rojas' "transmission" for talking about skills. Both terms are tricky as they lead us to think that contemporary individuals go to—so to say—the tree of tradition, and from there they grasp— with the help of an instructor—a certain skill, as if this is a finished, ready-made set of actions. And certainly neither Rojas, nor Mauss (2009), nor Ingold (2001) stands for such understanding of the relation between skills and tradition. Quite the contrary, as properly elaborated by Rojas in his chapter, developing a skillful performance of a musical instrument is done within the mesh of tradition, but this does not imply that such appropriation is "sheer individual imitation" (p. 000) of what has been done before.

Although not mentioned by him, the model of—active—internalization/externalization proposed by Valsiner (1997, 2006b) could offer a semiotic parallel[4] to clarify the approach outlined by Rojas. This general model sheds light upon the indissoluble unity between the person and his or her environment—i.e. inclusive separation—, but specifically brings to the fore the *constructive* role of the person in the internalization/externalization process. This is constructive rather than just active, as human beings not only *choose* from a culturally limited set of ready-made ways of doing, thinking, and feeling, but are capable of "*construct-ing new choices*" (Valsiner, 1997, p. 290, emphasis in the original)—precisely by transforming those cultural suggestions. This constructive nature supports Rojas' position and clarifies why apprentices develop a particular style of performance in spite of addressing common musical themes. At the same time, it makes clear why the tutor needs to tailor his or her guidance to every apprentice rather than using a fixed pedagogic method. Additionally, the multilayer graphic model presented by Valsiner (2006b, p. 14) on internalization/externalization offers a perspective on the "psychic deepness" involved in this process. In brief, it makes visible that internalization/externalization is not just a matter of binary *in/out*. On the con-trary, much of the constructiveness involved—both of the person and the environ-ment—has to do with how deep into the personal-sense structure is something internalized; or how related some externalization is to this generalized core of meanings.

Ultimately, Rojas' reflections on intergenerational reprise bring forth tui-tion as a vivid example of a *junction of developmental scales*: a juxtaposition between micro, personal, and cultural experiences. Only when all this is consid-ered together, is it possible to grasp the full significance of the tuition relationship, and to better understand its relevance for the complexity of human development.[5]

Concluding remarks

When we think about which form could properly represent development, we prob-ably think of something like an ascending arrow. This arrow portrays not only the temporal dimension but also the upward direction that we naïvely ascribe to development—when actually phenomena like aging or extinction are developmen-tal too, and so it is not possible to conflate *growth* with development. Despite this, if we see a sales chart with an ascending arrow, we would assume that business is now bigger than before, and so is developing properly. Likewise, a similar chart representing the height and weight of a newborn should lead us to conclude that the baby is healthy and developing accordingly, since every week he or she is growing stronger. As natural as this common understanding of development is   and it is mostly correct in these cases—, it is nonetheless misleading for grasping the whole of what developmental phenomena involves.

Following Rojas' ideas on reprise and the developmental nature of skills, prob-ably the most simplified yet accurate figure to represent development should be a *helix*. Although the direction of the helix (upward, downward, horizontal) should not be defined beforehand—as it is not possible to predict the direction development (Valsiner, 2006a)—, this figure manages to capture the three features of develop-ment mentioned above. In the first place, it depicts the recursive nature of devel-opment, which, as seen, does not lead to replication but to novelty. A helix also portrays the irreversible nature of development given by the irreversibility of time—thus showing that it is possible to go through similar moments of development, but never to return to an *identical* previous one. Additionally, an extended helix could be helpful in representing how micro- and ontogenetic development actualizes previous socio-cultural elements; for instance, the apprentice performing and reprising in the present a musical theme created 200 years ago.

Trying to define the most accurate way of representing development certainly is an over-ambitious aim for this commentary. It is, however, a useful exercise to see the ways in which Rojas' chapter on skills expands the understanding of development beyond traditional accounts—centered in finding stages along a straight line.

Notes

1 On a side note, it is interesting to observe how all these skills—developed through repetition—also remind us how development might be, in a certain sense, reversible. As long as we stop doing any of those mentioned above, our dexterity starts to decay slowly but steadily.
2 Although it could be easier to say that microgenetic phenomena occur in timeframes of seconds, and eventually minutes, such translation into absolute time could easily turn into a misleading reduction. Misleading, as developmental scales are precisely conceived as ad hoc measures of length that fit to the particularities of different phenomena (see Cornejo & Olivares, 2015).
3 It is crucial to keep in mind that, although composed by the three actors/elements mentioned, the Organon Model proposed by Karl Bühler is a *functional* model. In this vein, the actors in the model are relevant in terms of the communicative functions they perform: expressive function for the sender; conative, or appealing, function for the receiver; and representation function for the objects and state of affairs.
4 One possible tension—depending on the theoretical stance within semiotics—arising from this link comes from the fact that musical tuition deals not only with linguistic meanings and valuations. Although most semiotics theorizations on human experience include the affective factor, it is not entirely clear how they could deal with the inclusion of bodily skills, which could be only indirectly addressed by linguistic accounts.
5 The latter, however, leads to an open question that goes beyond the scope of this commentary: to what extent does the developmental junction presented by musical tuition apply to other developmental phenomena? Is it a particularity of tuition in general? If not, why is it so salient in those interactions?

References

Bergson, H. (1911). *Creative evolution.* New York, NY: Henry Holt. (Original work published in 1907)
Bühler, K. (1990). *The theory of language: The representational function of language.* Amsterdam, Netherlands: John Benjamins.
Cornejo, C. & Olivares, H. (2015). Living and observing: Two modes of understanding time. In L. M. Simao, D. Silva Guimaraes, & J. Valsiner (Eds.), *Temporality: Culture in the flow of human experience* (pp. 95–114). Charlotte, NC: Information Age Publishing.
Ingold, T. (2001). From the transmission of representations to the education of attention. In H. Whitehouse (Ed.), *The debated mind: Evolutionary psychology versus ethnography* (pp. 113–153). Oxford, UK: Berg.

Mauss, M. (2009). *Sociologie et anthropologie* [Sociology and Anthropology]. Paris, France: PUF. (Original work published in 1950)

Polanyi, M. (1958). *Personal knowledge: Toward a post-critical philosophy.* Chicago, IL: Chicago University Press.

Valsiner, J. (1997). *Culture and the development of children's action: A theory of human development* (2nd ed.). New York, NY: Wiley.

Valsiner, J. (2006a). Developmental epistemology and implications for methodology. In W. Damon & R. Lerner (Eds.), *Handbook of child psychology*, 6th ed. (Vol. 1, pp. 166–209). New York, NY: Wiley.

Valsiner, J. (2006b). The semiotic construction of solitude: Processes of internalization and externalization. *Sign Systems Studies, 34*(1), pp. 9–35.

Wagoner, B. (2009). The experimental methodology of constructive microgenesis. In J. Valsiner, P. Molenaar, M. Lyra, & N. Chaudhary (Eds.), *Dynamic process methodology in the social and developmental sciences* (pp. 99–120). New York, NY: Springer.

Werner, H. & Kaplan, B. (1963). *Symbol formation: An organismic-developmental approach to language and the expression of thought.* New York, NY: Wiley.

Representing Development

The social construction of models of change

David Carré, Jaan Valsiner and Stefan Hampl

Any science is based upon a core set of assumptions that are presented through a complex of social representations. These set up the general vision of the world, i.e. the set of axioms on which the whole of the inquiry is further pursued (Branco & Valsiner, 1997). Developmental Science is no exception to this. Yet it has a special place, as it has questioned the social representations systems about the phenomenon of instability over time, i.e. change, within the societies in which it emerged. Social representations, as a general rule, try to make familiar the unfamiliar by turning unstable phenomena into a series of static forms, i.e. assimilating novelty within already existing structures.

As seen throughout this volume, however, addressing the notion of development and its representations calls for a multiple, and eventually chaotic, range of perspectives. Moving from historical perspectives—going back to up to 200 years (Chapters 1, 2 and 3)—, to contemporary issues (Chapters 4, 5, 6 and 7), to alternative, future-oriented views about development (Commentaries), it is not difficult to lose sight of the broader perspective—and thus concluding that development is something 'just too big to handle'. Nevertheless, the rationale behind the manifold contributions composing this volume is the exact opposite: if development is to be addressed, this needs to be done through the *multiplicity* of its representations. Therefore, the whole set of these representations needs a meta-theoretical analysis in order to construct theories of development. In fact, at the present time there has been considerable confusion about what kinds of theoretically oriented stories could qualify as *theories* (in contrast to *accounts*[1]) of development, as chapters 1 and 2 in this volume show.

Representations and their roots

The most basic opposition in representations to deal with development is that of

CHANGE <in relation with> DEVELOPMENT.

Questions like, "Is any change development?", "Does development always show itself in manifest change?" or, "Can development occur without any phenomenological manifestations?", are all usual in the sciences of development. The cells in our bodies, for instance, change all the time, but such process is not visible in the form of our bodies from day to day. Alternatively—in the reverse direction—our genome mutates all the time, but this is immediately repaired, or undone, by specific gene mechanisms. Constant change that is corrected is still change—but is it development?

These kinds of questions—though natural—are in principle misguided. Instead of asking an ontological question (is X = Y?), the suitable question would be, what kind of *relationship* exists between the opposites (X and Y). Furthermore, the relationship here needs to be functional, not formal. A functional relationship is conditional as it specifies the catalytic conditions (Cabell & Valsiner, 2014) under which one of the posited opposites (X) transforms into the other (Y)—and possibly vice versa. Chapters 3 and 4 exemplify this point thoroughly.

The relation between change and development was already worked out in the 1920s by Aleksei Severtsov (Sewertzoff, 1928). His model of linkages between temporary changes (*idioadaptations*) and developmental transformations (*aromorphosis*) sets up the representation of development in a phylogenetic framework (Figure C.1).

Severtsov's scheme is fully based on phylogenetic development of species— not of individuals. Interestingly, it involves the axiomatic acceptance of the HIGHER <> LOWER organizational levels in biological evolution. As Figure C.1 depicts, at some stages of evolution the existing form of a species (A) acquires several progressive characteristics that lead to the species transformation into the line of higher forms ($a_1 \ldots a_2$). The emergence of new forms leads to new relations with the surroundings—new forms of adaptation co-exist with descendants of the previous ones (a_2 with b_1, a_4 and a_5 with b_2). Thus, the newly emerged forms (a_2) develop into various sub-species (bifurcations S...s). In turn, each of the co-developing forms is challenged by the adaptation pressures (planes P, Q, R), where some (R) guide the evolutionary process towards higher levels of organization, while others (Q) maintains the "lagging behind" species (b_2) at its current level. Furthermore, the organizational level can even become lower (B_1) under environmental pressure (P). In this vein, evolution might also involve involution.

Ideological canalization of social representing

For Severtsov—as well as for most other evolutionary theorists—the notion of the HIGHER–LOWER distinction in evolution was a natural, axiomatic given. *Homo*

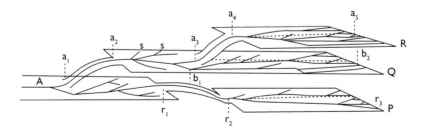

Figure C.1 Account of change and development by Sewertzoff (1928, p. 64)

sapiens is undoubtedly a more complex biological species than the Ebola virus— although the latter can efficiently eradicate the former, rather than the other way around. Such contrast, however, has not been an axiom in the psychological discourses on development over the 20th and 21st century. Within them, the social imperative of egalitarian societies, promoted by political forces, have problematized any claim considering some psychological form "higher" in contrast to other "lower" forms. The result is an increasing difficulty for developmental sciences as new forms that emerge can be observed—and labeled—to be *more* complex. Greater complexity, however, does not equate to *higher* forms of organization, since the latter is a transformation not in terms of quantity in comparison to the previous form, but in terms of quality, as shown in chapters 6 and 7.

This terminological and conceptual limitation shows a social constraint of the meta-theoretical kind, supported by the dominance of quantification as the socially set norm for considering psychology as "science" (Toomela & Valsiner, 2010). Yet the result of removing such qualitative transformations from the methodological repertoire of psychology has been to bring its own development as science to a standstill. Accordingly, we can observe the recurrent change of fashionable tendencies—from behaviorism to cognitivism, and further to ecological and positive psychologies—but little qualitative innovation of the discipline. Therefore, lateral extension of ideas has replaced actual development in psychology, which is likely to lead to the extinction of the discipline as a basic *Wissenschaft*. Hence, during the past few decades we have observed efforts of reducing psychological phenomena either downward (to physiology, or genetics) or upward (considering persons as texts) in terms of abstraction.

Development as an open-systemic phenomenon

Development is only possible in the case of open systems that have clearly defined properties. They exist due to their full dependence upon relations with their environments—immediate contexts for living, or *Umwelt*. If these relations are externally and suddenly intervened, systems become extinct. As a result of this strict condition, development produces increased variability (*variability amplification* in Maruyama, 1963), and cannot be predicted from initial conditions of organization.

Implications from these defining characteristics of open systems for the study of development are obvious. First, measurement of ontologically defined characteristics (e.g., intelligence, personality, etc.) is irrelevant for developmental science in its psychological realm—even if it may be a respectable pastime for non-developmental psychological science. Second, any study of development needs to consider time as central for its representations. Comparisons of human age groups—children with adolescents, adolescents with adults, adults with old age persons—do not reveal processes of development: these are accounts of developmental outcomes. Regrettably, as chapters 3 and 6 and commentaries 2, 3, 4 and 6 reveal, disciples from life and human sciences have followed an indisputably non-developmental path.

Development as an abstract notion

It is easy to assume, for instance, that studying the development of embryos (Chapter 3) has nothing to do with understanding how musical skills are appropriated (Chapter 7). The question for both investigations, however, seems to be the same: how is it that A gets irreversibly transformed into something B, while partially remaining the same? While the concrete descriptions may differ, both phenomena reflect a common developmental nature: they transform along with the environment (enzymes for embryos, tutors for apprentices) and across their own time-scales. For development, *time is time-for-the-organism*; we can certainly use standard metric time for comparison, but not in place of looking for an absolute scale (see Commentary 6).

This volume is not intended to be the last, concluding word on the subject of development. On the contrary, it aims to work as a sort of mirror for those concerned with any developmental issue. Why a mirror? Simply because this book presents a series of representations of development—other than stage-orientation ones—that we hope might serve to encourage the reader to acknowledge his or her own orientation within this entangled field. Development in itself is a summarizing notion, as it condenses our experience of observing, living, and sometimes even suffering, the world changing around—if not within—us. Exploring how this has been and is represented allows us new freedom to construct models of development. These are models that could break through the ideological and normative limits that, coming from both common and scientific language, have constrained our understanding.

Note

1 Our distinction of *theory* and *account* is specifiable on the basis of the well-revered work of Jean Piaget: his theory of development is that of progressing equilibration (*equilibration majorante*), while his account of development is depicted by his "theory" of stages. The stage *account* is descriptive of development, but it cannot explain development. A *theory* is a system of abstract ideas that explains the phenomena in their full complexity, thus including their absence.

References

Branco, A. U. & Valsiner, J. (1997). Changing methodologies: A co-constructivist study of goal orientations in social interactions. *Psychology and Developing Societies*, *9*(1), 35–64.

Cabell, K. R. and Valsiner, J. (Eds.) (2014). *The catalyzing mind: Beyond models of causality*. Vol. 11 of *Advances of theoretical psychology*. New York, NY: Springer.

Maruyama, M. (1963). The second cybernetics: Deviation-amplifying mutual causal processes. *American Scientist*, *51*, 164–179.

Sewertzoff, A. N. (1928). Directions in evolution. *Acta Zoologica*, *12*, 59–93.

Toomela, A. and Valsiner, J. (Eds.) (2010). *Methodological thinking in psychology: 60 years gone astray?* Charlotte, NC: Information Age Publishers.

Index